Introduction

When my other series - Old Paris|
- flopped because it was academic
Not only with the interesting stuff f
grab the reader. People who quite
body ought to make a collection of
but nobody ever does. So here it i:
parishes as the chapter perimeters because they were static for when we
have statistics. Staffordshire had 166 ancient parishes; for dimension rat-
ings 169.

For such a densely-populated area as the Black Country and not being
intimate with the local press on an ongoing-basis it was difficult to make
a truly comprehensive work. Nevertheless newspaper cuttings relating to Amblecote, Codsall, Wombourne, Trysull, Tipton, Wednesbury,
West Bromwich, Smethwick were helpful in Brierley Hill, Stourbridge,
Smethwick, Coseley, Wolverhampton and William Salt libraries. Many
thanks to those who assisted me in these libraries. I would especially like
to thank those who compiled the very valuable albums of cuttings. It is
a pity so few are done, currently. I am sure there are far more claims for
future editions. Please do not hesitate to get in touch if you find a mistake
or think a new claim ought to be included in the next edition. Critics
will also say the facts - about 80% are new and not in the Encyclopaedia
- don't tell a proper story of the parish, but what I found by chance as information randomly accumulated (and was not searched for) unforeseen
themes emerged. For instance:

Amblecote - parish of covert harshness. Bobbington - parish of small
interests. Bushbury - avoidance and transport. Clent - enduring legacies.
Codsall - lone craftsmen. Darlaston - parish of the wily or daft. Enville
- the lord manicured the landscape about him, but by design or nature
a hoary primitiveness prevails at the peripheries. Himley - speed and
tragedy. Kingswinford - a nexus of communities who don't do things by
half, whether kindness, happiness, humour, feast, conspiracy, enterprise,
or engineering feats. Kinver - beneath the loveliness is a gruesomeness.
Patshull - people have an ambivalent regard for their fellows. Pattingham
- parish of rural brawn. Penn - parish about which nothing is quite reso-
lute. Rowley Regis - blood, earth, wind and fire. Sedgley - a slovenly people, contemptuous of others, impervious to their views, in communities
diffident towards one another. Smethwick - world cometh, world bound.
Tettenhall - harebrained men, talented women. Tipton - parish of the
poor and oversized, who revere courage and service. Trysull - alertness.
Upper Arley - spawns heroes. Walsall - parish of indulgences and show-
manship. Wednesbury - parish that nurtured invention. West Bromwich
- men in bonded harmony, women in militant isolation. Wolverhampton
- parish of blinge and promenading, whether its buckles, ghosts, tramps,
politicians, militia, criminals, cyclists, and motor-cyclists. Wombourne
- crafty or just plain batty!
Abbreviations for references are not listed - readers can consult The Staf-

fordshire Encyclopaedia Website at http://www.the-staffordshire-ency-clopaedia.co.uk/ Many thanks to Mad Cat Toys for the Sunbeam image (page 154); their website can be visited at http://www.madcattoys.com

There are 3 more volumes planned, covering the rest of Staffordshire (Staffordshire Moorlands, volume 2, came out in 2007). Many thanks to Jim Sutton for translation of a medieval document, Stan Hill for his help, and the Black Country Society for marketing this book.

Tim Cockin. Barlaston. April 2008.

THE BLACK COUNTRY SOCIETY

THE BLACK COUNTRY

The term 'The Black Country' was first used in the mid 19th century to describe the area on the South Staffordshire Coalfield, where the 'thick coal' lay.

The 1850s and 1860s saw the peak of mineral and iron production and the area would have been at its blackest then.

Over 150 square miles some 100 small industrial communities developed and by the turn of the century a couple of dozen of them were of sufficient size, perhaps when linked with some of their neighbours, to have their own municipal councils.

There were never any precise boundaries for the Black Country for the term was not official, not to be found on Ordnance Survey maps, for example.

However, 20 years campaigning by the Black Country Society and others, seemed to bear fruit regarding the name, for in 1987, the Government sponsored body 'The Black Country Development Corporation' was established with a 10 year life, later extended by one year. What was once a nickname was elevated to be included to describe an official body.

By 1974 all the townships of the Black Country, by whatever definition, were absorbed into four Black Country Metropolitan Boroughs; further official acceptance of the name.

THE BLACK COUNTRY IN 2000

Website address: www.blackcountrysociety.co.uk

The Black Country Society was founded in 1967 by enthusiasts led by the late Dr. John Fletcher, who felt that the Black Country did not receive its fair share of recognition for its great contribution to the industrial development of Britain and the world.

The Society grew out of the Dudley Canal Tunnel Preservation Society which had successfully campaigned to save Dudley Canal Tunnel, that had been threatened with closure by British Waterways and British Rail.

The Tunnel is now a major attraction adjoining the Black Country Living Museum.

The Society's stated aim was 'to foster interest in the past, present and future of the Black Country', and its voice, at a specially called meeting on 6th October 1968, was one of the

2

earliest calling for the establishment of a local industrial museum.
Since the establishment of The Black Country Living Museum, the Society and individual members have continually supported it.

THE BLACKCOUNTRYMAN

The Blackcountryman is the society's quarterly magazine. In the 160 issues published in the past 40 years there have been over 2,100 authoritative articles on all aspects of the Black Country by historians, researchers, teachers, students, subject experts and ordinary folk with an extraordinary tale to tell. In addition, some 620 books written during that period on Black Country subjects have been reviewed in the magazines.
The whole 40 volume collection constitutes a unique resource for teachers, students, researchers and anyone with a general interest in the area.
Several local libraries have complete sets and an index available for reference.
Some 2,000 magazines are printed each quarter, each of the 2,000 members has a copy delivered and there are several sales outlets.
The magazine is non-commercial and nobody receives payment for their articles and this publication is the most important function of the Black Country Society.
The 'contents' page of each 84-page A5 magazine lists 25 items including details of the programmes of three branches, walks and excursions,, substantial articles, several lighter ones, Black Country humour, poetry, correspondence, and book reviews.
There is a coloured cover and about 20 photographs (some in colour) in each issue.
Two national history publications have named *The Blackcountryman* as a leading magazine in the field of local history.

Editors of The Blackcountryman
Harold Parsons 1967-1988
Stan Hill 1988-2001
Dr. David Cox M.A. 2001-2005
Mike Pearson B.A. (Hons.) 2005-

BLACK COUNTRY SOCIETY MEMBERSHIP RATES

Individual or Group £12.50 pa
Family (in 2 adults) £15.00 pa

Send cheques payable to: The Black Country Society, to:
Miss Linda Button, Membership Secretary, 25 Foxhills Park, Netherton, Dudley DY2 0JQ. Tel 01384 213479.

BENEFITS:
'THE BLACKCOUNTRYMAN' is delivered to each member.
Reduction on Society publications' prices.
Access to Society's Programme of Summer Walks & Excursions.

SOCIETY SALES

The Black Country Society has a range of inexpensive Black Country publications for sale. Now available:

Black Country Tea Clothes - 3 patterns - 'Man', 'Woman', 'Black Country Alphabet' each £3.30p.

For full list of items available send sae to The BC Society, P.O. Box 71, Kingswinford DY6 9YN.

The Black Country
Did you know that...

'**Cradle of the Industrial Revolution**' Refers to the Black Country (TB Oct 4 2001 p16). '**Iron Country**' Former reference to the Black Country area coined by William Cobbett in 1830 (TB Jan 29 2004 p10). **First appearance of the name Black Country (lower case)** 1834 '...in the densely populated black country...' in Memoirs of CM Young. CM Young, 1871, p212 (OED). **First appearance of Black Country (upper case), first book with Black Country in its title** 1846 in the novel 'Colton Green: A Tale of the Black Country, or the Region of Mines and Forges in Staffordshire' by Rev W Gresley. That the term was colloquially prevalent much earlier is suggested in The Christian Witness and Church Members Magazine c1856, p537 '... they preached in what was called 'The Black Country', including Oldbury, Greatbridge, Walsall, Tipton, Gornal, Wolverhampton and Bilston...' (E&S March 2008, David Horovitz correspondence). '**Queen of the Black Country**', '**Historical capital of the Black Country**', **heart of the Black Country** Is a reference to Dudley (MR2 p120) (TB Nov 12 1998 pp14-15. Sept 28 2000 p24). '**Capital of the Black Country**' Wednesbury (see). **First appearance of Black Country dialect in a publication** Knights Quarterly Magazine, and then reprinted in The Mirror, a weekly, Saturday Oct 18 1823; the article was about the Staffordshire collieries and the dialect in particular (TB June 29 2000 pp4-5). **The translator of the Bible into Black Country dialect** Kate Fletcher, born Bilston c1927, midwife and nurse. She moved to Kinver in 1976 (Preface in Old Testament part 1, and The Gospels in Black Country Dialect). In 1967 Miss Linda Payton of Gospel Oak Road, Tipton, Dudley librarian and Black Country Society member, was translating Jonah and the Whale (E&S April 24 1967 photo). **The Black Country dialect authority** Conrad Everson, of Iverley, Kinver (see). **Britain's worst accent** The Black Country accent, as voted in a BBC survey, 2005 (BBC website). The accent is unique (BCM Autumn 2006 p37). **Most grotesque Black Country accent** Halesowen (VB p41). **Nowhere more typical of the Black Country** Tipton, according to Robin Pearson in Tipton (1904) the Godfrey edition of the Old Ordnance Survey Maps, 2003. **Last men to sell their wives in the Black Country** Samuel Lett, but some say 'Rough Moey' (Q&ABC no. 157), whilst another contender is Job Green of Rowley Regis (see) in the 1840s. **Most Black Countrymen killed on single day in WW1** Many of 300 of the 4th Worcester Battalion who lost their lives on Aug 15 1915 at Gallipoli were from the Black Country; this number of 300 may be the greatest loss to one battalion on one day in WW1 (TB Nov 15 2001 p25). **Most famous Black Country dish** Frumity alias frumenty (FOS). '**White Shirt-Black Country**' **footballers** Are those 54 Black Countrymen who have played football for England (White Shirt - Black Country. Patrick Talbot. 2004) (TB May 20 2004 p4p) (BCM Autumn 2006 pp7,21). **Worst weather month in the Black Country** Feb 1947, with Edgbaston Meteorological Ob-

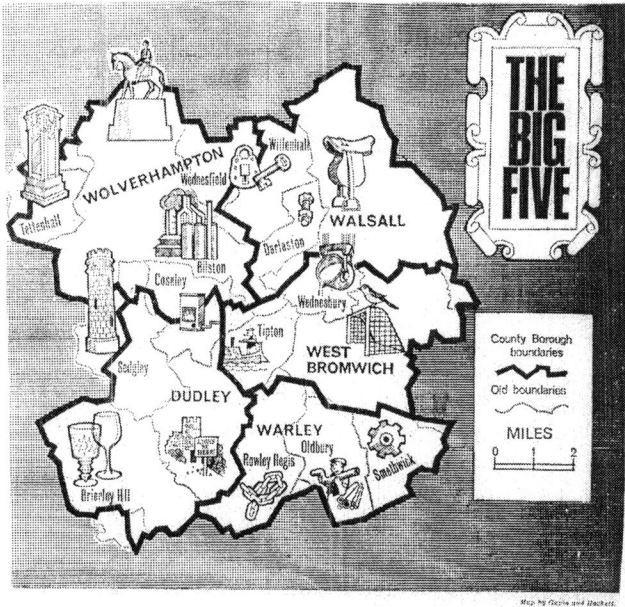

How the Black Country urban districts, municipal and county boroughs were grouped into new county boroughs in the new county of West Midlands, 1974

servatory recording a mean minimum temperature of -3.7C, snowing practically every day somewhere or other in the Black Country, and 12 consecutive days of continuous frost (TB Jan 25 2000 p16) (BCM Spring 2007 pp23-25). **Most Black Country blast furnaces ever** 283, or at least over 200 at height of C19 iron production; the unusual thing about lighting them was the first fire had to be lit by a woman or a girl (Q&ABC nos. 126, 167). **Last Black Country colliery to close** Baggeridge Colliery, closed 1968 (SL p265). **'No. 1 in the field of spring-making in the world'** The Black Country (TB June 15 2000 p21). **'Jew's Harp capital'** The Black Country (TB Feb 3 2005 p16). **Most musical place in all England** The Black Country according to Lewis Ingram in Leisure Hour magazine, who visited the region in the 1850s:- ".. the love of music (is) apparent even among the humblest classes, there is no other part of England which can in the least compete with it.." (TB June 28 2007 p18). **'Black Country's foremost historian'** FW Hackwood (TB April 26 2001 p20). **'The Black Country's best known author'** Francis Brett Young (1884-1954), born Halesowen, who published 45 novels, in the opinion of Black Country stalwart, Stan Hill (BCM Spring 2006 p78). **Catherine Cookson of the Black Country** Meg Hutchinson of Wednesbury (see). **'King of the Black Country'** Harry Cabbage, according to a modern ballad by Aristotle Tump alias Harry Taylor, founder and first editor of The Bugle (TB Aug 21 2003 p9). **Artist of the Black Country** Ewart Chapman of Old Hill, later residing at Sleeping Mill, Cookley near Kidderminster (Q&ABC no. 185). **Artist who records the Black Country's industrial decline** Arthur Lockwood (E&S Nov 24 2005 p8p). **Cartoonist of the Black Country** Clebak, alias Charles Leslie Baker (Q&ABC no. 189) (Evening Mail Nov 2 1971). **Picasso of the Black Country** alias the Mario Lanza ghostwriter or scribler, see Tipton. **'Horse of the Black Country'** 'Sleipnir' a large sculpture of a horse - perhaps largest in the Midlands - by the canal at Brierley Hill, by Steve Field, made by Apollo Engineering in 1998 (BCM Autumn 2003 pp31-33). **'the White City of the Black Country'** Aldersley Stadium, as described in one venue programme (TB May 17 2007 p35). **'The Blackcountryman' locomotive** Was a Class 31 diesel based at Bescot. The naming ceremony took place on Aug 30 1992. The nameplate was unveiled by Black Country comedian Tommy Munden. It was removed in 1998 (Stan Hill's Brierley Hill and Life. 1999. p46). **The Blackcountryman Inn** In 1975 The Britannia, Lower Church Lane, Tipton, changed its name to this at the request of its regulars, so by giving it a unique name (E&S Dec 3 1975). **England's other Black Country** Another region perhaps at one time dubbed 'The Black Country' was an industrial area covering Riddings near Alfreton, Derbys, for there is a book by Rev WE Littlewood titled 'Down in Dingyshire, or Sketches of Life in the Black Country' (1873); he was vicar of Riddings in 1871. However, the subtitle of the book was enough to initially dupe The Bugle in believing Littlewood was writing about the Staffordshire, Worcestershire Black Country (TB June 22 2006 p16. July 6 2006 p18. July 27 2006 p4).

Humour & comradeship...

First popular exponent of Black County humour Billy Russell (1893-1971), comedian, who grew up in Dudley (MR2 p123). **The Black Country Three** A folk group who celebrated the story of 'The Making of the Region' in rhyme and song, of its hardships and cruelties inflicted upon the workers. In 1966 they accompanied poems written and read by Dr John Fletcher, historian of Wednesbury, at the Mermaid Theatre, London (Midland Chronicle etc. Dec 2 1966 p15). **'one of the largest sub-regional societies in the country' 1988** The Black Country Society with some 2,500 members (Stan Hill's Brierley Hill and Life. 1999. p45). **First meeting of the Black Country Society** Jan 1 1967, the triumvirate founders were:- Dr John Fletcher (1940-96), John Brimble (1940-2006) and Harold Parsons (1919-92); the first committee meeting was on March 29 1967 at Druids Heath Inn, Coseley; their quarterly journal 'The Blackcountryman' first appeared in Jan 1968 (Stan Hill's Brierley Hill and Life. 1999. p40). **'Black Country Nights'** Black Country Society social evenings with entertainment of a Black Country theme in the 1970s, inspired by the then current 'Welsh Nights' organised by Welsh teachers in Dudley borough. The first 'Night' was held at Dudley Teachers' Centre in Oct 1971: John Fletcher and Jon Raven performed and Barbara Cracknell made a huge cauldron of groaty pudding to her grandmother's recipe. About 12 more 'Nights' followed (Stan Hill's Brierley Hill and Life.

1999. p41). **The 'Queen of Black Country humour'** Dolly Allen of Wordsley. **First-known mention of Enoch and Eli** By the musical hall comedian Ernie Garner (d1936) in the late C19; alternatively written Aynuck and Ayli in Black Country dialect (TB Feb 1975 p17. Nov 8 2007 p10). **Highest concentration of Enochs and Elis** The Tipton district, according to The Bugle (TB Sept 1997 p17). **Traditional home of Enoch and Eli** The Gornals, according to Mike Raven (MR p162). **Female equivalent to Enoch and Eli** - perhaps Clara and Ada (TB April 5 2001 p5). **Most famous duo who played Enoch and Eli** Alan Smith (Enoch), with three successive Elis - Harry Felton (1964-65), John Guest (1965-86), John Plant of Netherton (1986-2007) (TB March 29 2007 p26p of John Plant. Nov 8 2007 p10).

The Black Country Bugle...

Country's most idiosyncratic nostalgia journal 'The Black Country Bugle: The Voice of The Black Country', published by Mercia Publicity from April 1972. (The Times Dec 11 1972). **First editor and originator** Harry Taylor (1932-2003), who often wrote under the pseudonym of Aristotle Tump, with the help of business partners David James and Derek Beasley; Taylor had formerly edited The Circular in Halesowen (TB July 2003 p1p). **First Bugle annual** Dec 1973. **Original home** 91 Stourbridge Road, Halesowen to 1983, then at Brettell Lane, Amblecote to 1989, then at 41 High St, Cradley Heath (TB April 5 2007 pp18,21). **Bugle's three greatest on-going investigations** Perhaps: 1) Who put 'Bella' (a female skeleton) in the wych elm in Hagley Wood near Stourbridge (murder story), 2) Who put the pig on the wall at Gornal (folklore), 3) Jack Judge of Oldbury (unravelling biographical details). **500th edition** March 28 2002 (TB March 28 2002 pp1,18-19).

Amblecote
Did you know that...

Amblecote's top folklore According to tradition the Starving Rascal Inn, originally the Dudley Arms, is so called after a licensee once turned away a starving beggar, whose frozen body was found the next day close by the inn. The house became known as the Starver. Courage brewery changed it to the Starving Rascal. Its sign shows on one side the beggar turned away and on the other the beggar's ghost being welcomed by a new licensee (BCM Jan 1983 pp55-56p) (GPCE p24). **What Amblecote is famous for** Glass making. The **name Amblecote first appears** in Domesday Book, 1086. **One of the first glasshouses in Amblecote** Built at Holloway End in the earlier C17 (VCH vol 20 p49). **Best clay in England** Reputedly, that at Amblecote; used by immigrants from the Lorraine region of France to make glass pots by the 1620s (VCH vol 20 pp58-59). **'best makers of glass in the world' 1878, Grand Prix for glass winners 1878, 1889** Messrs Thomas Webb & Co. of Dennis Glassworks, at the Paris International Exhibitions 1878, 1889; the quote is from the 1878 catalogue (Thomas Webb crystal website 2008). **One of the oldest**

The Starving Rascal inn sign, Thomas Webb (d1869) of Messrs Thomas Webb & Co., and Coalbournbrook Glassworks. The motto 'commune bonum' in the Amblecote Urban District badge means 'the good of the community'.

cricket clubs in the Midlands Amblecote Cricket Club, dating to c1865 (County Express April 3 1965 p18). **First First Class County Cricket match played** When Worcestershire played Leicestershire at Stourbridge cricket ground at High Street, Amblecote on June 28 1905, lasting 2 days, with a Worcestershire win. In total there have been 61 first class matches on the Amblecote ground, the last in 1981 (TB June 16 2005 p35). **Smallest urban district in the country** Amblecote UD when formed in 1894 with 665 acres (VCH vol 20 p49) (WMVB p15). **First powered flight in the Black Country** When Stanley Spencer, an early aeronaut, took off aboard his airship from Corbett Hospital fete in Aug 1905 (TB June 30 2005 p4). **Highest selling exhibition of current contemporary glass in the country** British Glass Biennale at Ruskin Glass Centre, Wollaston Rd, Amblecote (BBC website 2006). **Smallest dairy in the country** Believed to be Cartwright's Dairy, 10 John Street, Amblecote, started by George Cartwright in 1931, closed April 1996 (Stourbridge Chronicle Sept 13 1996). **Highest concentration of glassmakers in Staffordshire 1921** Amblecote, where 219 out of every 1,000 males aged over 12 were employed in the glass industry, according to the 1921 census (VCH vol 20 p60). **UK's first International Mask Festival** Was held at The Glasshouse Arts Centre, Amblecote, and Stourbridge Town Hall Oct 19-27 2007 (TB Sept 6 2007 p21).

People...

Amblecote's hero Lt Cpl Joseph Darby (d1959), 9th Lancers, of Amblecote, wounded in the battle of Mons and taken prisoner by the Germans, escaped with others to occupied Brussels, eventually making their way to Holland where they were believed to be British civilians and returned to England to fight in the War (TB Jan 20 2005 pp16-17p). **Royal Society of Arts prizewinner** George Ensell of Coalbournbrook, glassmaker, was awarded £50 in 1778 for his sheet glass, the secret of which he is supposed to have brought back from Germany. In 1780 he perfected a new tunnel type of leer for annealing which largely replaced the old kilns (VCH vol 2 p228). **Midland Horticultural Society Medalist 1875** Walter Jones of Titan Works (engineers of heating and ventilation products), High St, Amblecote, for inventing an improved expansion joint. **Man who designed and produced the first 8,000lb bomb** AC Brookes, MBE, residing at 'Homestead', Amblecote, in 1944 (West Bromwich, Oldbury & Smethwick Midland Chronicle & Free Press May 26 1944 p4). **UK's best Small Site Supervisor (West Region) 1989** Tony Gregory, a Stourbridge builder, for his work on Stamford Green (30 houses/ bungalows), off Stamford Road, Amblecote. The award is a category in the Pride in the Job contest (begun 1981) in a regional final of the National House Building Council's annual awards (County Express Nov 30 1989). **Most sets of twins in one school in Staffordshire** Peter's Hill Primary School, just S of Hillfields Rd, had 12 sets of twins in May 1994 (SNSV vol 1 p259) (Daily Express May 26 1994 p27p). **First female awarded the Military Cross** Michelle Norris, 19, Royal Army Medical Corp, Prince of Wales', of Amblecote, June 11 2006 (BBC Midlands Today Dec 22 2006). **World authority on glass** Stan Eveson (1914-2004) of Collis Street, Amblecote, former director of the Thomas Webb glassworks, and 'one of the last outstanding figures in (Stourbridge) the town's glass industry' (E&S Feb 21 2004). **Amblecote's kindest** Ernest Stevens (1867-1957) and his wife Mary (nee Collins) (1869-1925), wealthy galvaniser of Quarry Bank and Stourbridge, where they were great benefactors. In 1928 Ernest gave a new pavilion to Stourbridge Cricket Club at their War Memorial Ground in Amblecote; and both were keen supporters and benefactors of Corbett Hospital (TB Oct 4 2007 p3p) (Ernest & Mary Stevens: The Continuing Legacy. Roy Peacock. 2007). **Strange but true!** Mrs Ada Hill of Lye, Stourbridge, brought a writ for libel on Dec 7 1973 halting distribution of 'A cage of shadow' the autobiography of her son Archie Hill, published by Hutchinson & Co, based in and around Amblecote, because she felt there were 'many derogatory remarks' about herself, and her character, though disguised, was clearly identifiable (County Express Dec 21 1973). **Amblecote's poorest** Oldswinford parish vestry provided a number of small houses for a parish workhouse in 1728, replaced by a new building in 1738 (BCM Spring 2007 p5). From 1836 the poor went to Stourbridge union workhouse (later Wordsley Hospital), Stream Road, Wordsley. **Choicest quote** DR Guttery in his From Broad-Glass to Cut Crystal: A History of the Stourbridge Glass Industry, 1956, writes 'Only in one very small area of the coalfield along the boundary between the two Swinfords is the famous fireclay (This fireclay was first mined in Amblecote and for long was known as 'Amblecote Glasshouses Pot Clay'; now it is 'Stourbridge Fireclay'.) mined; it was there the Lorrainers built their glass-houses.'

Church...

At Amblecote is Holy Trinity, **one of 4 such county dedications** (of ancient parish churches); **21st last ancient parish county church built** 1841-2 (if Amblecote is accepted as an original parish!). **Only church in the country faced with firebrick** Believed to be Holy Trinity, consecrated 1844 (TEBC2), but Quarry Bank church, consecrated 1847, was built with firebricks which came from Messrs Harper & Moore (info Stan Hill). **Most intriguing thing** A tapestry depicting 'Rebecca at the Well' given to a housemaid for her 21st birthday, 1920, by her employer, she in turn gave it to the church. It was painted by a Rebecca Beckley or Buckle, the employer's mother-in-law, and the Rebecca may be a representation of herself (TB Sept 26 2002 p21p). **The hidden memorial** That to Ensign Lyndon John Greer, killed at Cawnpore 1857; the monument, normally hidden from view, was exposed for a lecture on Sept 12 2007 (TB Sept 6 2007 p19p). Also note the memorial to Rev John William Crier (d1866 aged 55) first incumbent of Amblecote, who died suddenly after preaching in the church on Sunday Jan 28.

The area...

Amblecote was the **county's 154th largest parish** (actually a township of Old Swinford, a Worcestershire parish covering Stourbridge), consisting of 665 acres; **5th farthest parish away from the county town**, 23.1m; **extremist length** 1.2m, making it **14th shortest parish in the county**; **extremist width** 1.4m, making it **22nd= narrowest parish in the county**. **Chief settlement** Amblecote, a village and now suburban conurbation near Stourbridge. **Geology** AMBLECOTE - Middle Coal Measures (E), Bunter (Amblecote village and W), Permian (thin central band). **Highest point** Amblecote Bank at 433 feet. **Lowest point** 223 feet by the Stour at Platts. Amblecote was **56th most-populated Staffordshire parish in 1801** with 1,002; **59th in 1811** with 1,079; **61st in 1821** with 1,157; **61st in 1831** with 1,236; **50th in 1841** with 1,623; **46th in 1851** with 2,053; **41st in 1861** with 2,613; **41st in 1871** with 2,771; **43rd in 1881** with 2,808; **42nd in 1891** with 2,876; **39th in 1901** with 3,128.

Bentley & Bilston See Wolverhampton...
Bloxwich See Walsall...

Bobbington
Did you know that...

Bobbington's top folklore Halfpenny Green got its name as there was a well in the centre of the green for which withdrawers of water were expected to pay half a penny (N&Q Series ii 22 Aug 1857 iv p147). Others say the name is derived from rents (VCH vol 20 p65). The halfpenny was introduced in 1279. **Last day of ^{1}/2d. date-stamps** A special date-stamp was franked on 8,000 items posted in the country wall letter box by the Royal Oak Inn, at Halfpenny Green between 4.30pm on July 30 and 7.30pm on July 31 1969 to mark the last day of the halfpenny as legal tender. In addition, 42,000 items sent from Stourbridge Post Office on July 31st 1969 were franked with the same date-stamp. The date-stamp reads "Halfpenny Green, Stourbridge, Worcs." round the rim and "Last day of ^{1}/2d. 31 July, 1969" in the middle (County Express July 25 1969). **Last day of ^{1}/2d. special commemorative covers** In July 1969 Pin Green Scout Group, Stevenage, issued commemorative envelopes with their own special postmark to celebrate the end of the halfpenny and to raise Scout funds. Bobbington Post Office was sent 1,000 of them, and had the busiest period in its history dealing with 2,000 letters July 28-31. So popular were the envelopes Pin Green Scouts came to Halfpenny Green July 30-31 and sold more from a tent by the Royal Oak Inn. By Aug 22 1969 Stourbridge Post Office had sent and franked 69,626 envelopes, and the scouts had raised £500. Halfpenny stamps were withdrawn on June 30 1969 (County Express July 25 1969. Aug 1 1969. Aug 22 1969). **Only vineyard in Staffordshire** At Upper Whittimere Farm, started by Martin and Elaine Vickers in 1983 (PONP pp144-146). At the UK Wine of the Year Competition held by the UK Vineyard Association their 'Penny Black 2004' won Silver medal in 2005; other wines have won Bronze medals in 1990 (x2), 1991, 1992 (x2), 1993, 2004, 2005 (x2); whilst others received High Commendations in 2004 (x3). At the South West Vineyard Association annual wine contest a wine received a commended in 1990, and a Silver medal in 1991. At the 1992 Wine Magazine International Challenge their '1990 Huxelrebe' received a commendation (info certificates at Upper Whittimere Farm, 2008). **Staffordshire Best Kept Village winner (Small Village category) 2000** Bobbington, having won that year the South Staffordshire District (Small Village) category. **What Bobbington is famous for** Halfpenny Green Airport and a vineyard. The **name Bobbington**

A fanciful image of Bobbington: in the distance is the Black Country!

first appears in Domesday Book, 1086.

People...

Bobbington's most famous old worthy, producer of one of the earliest English examples of a Christmas card, contributor of the first double acrostic to the Illustrated London News Rev Edward Bradley, born Swan St, Kidderminster 1827, died Dec 12 1889, clergyman, novelist, illustrator and antiquarian; attended the new university at Durham. In 1846 he adopted the pseudonym 'Cuthbert Bede' based on the two Northumbrian saints. In 1847 Lambert of Newcastle published his design for a Christmas card, one of the earliest English examples. In 1856 he contributed the first double acrostic, forerunner of the modern crossword puzzle, to the Illustrated London News. His best-selling novel 'Mr Verdent Green' appeared in the late 1850s. Curate of Bobbington 1857-59. 'The Folk-lore of a Country Parish' (reprinted from Once a Week journal 1860), which contains much village folklore. It appears in a collection, published 1862, beginning with the novelette 'The Curate of Cranston', set in Bobbington:- After two years as a junior curate at Smokehampton (Wolverhampton) with his mother and cousin Margaret, Hugh Raymond takes up the curacy of Cranston. Whilst contemplating his lonely lot there one Christmas - too poor to return to Smokehampton to be with Margaret with whom he had fallen in love - he is called out to baptise twins in a hovel on the heath (the airfield area). Returning across the swamp he mistakes the sheet of a collapsed fire-balloon for the ghost of a murdered woman. The next Christmas, more happily raised to the rectory of Fairville (Enville), Hugh retells this story to his fiancee and mother (VCH vol 20 p67). **Unique equestrian competitor** Tracey Morley Jewkes of Whittimere Farm, sufferer from progressive rheumatoid arthritis, for competing in British Dressage, Paralympic Dressage, and British Eventing (TB May 4 2006 p31p). **Bobbington's most scorned woman** Elizabeth, wife of William Pratt of Bobbington, whose father John Ridge of Claverley, Shrops, brought a case of libel against Humphrey Elliots at the court of Star Chamber in 1621. The Bill of Complaint alleges Elliots plotted in Aug 1619 to marry her when she was aged about 17 and single, trying to secure for himself her large dowry. That he placed one Edward Hinkes as a servant in Ridge's household to entice her to court him. But shortly Hinkes acted for himself and got false witnesses to swear he had married Elizabeth. A number of Claverley villagers allegedly proceeded to spread rumours she was pregnant by Hinke, so tarnishing her virtue. At the same time a group of touring actors returned to the area and performed a play which seemed to mirror the story and mock Elizabeth. The case proved in favour of Elliots (Records of Early English Drama, edited by J Alan Somerset, 1994. WSL CB/Bobbington/1). **Woman who has her sketch book in the Staffordshire record office** Edith E Marion whose pencil sketches may show Bobbington scenes and old buildings, c1940 (D3373/6). **Bobbington's earliest recorded will** Belongs to William Marche ats Shakulton and is dated April 30 1558. **Bobbington's poorest** The parish was renting two thatched cottages (one a bakehouse to the other) and a garden for a workhouse, called the Forest House by 1826. In 1836 John Low of Commonside was removed to it at an expense of 5 shillings. In 1843 a parishioner was removed to Tettenhall workhouse. In July 1852 it was resolved to sell the cottages, the 'bakehouse' one then being described as a 'hovel' (D5148/3/1). In the new poor law system Bobbington was part of Seisdon Poor Law Union. **First persons in the parish register** William Newe and Dorothie Whorwood married Aug 13 1572. **Choicest quote** Rev Edward Bradley in his 'The Curate of Cranston' (1862, pages 1, 6) writes 'You would more readily have found Cranston in the County Map, than in the County itself. It was a leading peculiarity of its situation that it was eight miles distant from everywhere - from every town, at least ... Down in Cranston itself, the houses were dotted about irregularly, chiefly in detachments of twos and threes, with here and there, an attenuated farm-house, in keeping with the poverty of the district; and over everything was an air of damp, decay, and mildew. In the very centre of the swampy hollow, was the Church. It dated from early Norman days, and, after flourishing for many centuries, had begun to give way before the storms of time...'

Halfpenny Green Airfield...

First aircraft to land there March 1941 (TB Nov 2 2000 p26). **Halfpenny Green airfield's worst disaster** occurred on Aug 28 1972 in the 1972 Goodyear International Trophy Race when a plane crashed in Six Ashes Road killing Prince William of Gloucester (WMA vol 1 pp152-174a) (VCH vol 20 p67). **British skydiving record** Paul Hibberd, aged 26, of Cookley, near Kidderminster, who parachuted from more than 10,000 feet from a hot-air balloon on May 28 1978 landing in the middle of the airfield 6 minutes after his jump (E&S May 29 1978 p). **First British woman hand-glide pilot to be launched from a hot air balloon** Judy Leden, 20, of London, who glided from a balloon more than 5,000 feet high over the then Airport on Feb 22 1983 (E&S Feb 22 1983 p1p). **World record for most stacked hot air balloons** Five balloons in mid-air for a minute over Halfpenny Green airfield on May 9 1991, beating the old record of four (The Times May 10 1991 p1p). **World airship speed record** set over the Halfpenny Green airfield when Jim Dexter and Mike Kendrick reached 94.7km per hour in early 2000 (Wolverhampton Chronicle March 10 2000 p15). **First jet to land at the airfield in almost 10 years** A Cessna Citation executive jet from Staverton airport, near Cheltenham, on March 10 1978 (E&S March 10 1978). **'Quietest and greenest' airport in the UK** How chief executive of Wolverhampton Business Airport, Paul Whelan, described his proposed expansion of the airfield in May 2003, trying to make it a regional passenger-carrying airport (E&S May 9 2003 p23).

Church...

At Bobbington is Holy Cross, **one of two such county dedications** (of ancient parish churches); **8th= oldest county church** dating from 1100. **Most notable thing** Effigy of a man on slab in the porch - said to be Philip Fitz-Helgot d1213. The parish chest, C12, hewn out of a solid oak log, and containing two compartments, the lids of which are almost covered with wrought-iron bands (LGS p87). **In the church-**

yard Two of the most ancient yews in the county (LGS p87), and a stone coffin by the main footpath, taken from under the church.

The area...

County's 113th largest parish, consisting of 2,189 acres; **19th= farthest parish away from the county town,** 19.9m SSW; extremist length 4.2m; **extremist width** 3.8m. **Chief settlement** Bobbington, a small village which follows the cup-shaped road. **Geology** BOBBINGTON - Bunter (N third), Premian (S rest). **Highest point** Tuckhill at 574 feet. **Lowest point** 253 feet at Halfpenny Green. Bobbington was **114th most-populated Staffordshire parish in 1801** with 381; **119th in 1811** with 366; **119th in 1821** with 393; **117th in 1831** with 426; **117th in 1841** with 396; **118th in 1851** with 385; **116th in 1861** with 401; **115th in 1871** with 396; **119th in 1881** with 373; **120th in 1891** with 345; **122nd in 1901** with 303.

Brierley Hill See Kingswinford...

The opening of the Liverpool and Manchester Railway, 1830. The Jack of Hilton.

Bushbury
Did you know that...

Bushbury's top folklore The ghost of a cavalier on horseback reputedly haunts the lanes about Northicote Farm - possibly he is a royalist aristocrat in hiding after the battle of Worcester (1651). In 1983 a driver reputedly swerved to avoid him and overturned his car (info Carol Arnall). Another story concerns the Friar's Stone in Bushbury church (or possibly Friars Tomb). It was opened up prior to 1680 and reputedly caused such a localised earthquake which made the pewter in peoples houses clatter and the cauldron at Bushbury Hall leap from the ground (NHS p143). **Essington's top folklore**

That buried treasure lies somewhere in or near Essington Wood, one mile NE of Essington. A Spanish agent, Emilio Ripoll, working for revolutionary forces, trying to eject the Spanish from Cuba, came to England in c1900 to procure arms. But before being captured by pursuing counter forces he hid the money (French Francs, Spanish Pesetas and French gold coins - Louisdors) in the vicinity of Essington Wood. Ripoll could not precisely remember where. From prison he wrote to Thomas Cope, landlord of the Old Mitre Inn, to ask his assistance in locating it. Cope eventually declined to help although the family kept the correspondence. The buried treasure, if it really does exist, has never been found (TB March 1993 p17ps of the pub and letter). **Strangest jocular tenure service custom in Staffordshire or in country** Perhaps that involving the lord of Essington who took a goose every New Year's Day to the lord of Hilton and drove it round a fire three times whilst a little hollow brass figure kneeling called 'Jack of Hilton' blows fire (SCSF p5). **What Bushbury is famous for** Being a hiding place of Charles II after the battle of Worcester, railway engineering, and Goodyear tyres. The **name Bushbury first appears** in 994. **'Among the stateliest' great houses of Staffordshire** Moseley Old Hall (Staffordshire Handbook c1966 p15). **Unique derivation for a surname** Oxley will be from Oxley in this parish (PDS). **Only surviving post mill in Staffordshire** At Windmill Farm, W of Essington village. **'The Bushbury Bother'** Appears to have been the column in Midland Evening News about 1898-1904 for Bushbury news. It was sometimes called 'A Bushbury Bother' and was aptly named as invariably the stories were about some bother from heated vestry meetings to school board squabbles to loss of public footpaths (SRO D5403/2 - Album of newspaper cuttings relating to Bushbury). **Staffordshire's first motor car speeding offence** Perhaps Joseph Lisle along Stafford Road in June 1899 accompanied by his father E Lisle of Moseley Hall. Allegedly, 6 mph over the national speed limit, travelling at 20 mph they made Mr Webberley and his daughter of Chapel Ash swerve and fall off their horse and cart into a ditch, and were fined 40s and costs. In Sept 1901 Lisle, then a motor-maker, was caught again by three policemen timing his speed to 20 mph at midnight along Stafford Road. He was fined 20s and costs (SA June 17 1899 p7 col 7. Sept 28 1901 p7 col 4). **Oldest taxi firm in Wolverhampton 2003** Bennett's Taxis, of Bushbury, founded 1940 by Jack Bennett (d2000), and finished operating in 2003 (E&S July 3 2003 p12). **First houses built of Fallings Park Garden Suburb** 18-28 Victoria Road, designed by Wolverhampton architect WJ Oliver, and were complete when officially opened by the Bishop of Lichfield on Feb 26 1908 (TB May 12 2005 pp14-15). **One of the most deprived parts of Central England** The Low Hill Estate (take a brain sip website 2006). **First school in the country to be failed by OFSTED** Northicote Secondary School in Northwood Park Road, 1993. **'one of the worst schools in England and Wales'** Moreton School, Old Fallings Lane, but had improved by 2003 so as to no longer deserve the title (BBC website). **UK's Number 1 Sandwich Manufacturer 2006-7** Freshway, Stafford Court, Stafford Road, Wobaston. **Highest score in 24 hours of bowling by 1994** was 212,692 achieved by a team of six at Strykers Pleasure Bowl, Bushbury on June 20-21 1992 (GBR 1994 p244).

People...

Bushbury's most famous old worthy Thomas Whitgreave (1618-1702). Recusant and protector of Charles II. Lawyer by 1645, but unlikely to have been able to practice as he was a Catholic. Charles II sheltered at his home Moseley Old Hall after the battle of Worcester, 1651. Also there were his mother, the Benedictine John Huddleston and three pupils. As a reward, he was granted an annual pension, 1666, later commuted to his son; reprieved from prosecution for recusancy by royal order; exempted from punitive legislation following the Popish Plot; and made Gentleman Usher to Queen Catherine of Braganza. Known in his family as 'the Protector' he was buried in Bushbury church, where on the south wall of the nave is a tablet commemorating him (Staffordshire Catholic History 1980). **World's first railway casualty** William Huskisson (1770-1830), M.P. for several constituencies, including Liverpool; son of William Huskisson (d1790) - the Huskisson's held the Oxley estate, Bushbury, until 1793. The incident happened at the opening of the Liverpool and Manchester Railway, Sept 15 1830. Huskisson rode down the line in the same train as the Duke of Wellington. At Parkside, close to Newton-le-Willows, Lancs, the train stopped to observe a cavalcade on the adjacent line. Several members of the Duke's party stepped onto the trackside to observe more closely. Huskisson went forward to greet the Duke. As Huskisson was exiting his car, George Stephenson's locomotive Rocket approached on the parallel track. Huskisson was unable to get out of the engine's way in time, and his left leg was crushed by it; he died a few hours later from the wounds. A curious fact about Huskisson is that some years before his death, he narrowly escaped being killed when a horse fell on him during his honeymoon (Wikipedia 2007) (W p170 note) (The England. Spring 1994 p57p). **First person to use wills for genealogical information for a publication** Sir William Dugdale in his 'Baronage of England', early C17, when he made use of the records of the Prerogative Court of Canterbury. In 1623 he married Margery, 2nd daughter of John Huntbach of The Showells, Bushbury, and spent the first year of his married life there (HOWM pp96-97) (Wills and their Whereabouts. Anthony J Camp. 1974. pxxxi). **'bred some of the best horses of his day'** Eskricke Philips (d1871) of Bushbury Hill, according to Sportsman journal, he was the owner of of the celebrated stallions Sir Hercules, Lifeboat, Gunboat, Koh-i-noor. The Sportsman notes however he was no gamester, and even when his horses were morally sure to win, he seldom invested more than a "pony" (SA April 15 1871 p7 col 7). **Bushbury's villains** Samuel Taylor of Bushbury who so beat his wife, Mary, that her life was in danger and a petitioned March 8 1775 her local JPs to abstract sureties that he would reframe from beating her again (D3362/6/1). Rev F Aston, who high-handedly dismissed the much-respected headmaster of the National School in Bushbury

Lane, Francis Burton, on Dec 7 1897, despite parishioners' protests. **UK's youngest recipient of an ASBO to 2003** Luke Straker (b1992), of Old Fallings Crescent, Low Hill, who terrorised people on his housing estate, who received a Anti-Social Behaviour Order in Jan 2003 (E&S Jan 13 2003 pp1,5. June 6 2003 p5). **Bushbury's vagabond** Sarah Poulton (b c1739), born Reading, was bound to a William Mansfield of Bushbury, because her father was a Bushbury native, in c1747. Some years later she was apprenticed to a buckle-maker in Wolverhampton but ran away from him. After numerous casual jobs - some without Mansfield's knowledge - she ended up begging in Bristol, from where she was forcibly removed to Bushbury her parish of settlement in Dec 1761 (D3362/5/3). **First serving head teacher of a state school ever to be knighted** Geoff Hampton of Northicote Secondary School, 1998 (BBC Radio 4. World at One. Nov 1 1996) (I Jan 26 1998 p13) (Who's Who 1999). **Collection Crew of the Year 2007** Les Dewsbury, 52 of Wednesfield, and Roger Collins, 57 of Finchfield, refuge collectors in the Bushbury, Heath Town, and Low Hills areas. The award was made at the national Awards for Excellence in Recycling and Waste Management (E&S Oct 27 2007 p12pcs). **Bushbury's kindest** Francis Collie who left rental to the poor of the parish to be distributed at or before the Saturday next before Good Friday to 30 poor inhabitants, 1625. **Essington's saddest** William Nicholls, an awl-maker who lived alone in a cottage at Hobble End, Newtown, who had died unnoticed in 1898 and was subsequently gnawed by rats. The old man had lived in abject poverty, with only a few potatoes to eat, and was apparently of weak intellect. He had refused to go to the union workhouse (SA April 2 1898 p7 col 5). **Bushbury's poorest** A receipt survives for milk delivered to a workhouse in Bushbury in the early C19 (D3362/5/3). In 1838 a house belonging to Bushbury poor, perhaps the former parish workhouse, stood at a road fork in the present Bee Lane and Primrose Ave area (WSL. SMS 417, tithe map). From 1836 until 1870s the poor went to union workhouses at Penkridge, and then at Cannock. **Bushbury's earliest recorded will** Belongs to William Stoke, and is dated April 3 1538. **First person in the parish register** Henry Gravenor, brother to Mr Walter Grauvenor, buried Feb 5 1561. **Choicest quote** Author and comedienne, Meera Syal (b1963), was brought up in Essington. It is Tollington in her autobiography 'Anita and Me' 1996 in which she aptly describes the place of her childhood 'We were heading in the opposite direction, northwards down the hill, away from the posh, po-faced mansions and towards the nerve centre of Tollington, where Mr Ormerod's grocery shop, the Working Men's Club, the diamond-paned Methodist church and the red brick school jostled for elbow room with the two-up-two downs, whose outside toilets backed onto untended meadows populated with the carcasses of abandoned agricultural machinery'.

Goodyear Tyres...

First tyre produced at Bushbury Dec 1927, Goodyear having bought the Macfarlane & Robinson hollow-ware site in July 1927. **Britain's 2nd largest producer of aircraft tyres by 1940** Goodyear Tyres. **One of the largest employers in Wolverhampton 1971** Goodyear Tyres with more than 5,000 people. The plant closed in 2000 and relocated to Tyre-Fort, Birmingham (Documenting the Workshop of the World. Nov 2007).

Churches...

At BUSHBURY is St Mary, **one of 23 such county dedications** (the **most common dedication in the county**); **61st= oldest ancient parish county church** dating from the C13 or roughly 1250. **Most notable things** In the alcove near the altar (Founder's Arch) - defaced recumbent effigy of Sir Hugh de Byshbury in priest's attire and hence the figure has become known as the Friar's Stone. In the SE corner of the chancel is a badly preserved incised slab, depicting the figure of a lady - Jane (d1608) wife of William Allicock daughter of Sir William Smith of Sibbertoft Knt (SHOS vol 2 p179) (GNHS p177). In the lower part of the chancel an incised slab depicting Francis Colley (d1626) in a canonical gown, vicar of Bushbury for 38 years; there was also an incised effigy on a slab to his son John d1593 (SHOS vol 2 p179). Notice the memorial to William Huskisson (d1790) and his wife Elizabeth (d1774 aged 31), parents of the world's first railway casualty (see above), also that of their 2nd son Richard who died in Guadaloupe 1794 (SHOS vol 2 pp179-180) (SMC p170) (GNHS p177). **In the churchyard** The grave of Sarah and Lewis Clutterbuck is known as 'the witches grave' for its sinister stone carving marks (TB Jan 13 2005 p11). **Bushbury's longest-serving vicar** Thomas Hall, serving at least about 37 years, c1693-c1730. At LOW HILL is The Good Shepherd (1955). At FORDHOUSES is St James (1967). At ESSINGTON is St John the Evangelist (1932-3); the foundation stone was laid by Mrs JC Forrest in remembrance of John Charles Forrest 1932. At OXLEY is The Epiphany (1960). At COVEN HEATH is a Mission Church.

The area...

Bushbury is the county's 39th largest parish, consisting of 6,574 acres; **65th closest parish to the county town**, 10.9m S; **extremist length** 6.5m, making it **13th= longest parish in the county**; **extremist width** 7.4m, making it **7th= widest parish in the county**. **Chief settlement** Bushbury, a hamlet; but there were other focal centres, equally as big; all are now entirely engulfed by Wolverhampton suburbs; the other township, Essington, farmed and coal-mined. **Geology** BUSHBURY - Keuper Sandstones (W half), Bunter (Low Hill-Bushbury village-Moseley Hall, and extreme E), Permian (Old Fallings-Bushbury Hill); ESSINGTON - Keuper Sandstones (extreme W), Permian (Essington village), Upper Coal Measures (E of M6), Middle Coal Measures (far E). **Highest point** 623 feet NE of Essington Hall Farm. **Lowest point** 335 feet at Coven Mill. Bushbury was **64th most-populated Staffordshire parish in 1801** with 857; **54th in 1811** with 1,143; **58th in 1821** with 1,229; **60th in 1831** with 1,275; **55th in 1841** with 1,509; **54th in 1851** with 1,632; **50th in 1861** with 2,051; **48th in 1871** with 2,283; **38th in 1881** with 3,065; **36th in 1891** with 3620; **35th in 1901** with 5,059.

Clent & Broom
Did you know that...

Clent's top folklore The legend of St Kenelm. Kenelm was proclaimed king of Mercia aged 7 or 8 when his father, Kenulf (or Cenwulf) died. But this made his sister, Quendreda - wishing to be queen herself - jealous. She persuaded her lover Ascobert to take him into a wooded furrow on Knoll Hill, near Clent, and be killed. Ascobert buried the body at the murder scene; a place only discovered when a dove rose from Kenelm's severed head and travelled to Rome where it dropped a scroll on the high altar of St Peter's or some say at the Pope's feet with the Latin words

> In Clent Cow-pasture under a thorn
> Of head bereft lies Kenelm, King born.

As soon as messengers, sent to England to find the body, found it at nearby spring (St Kenelm's Well) reputedly burst open. Kenelm's body was taken for burial to Winchcombe Abbey, Glous (a foundation of his father), where in later years at the saint's shrine, miracles are said to have taken place (CCION no. 5 pp1-5). **Earliest guide to the Clent Hills** 'Guide to the Clent Hills' by William Timings, 1835 (TB June 28 2001 p25). **Only parish council in the country to have its own coat of arms** Clent, presented to the parish council in 1999 to mark the Millennium; the coat of arms carved in lime by John Harrison of Malvern hangs in the Parish Hall (BCM summer 2000 p78) (CCION no. 14 pp2,14). **Only Staffordshire garden designed**

St Kenelm, Clent coat of arms, Jack, the Woodman statue

by Gertrude Jekyll Field House, Clent, when Arthur Kendrick engaged architects Forbes and Tait to redesign the grounds, they in turn commissioned her, 1919, producing notably the Italian Garden (CCION no. 11 pp7-10). **Jack, the Woodman** 10-foot high stone statue in the garden of The Woodman Inn, Clent from 1964 to 1969, when poorly protected from the weather it was demolished, save the axe was kept as a memento. From 1891 the statue had stood in a first-floor niche alongside the main entrance to The Woodman Inn, Easy Row, Birmingham. On demolition of the pub in 1964 Mitchells and Butlers brewery relocated the statue to Clent (County Express July 25 1969. Sept 26 1969). **What Clent is famous for** The amazing panoramas from the top of the Clent Hills, and associations with St Kenelm. The **name Clent first appears** in Domesday Book, 1086.

People...

The Nine worthies of Clent Following medieval conceit to esteem nine worthies Ralph Brocklebank identifies nine obvious candidates for Clent and most have memorials in the church:- **1.** John Cox (1630-1705), of the Gate House, the forerunner of Clent Grove, on the site of the present Home Farm. He served as Trustee on various village charities. **2.** John Amphlett (1656-1705), founder of the Clent Charity School. **3.** William Waldron (1697-1764) of Walton House, owner of much land at Clent and Clent Hall. **4.** A member of the Durant family (they had acquired Clent Hall from the Waldrons) built the Infants School in 1868 and bequeathed it to the village. **5.** Charles Henry Crompton-Roberts (1832-91), inherited Field House by marriage; had a distinguished career as JP, Sheriff and MP in South Wales. **6.** John Amphlett (1845-1918), author of 'A Short History of Clent' (1907, see below). **7.** Sir George Ferguson Chance (1854-1933) of Clent Grove, Sheriff of Worcs 1910, gave land for the Parish Hall, and the Church of England Children's Home, Summerfield Rd. **8.** Richard Stuart Todd (1871-1954) of Clent Grove, later of Clent House Farm, Woodman Lane; Sheriff of Worcs 1926. **9.** Michael Henry Wilson (1901-85), polymath Quaker of Birmingham who set up Sunfield Children's Homes at Clent Grove from 1932 (CCION no. 20). **Strange but true!** The house of John Nickolls of Clent was robbed. Nickolls wrestled a gun off one of the thieves who then foolishly called out to his accomplice "Wassell, Wassell, come up". Hearing a man named Wassell was imprisoned at Wolverhampton Nickolls went to the gaol there and identified him. Joseph Wassell of Stourbridge (b c1767) was hung at Stafford on March 27 1790 (WSL crime bill poster). **The 'Blind Bard of Clent'** Nathan Withy, who resided in the 'Cottage in the Dale' rent free at the benevolence of Lord Lyttelton in c1805, styled himself as this; he may have been the author of 'The Hills of Clent' published in the journal 'The Phytologist' 1858, which begins 'Here sweetly smile the hill and dale,

The landscape all around;

Two towering mounts:- the fruit vale,

Clent Hills, with fir-trees crown'd'. He styled his daughter the **'Shepherdess of the Clent Alps'** (Guide to the Clent Hills. William Timings. 1835) (CCION no. 13 p1) (Clent Celebrated. 1999. pp4-5) (BCM

Spring 2003 p33). The **Lone Ranger of the Clent Hills** George Weston (b1908), warden for the Hills from 1949, helped in his task by his dog, Flash. The Hills were owned by Clent Hills Conservation 1886-1957, Worcestershire CC 1957-9, National Trust 1959- (CCION no. 17. pp16-17p). **Clent's heroes** Three sons of James and Sarah-Anne Roberts of Hill Cottage (alias Ranger's Cottage) on Clent Hill, later of The Leasowes, Church Ave, Clent, who lost their lives in WW1:- Lance Corporal Major William Roberts, Royal Fusiliers (1885-1916 on the Somme), Pte Henry Roberts, Royal Marines Light Infantry (1889--1915, of wounds received at Gallipoli), Pte Arthur Roberts, Royal Army Medical Corps (1897-1917 killed in action). They are remembered on Clent War Memorial in the churchyard. Frank born in 1908 was too young to serve in the Great War (CCION no. 17). **Clent's villain** John Heath convicted of stealing clothes from Clent, 1723, who was deported for seven years at the Summer Stafford Assizes (CCION no. 18 pp1-5). **Clent's villainess** Nurse Elizabeth (Eliza) Brandish (1859-1927), born Morton in the Marsh, who created a stir in 1898 with national headlines like "Alleged Murder by Clent Nurse" when she was accused of murdering her illegitimate infant son Rees Thomas Yella Edwards. After his birth in 1895 she put him into the care of a Mrs Post. The following year Brandish became Clent village nurse. In 1898 with Mrs Post unable to care for him anymore Brandish collected him. The boy was last seen on a train journey back to the Midlands with his mother. Clent was so torn between those in support of Brandish and those not the vicar was forced to preach from the pulpit for compassion. The son's body was exhumed twice. After retrials, eventually Brandish was acquitted on lack of evidence (CCION no. 2 pp8-12). **Clent's kindest** John Amphlett who founded Amphlett's School, Clent, for six poor children by deed Nov 30 1704. It was later the Mixed Junior School, then Clent Parochial School. The site for the school from 1974, titled Clent Primary Parochial School, is in Bromsgrove Road (TB July 14 2005 p12). Alfred Roberts (1835-1904) of Field House, Clent, devoted himself to the welfare of others, both in own parish and the wider area, supporting the village's Sunday School, and the Parish Hall (1906) is to his memory (TB Oct 26 2006 p15). Cyril Coles, woodman, born Broome 1914 moved to Clent when an infant, who did good turns for everyone in the village in the way of building fences, felling trees, building garden furniture (TB April 8 2004 p11p). **Broome's kindest** John Harris, the elder, of Red Hill who by will dated 1701/2 gave rental on land for bread for three poor church-going labourers dwelling in Broome once a week for 40 weeks. This ran until it was transformed into a St Thomas' day dole for the poor. **Clent's favourite historian** John Amphlett (1845-1918), born Whitehall Mayes, Kent. Author of 'A Short History of Clent' (1890). Resided at Clent Cottage. Contributed 'Clent Place Names and Field Names', and 'the Parochial Records of Clent' to the Midland Antiquary in 1882 and 1884 (CCION no. 15 portraits). **Worst singer in Britain or the world** Mrs Hazel Saunders of Clent between at least 1981-86 (GBR 1981 p102. 1986 p95). **English Amateur Golf champion 1927, runner-up 1935, Walker Cup team**

captain 1928, 1936 Dr William Twedell (1897-1985), of Hackman's Gate, Broome (County Express Nov 7 1985). **First person in Clent parish register** William Nashe, buried March 2 1562; although Amphlett says John son of Richard and Elizabeth Bodlye, baptised Oct 25 1562, is the first legible entry (Short History of Clent). **Choicest quote (Clent)** Elihu Burritt, the American consul in Birmingham in his Walks in the Black Country and its green borderland (1868) dallied in Halesowen's ancient church and Shenstone's Leasowes before leaving Halesowen and proceeding saw 'As the Clent Hills were tinged with purple mist in which the setting sun was sinking in the West.' **(Broome)** John Noake (1816-94), antiquary, born Sherborne, Dorset. Journalist for Worcestershire newspapers from 1838. He very succinctly summed up Broom in his History of Worcestershire (1868) as 'No manufacturers, or public works, no local squire, no mansion, no Dissenters chapel, no church-rate disturbances, no Fenianism, or agitation of any sort, distinguishes this little slice of happy land.'

Churches...

At Clent is St Leonard, **one of 5 such county dedications** (of ancient parish churches); **37th= oldest county church** dating from 1170. **Note in the church** A small model of the church in a glass case. Tapestries covering furnishings with 1,078,782 stitches which took 13 woman 1,660 hours in 14 months were completed in 1958 (Birmingham Mail March 12 1958 ps). **In the churchyard** The graves of John Guthrie Gifford d1929 General Manager of Kenrick & Jefferson Ltd, West Bromwich; and that of Albert Webster accidently drowned March 31 1969. **Clent's longest-serving vicar (also vicar of Rowley Regis)** Thomas Walker, who served for 50 years, 1669-1719. **In Broome church** - Note the memorial to Anne Hill (d1804), which is by Flaxman. It shows a young woman seated in profile on the ground. Pevsner noted the beautifully paced and lettered inscription (BOEW p113). **Broome's longest-serving vicar** Edward Dudley, serving 48 years, 1810-58; he had been curate from 1802. At Holy Cross Green is R.C. St Oswald and Wulstan, opened Feb 28 1927 (CCION no. 16).

St Kenelm and his Wake...

Earliest mention of St Kenelm In the Vita Kenelmi Regis Merciorum manuscript (TB May 31 2007 p20). **Unique custom** The defunct St Kenelm's Wake or the Crab Wake in the churchyard of St Kenelm; the inhabitants pelted each other with crab apples, commonly known as Crabbing the Parson, for rarely did the clergyman escape being hit by crab apples as he went to and from chapel. **Last parson to be 'crabbed'** Rev John Todd (curate of St Kenelm's 1801-1833), for people were beginning to throw more than just apples by the period of his curacy. The custom was revived in 1958 (County Express July 12 1958).

The area...

Clent was the county's 108th largest parish, consisting of 2,365 acres; along with Broom it was surrounded by Worcestershire until transferred to it in 1844; it was **2nd farthest parish away from the**

county town, 26.1m S; its **extremist length** was 2.1m; **extremist width** 3.7m. The **chief settlement** Clent, a pretty hillside village, but Holy Cross and Lower Clent are more populous. **Highest point** Walton Hill at 1033 feet. **Best panorama in the county** Clent Hill in the Clent Hills, 1013 feet high, 0.5m NNE of Clent, claimed by George Bates of Stone Street, Dudley, in the County Express, Sept 1906, to take in Snowdon (CCION no. 7 pp2-5). **Lowest point** 262 feet by Sweet Pool. CLENT was **73rd most-populated Staffordshire parish in 1801** with 738; **79th in 1811** with 737; **73rd in 1821** with 885; **72nd in 1831** with 922; **75th in 1841** with 918; **77th in 1851** with 937; **75th in 1861** with 966; **78th in 1871** with 921; **77th in 1881** with 972; **77th in 1891** with 997; **75th in 1901** with 978. BROOM was **143rd= most-populated Staffordshire parish in 1801** with 99; **141st= in 1811** with 110; **140th in 1821** with 134; **144th in 1831** with 110; **141st in 1841** with 129; **142nd in 1851** with 143; **143rd in 1861** with 118; **143rd in 1871** with 136; **145th in 1881** with 129; **145th in 1891** with 109; **146th in 1901** with 108.

Allan Bennett, the National Sausage Champion of Champions 2004, and George Russell in 1938 holding one of his Lupins

Codsall
Did you know that...

Codsall's top folklore A stone slab, called Deadwoman's Grave, resting on the grass verge at the end of Husphins Lane, near Little Harriot's Hayes Farm, Codsall Wood, is thought to be over 200 years old. It is supposed to mark the site or grave of a murdered woman whose ghost haunts the locality. Near by was a cottage called Dead Woman's Grave. **What Codsall is famous for** Lupins, particularly the Russell strain of Lupin developed at Codsall by George Russell, affected by the medicinal springs in the Codsall Wood area (Staffordshire: Shire County Guide. Peter Heaton. 1986). The assassination here of Rex Farran by a letter bomb sent by the Stern Gang in 1948, although they had meant to kill his brother. **Unique green colour paint** Manders Paints of Wolverhampton especially produced Pendrell green for Frank Gaskell of Pendrell Hall, 1926. The **name Codsall first appears** in Domesday Book, 1086. Codsall. **Staffordshire Best Kept Village winner (Large Village category) 1972, 1974, 1983** Codsall; in 1993 Codsall won the South Staffordshire District (Large Village) category.

Church...

At Codsall is St Nicholas, **one of 3 such county dedications** (of ancient parish churches); **61st= oldest ancient parish county church** dating from the C13 or roughly 1250. **Most notable thing in church** Gilded table-tomb of Walter Wrottesley (d1630), - unusual as it has no effigies of Wrottesley's wives (LGS p116). **In the churchyard** Two of the very ancient yew trees historian Stebbing Shaw noted in SHOS were still surviving in the 1990s. There is also a sundial on old cross shaft. At Codsall Wood is St Peter (c1885). **Codsall's longest-serving vicar** Matthew Kemsey, curate for 46 years, 1800-46.

People...

Codsall's most famous old worthy Walter Wrottesley (1578-1630). Gentleman and lord of Wrottesley. Sheriff of Staffordshire 1598. Commissioner for collecting the Aid of the Fifteenth and Tenth granted by Parliament for the Spanish War, and Justice of the Peace for Staffordshire 1600-13. He was perhaps deprived from other public offices having Catholic sympathies, and may have been one of the gentlemen Sir Amias Poulett thought would be a bad influence on Mary Queen of Scots if she was imprisoned locally. At his death he held various manors, tithes and oblations including Codsall, as well as the prebends and site of Tettenhall Collegiate church. On the 11th December he was buried at Codsall under a "brightly painted and golded" altar tomb bearing an effigy of him wearing a helmet, and a gauntlet at his feet. **Codsall's villain, 'Codsall Will'** William Edwards, presumably of Codsall, an alleged accomplice of Thomas Powell. Powell murdered Ann Spencer at Gorse Cottage, Cannock Road, Essington in 1824. At his trial, he claimed he had been given the stolen clothes and 1/6d. which indicted him, by 'Codsall Will' to pawn at a pawn shop. Convicted, and sentenced to be hung, he still denied the murder, and implicated 'Codsall Will' to the last (TB June 22 2006 p26). **Codsall's hero** Lieut Raymond T Daniels of The Lodge, Codsall, 22, South Staffs Regt, who was award the M.C. for conspicuous gallantry and devotion to duty whilst in charge of a trench mortar battery. He attended Wolverhampton Grammar School and was employed in the Land Valuation Office, Dudley District. In the War he was twice wounded (ELSONSS p180). **Codsall's kindest** Barry Ellis, who died of Leukaemia aged 15 in Sept 1980 in the Children's Ward of The Royal Hospital, Wolverhampton. He was a pupil at Codsall High School. When he knew he was dying he withdrew all the money from his bank account and bought a bicycle for his sister, and presents for his parents and aunt. Then he sent £100 to Jimmy Savile's appeal for Stoke Mandeville Hospital. In a letter to Mrs Ellis, a nurse wrote "I have been on the ward for 11 years and no patient has ever moved me like your son... He had so much courage and dignity." (BBC 2 'The Easter Experience' April 17 1981) (E&S April 17 1981 p6p). **Codsall's bravest** Miss Irene Burgess of Parkes Ave, Codsall, 63, who saved the life of her neighbour Mrs Doreen Hughes, 45, whose clothes caught fire, turning her into a ball of fire in her garden. Miss Burgess' mother, Hilda, 85, also attended the incident. Irene was awarded a certificate for bravery from the Society for the Protection of Life, 1978 (E&S March 10 1978 p1p. April 11 1979 p11p). **19th President of the Royal Academy of Arts** Sir Charles Wheeler (d1974), sculptor, born in a cottage in Church Road, Codsall 1892, who served as President 1956-66. He designed the great bronze doors of the Bank of England, a figure of Ariel on the dome at the corner of Princes and Lothbury Streets, and the gilded springbok of South Africa House in Trafalgar Square, as well as works for Rhodes House in Oxford, India House, Aldwych, and the statute of Lady Wulfruna outside St Peter's at Wolverhampton (Staffordshire Handbook c1966 p41) (TB Sept 7 2006 p27). **Staffordshire's first motor car fatality** Perhaps Thomas Bedward, 63, farm labourer at Oaken Farm. On July 13 1901 he was putting straw on a rick in a field near the roadside when the sound of horns from two cars startled a horse which bolted bringing his ladder down. He fell to the ground and was later removed from the General Hospital, Wolverhampton, to Wolverhampton Workhouse who were not informed adequately of his condition, and he subsequently died of his injuries (SA Aug 10 1901 p5 col 3). **One of Codsall's best known public figures** Edith Cockerill (b1881), of Wood Road, pupil teacher from the age of 12, remaining a teacher at the same school until she was 60. She helped found Codsall Civic Society and was its first president; commandant of the Codsall Red Cross. She lived until at least the age of 96, never having a television, nor travelled much out of Codsall, and never aboard (Wolverhampton Chronicle Jan 14 1977 photo). **BBC TV's Young Scientists of the Year 1975** Wendy Heath, of Wayside Acres, and Jane Darling of Wilkes Road, both 15 of Codsall Comprehensive School (E&S Feb, March 1975, press cutting in Codsall Library). **National Sausage Champion of Champions 2004** Allan Bennett, 65, butcher of Station Road, Codsall with a winning recipe for a pork and caramelised onion sausage. In addition, he won four gold medals at the 2003 National Sausage Competition (E&S March 12 2003 p21p) (TB Feb 5 2004 p14p). **'one of Britain's oldest women', 'Black Country's oldest woman' 2003** Hilda Tudor (1895-2003) who reached her 108th birthday on April 3 2003, when residing at Springfield Residential Home, Oaken Drive, Codsall. Originally of Wellington, Shrops, later of Wolverhampton; the oldest women in the UK in 2003 was aged 111 (E&S April 4 2003 p15p. July 9 2003 p1pc). **Champion Shepherd** Colin House, 59, of Codsall Wood, who is blind (BBC Midlands Today 27 April 2007). **Codsall's**

poorest A poorhouse by the late C18, on the Wolverhampton road east of Codsall village, was probably the same as the workhouse mentioned in 1823, and a building near the Wheel Inn called Old Workhouse in 1861 (VCH vol 20 p86). From 1836 the poor went to Seisdon union workhouse. **First person in the parish register** John son of Laurence Corden of Oaken baptised Nov 1 1587. **Codsall's earliest recorded will** Belongs to Roger Rostones, and is dated July 22 1663. **Choicest quote** D Banks in the Free Village News, April 2002 (distributed free in the surrounding area), remembers Bilbrook of their childhood 'Back we go again to the village green, to take a walk back through time down Bilbrook Road, where Lane Green First School now stands. Not many buildings stood in this road sixty years ago; the 1930s saw the shops appear opposite the church, and a few more houses started to spring up in the years to follow on the same side as the shops. On the other side of the lane where the school stands now was nothing but fields stretching out towards Codsall, with the odd farmhouse scattered about.'

The area...

County's 90th largest parish, consisting of 2,994 acres; **73rd= closest parish to the county town**, 11.8m SSW; **extremist length** 3m; **extremist width** 3.2m. **Chief settlement** Codsall, a large commuter-belt (for Wolverhampton) village. **Geology** MOST - Keuper Sandstones with intrusion bands of Keuper Red Marls (NW fringes stretching S to Oaken Lawn and E to Codsall village). **Highest points** 482 feet at Kingswood Common and Codsall Wood. Church Hill (453 or 442 feet) is said to be the **highest point until Russia is reached** (St Nicholas' Church, Codsall: A Brief History) (SVB p57). **Lowest point** 341 feet on the boundary by Moat Brook near Bilbrook. Codsall was **84th most-populated Staffordshire parish in 1801** with 589; **78th in 1811** with 739; **72nd in 1821** with 903; **66th in 1831** with 1115; **68th in 1841** with 1,096; **66th in 1851** with 1,195; **69th in 1861** with 1,204; **69th in 1871** with 1,313; **66th in 1881** with 1,398; **63rd in 1891** with 1,436; **64th in 1901** with 1,452.

Coseley See Sedgley...
Cradley Heath See Rowley Regis...

Darlaston
Did you know that...

Darlaston's top folklore The story of how a pocket watch dropped by a traveller in a field near Darlaston frightened the local people - for they did not known what it was - has been passed down in Darlaston folklore. Those that heard the watch ticking thought it was a demon grasshopper and that judgement day had come (FTWM pp116-120). **'most luxurious and extravagant of the Black Country towns'** Darlaston, when gun locks were in demand in the Napoleonic Wars (TB Aug 8 2002 p10). **'one of the largest villages in Staffordshire'**

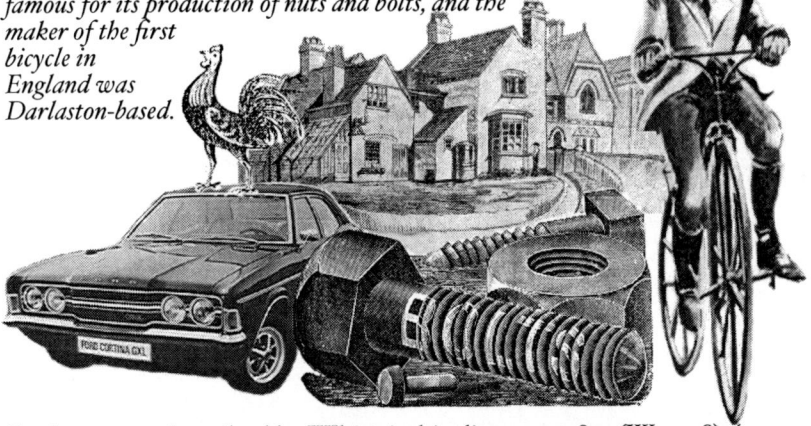

Old buildings in Pinfold Street. The cock represents the church weathercock. Those who tried to steal it earned the nickname 'Darlaston Geese'. The TV series 'Life on Mars' 1973 Ford Cortina sold to a Darlaston man. The town is famous for its production of nuts and bolts, and the maker of the first bicycle in England was Darlaston-based.

Darlaston, as described by White in his directory 1851 (W p598). **'no town of equal size and population in the three kingdoms so completely cut off from RAILWAY COMMUNICATIONS'** Darlaston according to The Staffordshire Advertiser in 1890, complaining the town, with 18,000 inhabitants, should have its own railway station, one nearer than that at James Bridge a mile off (SA Jan 11 1890 p4 col 6). **Most sinful and grossest indulgent wakes in the Black Country** Darlaston and Willenhall wakes in c1830s, according to Quaestor (E&S Nov 25 1937 - 100 years ago recalled by Quaestor). **The Black Country's traditional fool** The Darlaston man (HODW p173). **'Darlo'** How Black Country people pronounce Darlaston (Where I live: The Black Country BBC website). **Black Country 'King of all bonfires'** Perhaps that at Darlaston for George VI's coronation 1937, which was 50 feet to the top of the flag, approx 100 tons, 10 square yards (TB Jan 20 2005 p3p). **Best British Bred Trotting Pony 1993, 1995** 'Little Erster' a stallion trained by Horace Cox of Darlaston Green, 75. The title is awarded at the annual Prakas Race, Tir Prince, Abergele (TB Nov 1995 p6p). **World's first mobile cinema?** Possibly that which came to the bottom of Horton Street, The Green, in the early 1930s; a white screen would be fastened onto a house in St Giles' Square (TB Jan 1996 p6). **The plane Darlaston sponsored in WW2** A Handley Page - Halifax (BBC website). **What Darlaston is famous for** Making gunlocks. The **name Darlaston first appears** in c1154.

People...

Darlaston's most famous old worthy Thomas Pye (d1609). Vicar, schoolmaster and scholar in linguistics and polemical divinity. A native of Darlaston he became a chaplain of Merton College, Oxford, in 1581, having studied logicals and philosophy there. In 1590 he became vicar and schoolmaster at Boxhill, Sussex, where he is buried in the schoolhouse. He paid for the stone steeple of Darlaston church. The Staffordshire historian, Dr Robert Plot called him "pious Pye" and the Black Country historian, Frederick Hackwood, was apoplectic with indignation so very little had been written about him (Hackwood's Darlaston). **Darlaston's villain** Joel Lunn, a great thief and housebreaker. He was born in Darlaston, and apprenticed to a gun-lock filer. Many of his robberies occurred in the Pelsall, Walsall Wood, Shire Oak, Icknield Street areas. His wife Ester was also of ill-repute and got seven years transportation. He was hung at Stafford on March 20 1793 (WSL crime bill poster). Apparently, whilst awaiting execution he attempted to escape. The prison guards quickly put the ring-leaders in irons, and also apprehended some 'assistants' who were waiting on the outside of the prison walls with horses, hoping to make a quick getaway (TB April 1993 p17). **Darlaston's heroes** Pte E Baker of Darlaston whose M.M. was announced Sept 17 1917, and A/Cpl T Austin of Darlaston, 7th South Staffs Regt, whose M.M. was announced Jan 28 1918 (ELSONSS pp94,95). **Darlaston's 'Favourite' son** Bob Smith (1869-1956), shop keeper, philanthropist and character, known for his catchword 'favourite' which he applied to his many ventures and multitude of goods. In the 1890s he moved to James Bridge, probably to 39 Station Street, where he was a hairdresser by 1904. That year he is said to have built Favourite House in Church Street, Darlaston, and by 1908 he had moved to the Favourite House. Here he stayed until at least 1940, employed as a hairdresser, picture framer and general dealer; his Favourite Motor Trip Club ran trips to Brewood, Kinver, Bridgnorth and Bewdley. **Darlaston's pugilists** Jem Butler of Darlaston fought Joe Burton of Bilston in Jan 1827 for the Midland Collieries Championship; Butler won after 63 rounds! (HODW p166). Rough Mooey, landlord of the Mine Borer's Arms. "Despite having a wooden leg and only one eye, he was always ready for a spat, and he must have been a daunting opponent with his face pock marked and scarred by a pit explosion. His domestic life was equally quarrelsome and he eventually sold his wife at Wednesbury market" (The Black Country. Edmund Bealby Wright. 1996 p9). **Darlaston's coiner** John Duffield of Darlaston, convicted at the Staffordshire Summer Assizes in Aug 1819 and hung for 'stamping' on 'base' shilling pieces provided by a Birmingham coiner (TB April 5 2007 p24). **Strange but true!** Houses built on the Darlaston Wednesbury boundary at the junction of Walsall Road and Sparrow's Forge Lane, Fallings Heath, were questioned as to which parish they lay in for poor rates, in particular which parish was chargeable for a pauper in a house. The point was contested, and it was decided that the parish chargeable should be that in which the pauper's head lay in his bed at night. In addition, the houses were no obstacle when it came to beating the parish bounds, as a man was made to climb over them (HODW p167). **'The stupidest man in Staffordshire'** Ernest Care, used as a 'spy' by the prosecution in the case of Mary Ann Webb, landlady of the Wolverhampton House inn, Pinfold Street, in Spring 1900, charged with illegal gaming. Despite the defence calling Care 'the stupidest man in the county of Stafford' the defendant was fined 40s and costs (SA June 23 1900 p7 cols 5-6). **'The Omega Trio'** A travelling show of strongmen and acrobats from Darlaston comprising Jack Butler, and brothers Maurice and Harold (Leo) Phillips, c1910; Maurice was the compere (TB June 1 2006 p39p). **Only UK person to have served in four levels of Government, survived a record 13 recounts in 4 general elections** Harmar Harmar-Nicholls, native of Darlaston, a councillor on Darlaston UDC, MP for Peterborough, MEP for Manchester South, and sat in the House of Lords (57 Black Country People. Stan Hill 2002 p163) (BCM Summer 2005 p80). **Royal Antedeluvian Order of Buffaloes Grand Primo 1980** John Askey (1937-2003), IMI Refiners purchasing manager, and freemason of Darlaston (E&S Jan 16 2003 p13p). **CSA Centenary Trophy winner 1999, Oldam Trophy winner 1999** Mark Rickhuss, born Darlaston 1965, who swam the English Channel in 9 hours 18 minutes: the first trophy is for fastest swim by a British Person during 1999 and the second for the best British long distance swimmer of the year (TB Jan 20 2000 p17). **Olympic 4 x 100 relay gold medallist 2004** Mark Lewis-Francis, born Darlaston 1982 (Wikipedia 2008). **The man who bought the 1973 Ford Cortina which appeared in the TV series 'Life on Mars'** Paul Shedden of Darlaston, for £10,000 at an auction (BBC Midlands Today Oct 29 2007). **Darlaston's kindest** John Perry of Darlaston who left in his will a house in Blackmore's lane, and land in Kingshill Field to the poor; the charity existed by 1712, and was at some time paying for a bread dole distributed on New Year's day. **Darlaston's poorest** A parish workhouse at the corner of George St and The Green, Darlaston Green, opened in 1813. It closed on the formation of Walsall Union by c1838, when the building was demolished (HODW pp44, 155) (TEBC2). **First person in the parish register** John ____, son of William Bar(n?)ker, baptised Nov 4 1539. **Darlaston's earliest recorded will** Belongs to Robert Collins, and is dated 1527. **Choicest quote** Osborne in his Guide to the Grand Junction Railway etc, 1840, (3rd) writes 'To the west, about a mile from the line, is the town of Darlaston, a part of the mining district. The town is situated on a hill, and from a distance looks very well; but as we approach it, there is more appearance of actual wretchedness than in any other part of the mining district. The buildings are almost all small houses for the workmen, and their workshops; and the place is as ill constructed and rough in appearance as if there were no town within a hundred miles.'

Work...

First machine for forging nuts and bolts Invented by Thomas Oliver, a Darlaston man (Staffs County Handbook c1958 p56). **Founder of the Midland Counties Trades' Federation** Richard Juggins (1843-95), of 60 New St, Darlaston, sometime by 1890. He was one of the founders of the Nut and Bolt Association Trade Union in 1870, which turned into the National Amalgamated Association of Nut and Bolt Makers in c1872 (HODW p160) (SA Sept 18 1897 p5 col 1) (BCM Autumn 1981 pp6-8). **World-famous for the making of gunlocks** Darlaston (Staffordshire: Shire County Guide.

Peter Heaton. 1986), and **steel fasteners** Darlaston (TB Sept 20 2001 p14). **Maker of the first bicycle in England** Maurice Phillips (1843-1922) of Llanrhaedr-y-Mochant, Denbighshire, who came to Darlaston in 1865. His bicycle pre-dates by several months what was believed to be the first English bicycle, made by the Coventry Machinists Company in 1869. Maurice claims in Cycling Journal May 20 1887 'I certainly made the first and rode the first bicycle ever seen in England' (E&S Aug 21 1979). **'one of the largest industrial conglomerates in the world', one of the largest privately owned companies in Britain** Rubery, Owen & Co Ltd, founded by John Tunner Rubery at St George's Ironworks, Darlaston, 1884, and whose head office and main works were at Darlaston. The firm produced its first motorcar chassis in 1896; AE Owen invented the pressed steel chassis, enabling the construction of lighter and therefore faster vehicles. During the Chief Executiveship of Sir Alfred Owen (1908-75), the firm incorporated over 40 different divisions with a workforce of 16,000. One subsidiary company produced the bodywork for Donald Campbell's world-record-breaking Bluebird in 1963. The second claim was made c1958. It has been said: 'Strip down every car or truck ever built in Britain before 1980 .... and you will find a Rubery Owen part somewhere' (Staffordshire County Handbook c1958 p53) (MIW pp55,57,64p). **Darlaston's best known employers** Charles Richards & Son, Heath Road, which began life as a maker of simple domestic utensils, before branching out into nuts and bolts (TB Sept 20 2001 p1).

Churches and chapels...

At Darlaston is St Lawrence, **one of 4 such county dedications** (of ancient parish churches); **10th last ancient parish county church built** dating from 1871. **Why 'Darlaston has been immensely favoured above half a century in its parochial ministry'** Because 'It numbers among the past series of rectors the honoured names of a Waltham, Lowe, Fisk, and Kyle' (SA Nov 10 1849 p7 col 6). **Staffordshire's best church choir 1849** The author of Staffordshire Advertiser's 'Towns of South Staffordshire' series wrote "We know of no church in the county where we more enjoy and we trust profit by the devotional beauty of the National Liturgy, than in its choral and pastoral expositions in the church at Darlaston, choir and clergy are both above par,..' (SA Nov 10 1849 p7 col 6). **Darlaston's longest-serving vicar** William Dickin, who served 36 years, 1678-1714. Darlaston At **DARLASTON GREEN** was St George (c1851-2). After it was demolished 1974 the pulpit and sections of columns and capitals went to gardens at Tenbury Wells and Wombourne (BCM Jan 1976 pp34-39). **Man charged with stealing coal from under St George's** George Oates, colliery owner at Darlaston Green, charged on May 29 1863 with stealing 3,000 tonnes of coal from under the church, to a value of £1,000, the property of then incumbent Rev Manton Hathaway (SA May 30 1863 p5 col 3). At FALLINGS HEATH is All Saints (rebuilt 1962), Walsall Road. The old church of 1871-2 was destroyed in a landmine (BOE p297). It was **Lichfield Diocese Best Kept Churchyard winner 1993**. METHODISM

Birthplace of West Midlands Primitive Methodism Darlas-ton, after the visit of preacher Samson Turner, 1819 (TB April 25 2002 p26). **Perhaps the first purpose-built Methodist meeting place in the Black Country** The New Room erected Easter 1762 in Bilston Street (known as Meeting Street in the later C18). There were later Methodist chapels in Pinfold St, Slater St (surviving in 2000 as Darlaston Church), Great Croft St, Joynson St (surviving in 2000 as Kings Hill Church), Old Park Road, Bell St (of 1836, replacing the first Primitive Methodist chapel which stood in Willenhall St and between Stafford Rd and Rough Hay Rd; destroyed by wildfire 1908), and at Fallings Heath, and at Darlaston Green (TB April 13 2000 p13. April 25 2002 p26). ROMAN CATHOLICS **The first building lit by gas in Darlaston** St Joseph's RC chapel, Church Street, built 1793 (HODW p 138).

The area...

County's 148th largest parish, consisting of 800 acres; **54th farthest parish away from the county town**, 16m S; **extremist length** 1.7m, making it **29th= shortest parish in the county**; **extremist width** 2.2m. **Chief settlement** Darlaston, once a small-ish Black Country town, but now the whole parish is Black Country conurbation. **The part of the parish in no parish!** That part of Pinfold St nearest Wednesbury, which invariably escaped being levied for poor rates (HODW p167). **Geology** Entirely Middle Coal Measures. **Highest point** 470 feet at King Street. **Lowest point** 380 feet by the Tame at James Bridge. Darlaston was **18th most-populated Staffordshire parish in 1801** with 3,812; **17th in 1811** with 4,881; **17th in 1821** with 5,585; **16th in 1831** with 6,647; **16th in 1841** with 8,244; **15th in 1851** with 10,590; **15th in 1861** with 12,884; **17th in 1871** with 14,416; **19th in 1881** with 13,563; **19th in 1891** with 14,422; **19th in 1901** with 15,386.

Dudley Castle Hill
Did you know that...

Dudley Castle Hill's top folklore There are lots of ghosts who haunt the Castle, from ghostly couples to the 'Grey Lady'; from an elderly woman in sackcloth shift and grey shawl to an old woman who hung off the battlements on All Hallows eve with her black cat swinging from her body. A small ghostly dog has been seen by the Keep towers; a female skeleton by the limestone cave quarry; a small dog skeleton; a monk skeleton; a monk in black habit with a white crucifix; hooded figures; figures walking round a fire; poltergeist in the Zoo aquarium; footsteps; pickaxe sounds; piano sounds in the restaurant on the site of the old St Edmund's churchyard; horse hoof sounds; and an incredible chill. **First new canal tunnel in Britain for 130 years** That linking Dudley Tunnel and Singing Cavern under Castle Hill built 1984 (Dudley Canal Tunnel leaflet) (MR p135). **Earliest example in England of Tudor and Stuart domestic architecture** The residential portion of Dudley Castle (VB p47).

Earliest definite physical evidence for the use of animal-membrane condoms in post-medieval Europe Found in the Keep garderobe latrine, c1985, of 1647 (info Debbie Ford, Potteries Museum) (Post-Medieval Archaeology. vol 30 1996 pp129-142 ils). For **Thomas Newcomen's first steam engine** see Tipton. **Britain's friendliest open-air museum** The Black Country Living Museum, which is situated in the old parish of Dudley, Worcs. **World record for five forward spring jumps with weights** Was set by Joseph Darby (1861-1937) in the grounds of Dudley Castle on May 28 1890, when he cleared 76 feet 3 inches (TB Aug 5 2004 p13).

Dudley Castle and the Suttons...

'**one of the the best known Black Country landmarks**', '**the first Black Country tourist attraction in history**' Dudley Castle (TB Jan 10 2008 p23). **First Dudley Castle fete** 1850, becoming an annual event, and from 1908 known as Dudley Historical Pageant (TB Jan 10 2008 p23). **THE SUTTONS Fought at the**

Ghostly goings-on in the shadow of Dudley Castle, the elephant represents Dudley Zoo

battle of Blore Heath 1459 John de Sutton (1400-87), created 1st Baron Dudley by writ of summons to parliament in 1440 (SHC 1898 p283. 1912 pp314, 316, 317). **Had fifteen children** Edward Dudley (or de Sutton) (d1531-2), son of Sir Edmund (d1483); by his wife Cicely daughter of Sir William Willoughby, he had 15 children (SHC 1898 p283. 1912 pp317, 319). **Lord Quondam (alias 'once a Lord')** John Dudley (d1553), succeeded to the Dudley barony in 1532. He was lampooned as this on account of his foolish character and being a spendthrift (VB p46). **Mary I restored Dudley Castle to him** Edward Dudley (d1586), son of John (d1553) (SHC 1912 pp323,324). **Last Lord Dudley of the Sutton line, eloped with a collier's daughter** Edward Dudley (1567-1643), son of Edward (d1586), 5th Baron; his estates in the hands of sequestrators 1593, and he appears to have been a person of infamous conduct; married Theodosia Harington, but 'left that virtuous lady, his wife... and took to his home a lewd and infamous woman, a base collier's daughter, Elizabeth Tomlinson, who bore him eleven children', buried at St Edmund's, Dudley (SHC 1912 pp324, 327, 331. 1917-8 p376-7). **'Dud Dudley'** son of Edward (d1643), by Elizabeth Tomlinson (VB p47). **JUNIOR BRANCH Executed by Henry VIII** Edmund Dudley (1462-1510). Of Sussex, where he was MP and sheriff; on the Privy Council soon after the accession of Henry VII; Speaker of the 1504 Parliament; overthrown and executed by Henry VIII 1510 (DNB) (SHC 1912 p318. 1917-8 pp285-6). **Only Lord Lieutenant of Staffordshire beheaded** John Dudley (c1502-1553), son of Edmund (d1510); Viscount Lisle 1542; Earl of Warwick 1547; Duke of Northumberland 1551; father-in-law of Lady Jane Grey, whom he betrayed; executed Aug 22 1553 (DNB) (SHC 1912 pp284, 319, 321. 1917-8 p309).

Dudley Zoo...

First guide to the Zoo Appeared when it opened in 1937, costing 6d (TB Jan 17 2002 p15p). **'Two of the world's leading (architect) Modernists'** Lubetkin and Tecton who designed the Zoo, in the then 'theatrical' or 'staged' method of presenting the animals (TB Jan 17 2002 p15). **Britain's largest captive gorilla** (Western Lowland gorilla) Is 'Bukhama' (b1960) at Dudley Zoo, who was reportedly 500 lb in 1969, but has not been weighed since (GBR 1993 p27). **Worst zoo in England** Dudley Zoo as pronounced by Holiday Which Magazine in 2000.

People...

The MP who brought down Profumo George Wigg (1901-83), Labour MP for Dudley, who exposed John Profumo's affair with Christine Keeler, 1963 (TB June 26 2003 p16p). **Dudley's poorest** Dudley Poor Law Union, which included Rowley Regis, Sedgley and Tipton parishes, was formed on Oct 14 1836, used a new workhouse, built 1855, at Shaver's End (TB Jan 6 2005 p19). **Choicest quote** J.B. Priestley in his English Journey, 1934, said 'I climbed a steep little hillside, and then smoked a pipe or two sitting by the remains of the Keep of Dudley castle. The view from there is colossal.'

The area...

County's **165th largest or 5th smallest parish** (extra parochial), consisting of 67 acres; **27th farthest parish away from the county town**, 19.3m S; **extremist length** 0.7m, making it **6th= shortest parish in the county**; **extremist width** 0.25m, making it **4th narrowest parish in the county**. **Chief settlement** and **what Dudley Castle Hill is famous for** Dudley Castle and its zoo. **Geology** ALL - Silurian (Wenlock) Limestone. **Highest point** The Keep summit at 755 feet which has **one of the best views of the Black Country**. **Lowest point** Northern foot of Kettle Hill at 541 feet.

Enville
Did you know that...

Enville's top folklore A vagrant Billy Pitt and his mongrel dog were put in the parish stocks at Enville crossroads on a cold night. Pitt died of exposure and his ghost and the dog are said to haunt Enville Heath (TB March 1979 p5). **'one of Staffordshire's most charming estate villages'** Enville in a notice advertising one-day opening of Enville Hall gardens in 2004 (TB March 18 2004 p11). **Largest Spanish/ Sweet Chestnut in England** Reputedly one at Highgate Farm on the edge of Highgate Common. It has a girth of 26 feet (BCM spring 1999 p72) (LGS p137) (KES p96). **Strange but true!** At the Enville Wakes of 1847 the organisers decreed that a foothurdle race 'of'r a rich smart patterned waistcote' should be open to "men and lads of any size or colour, except black". No such colour bar was mentioned in a scripted notice of similar wakes events held in 1845, also once shown in a wall cabinet at the Cat Inn, Enville (County express Jan 9 1965 p19). **Largest unenclosed land in Staffordshire by 1930** (after Cannock Chase) Highgate Common (LGS p137). **Enville's first recorded pub** The Crown inn, recorded in 1642 (County Express May 11 1989). **Only pub in England not allowed to open on a Sunday** Cat Inn, Enville; dry on the Sabbath for 300 years until Oct 24 2004. **First drink on a Sunday at the Cat Inn** October 24 2004 (BBC Midlands Today Oct 24 2004). **What Enville is famous for** Enville Hall, its lords (the Greys of whom the most famous was Queen Lady Jane Grey), its amazing pleasure grounds, Cherry wakes, and cricket. The **name Enville first appears** in Domesday Book, 1086.

People...

Enville's villain Thomas Wyer, aged 23, committed Nov 6 1818 for cow and duck stealing from Edward Stokes of Enville, sentenced on Jan 13 1819 to be transported for seven years (Calendar of Prisoners). **Enville's bravest** Thomas Amphlett, 3rd son of Joseph Amphlett, councillor, engineer, merchant at Calcutta, in Bengal, for the East India Company. He was resident at Monghyn, in the Mogul's Court. He fell victim to the confusion of the times and was barbarously massacred by order of Cossim Ally Cawn in his return from Monghyn at Patna on Oct 3 1763 aged 27. He has a memorial in the church (SHOS vol 2 p274). **Enville's hero** Pilot Officer Ernest George Boucher of

Enville shot whilst descending in a parachute over Germany on Aug 5 1944. There was a memorial service for him in the church on June 24 1945 (Country Express June 30 1945 p12). **'one of the greatest patrons of cricket in England'** Lord Stamford (b1827) of Enville Hall, according to Richard Daft, the famous Notts cricketer in his book 'Kings of Cricket' (Staffordshire Cricket. William G Watson. 1924. pp19-20). **Best-loved schoolmaster** Edwin Bennett (d1905), born Horseley Heath, Tipton 1835, schoolmaster of the National School in Hall Drive c1855-1895, known as Enville Parochial School by 1879, later reverting to Countess of Stamford and Warrington School. He received unusually three testimonials on his retirement, one from current pupils, one from former pupils and one from the parish (TB July 28 2005 p16). **Enville's poorest** Poorhouses existing from probably the C17, certainly from 1718, were being used as almshouses by the later C18. In the early C19 the former Cock Inn was used as a workhouse (VCH vol 20 p113). From 1836 the poor went to Seisdon union workhouse. **Enville's kindest** Lady Dorothy Grey (d1781), eldest daughter of 3rd Earl of Stamford of Enville Hall, was a benefactor, building the village school for poor girls; she has a memorial in the church (SHOS vol 2 p274). **Enville's earliest recorded will** Belongs to Richard Lee, and is dated June 13 1533. **First person in the parish register** Joyce wife of Thomas Hale April 27 1627. **Choicest quote** Hon John Byng, 5th Viscount Torrington, wrote in his diary, 1793, (The Torrington Diaries 1781-94, vol 3 p226) 'Enville is a pretty village, and the church is nicely situated... From Enville - there are some pleasant lanes - up, and down riding, where I often turn'd to view the smoking heath.'

Church...

At Enville is St Mary, **one of 23 such county dedications** (most common dedication in the county); **23rd= oldest county church** dating from the C12 or roughly 1150. **'workmanship is the finest in the county'** Four choir stall misercords according to SA Jeavons in BAST. There are two on either side of the chancel. Late C15. They

Black cherries, the largest Spanish Chestnut in England, the conservatory of 1855 in Enville Hall grounds, a Victorian cricketer

depict i) Sir Ywain at the castle gate ii) a couple in a pew iii) dogs attacking a bear, iv) seated angel under a canopy. The elbow rests are also well carved (JMW pp50-51) (BOE p129) (CHMS p30) (KRC p19). **Best 12th Century sculpture in a church in the county** Enville (John Hunt, University of Birmingham), and **earliest stone figure/ effigy in the county**, a figure, and figure of a bishop, c1145 (BAST vols 69-71 p27) (JME part 1 p17). **Other memorials of note** Brass to Sir Edward Grey (d1528), showing his seven sons, 10 daughters and two wives in the S chapel near E wall (SHOS vol 2 p264) (GNHS p181) (GNHSS p32) (LGS p158) (JME part 1 p8 pl 1 (b)) (WAS 1st field study trip p9) (CHMS p37). Tomb with effigies to Sir Thomas Grey (d1559) with his wife Anne daughter of Sir Ralf Verney of Yendley, Bucks in the S aisle, but not in its original position (SHOS vol 2 pp272-3) (GNHSS p32) (SVS p273) (JME part ii pp20-21 pl9) (WAS 1st field study trip p9). Also note memorials to servants to the family of the Earls of Stamford of Enville Hall to Mrs Elizabeth Allden (d1765), a nurse, Samuel Rabey, a servant for above 40 years (SHOS vol 2 p275). **Note** Small statue of the Virgin Mary in a niche above the main doorway is a replica by a local man John Tonks to replace the one Parliamentarians took in the Civil War (County Express May 11 1989). **In the churchyard** Base of a preaching cross. Two stone coffin lids dug up in 1762 on one is inscribed a cross and 'Rogervs de Morfe'. A headstone which reads:-

'Christo duce,
sab cruce morior
P. Lafargue M.D.
Patria Profugus
anno 1711'

(SHOS vol 2 p275) (KRC p34). This is to Dr. Peter La Fargue (or Lafarque), a French Huguenot, tutor to the Grey Family d1711 (BCM Oct 1985 p29) (Church Guide. Geoffrey Smith. p12). Graves of Edwin Bennett, Enville's best-loved schoolmaster (see above), and Thomas Robins, who according to legend, was the last local man to be killed by a highwayman in 1769 (County Express May 11 1989). **Strange but true!** The rector of Enville in 1875 is said to have special powers which revived only those dying in his parish. He cured one woman, who seemed to be possessed by some evil spirit which was draining her blood away and reducing her to a skeleton, by every few days supplying her with port wine and soup until she recovered (STMSM July 1980 pp32,33).

Enville Hall...

Enville's most famous old worthy, "One of the finest female minds of the century" Lady Jane Grey (1537-54). Queen of England for nine days in July 1553, and related to the Greys of Enville Hall. She was the eldest daughter of Henry Grey, 3rd Marquis of Dorset and Duke of Suffolk, who in turn was uncle of Sir Henry Grey 1st Lord Grey of Groby (d1614) of Pyrgo, Haveringham-atte-Bower, Essex, whose younger son Ambrose Grey (d1636) inherited Enville. There is a tradition she stayed at a house at nearby Stourton. The claimed about her mind was made by Alison Weir, historian (Wikipedia 2006). **One of only two halls in C17 Staffordshire to face south** Enville (old) Hall (NHS pp40,41). **Earliest chinoiserie garden building in England** The Chinese Temple of 1747-50, on Enville Hall's Temple Pool island ranks one of the earliest recorded (VCH vol 20 p99). **Staffordshire's highest fountain** Perhaps that at Enville Hall, as it was claimed it could be seen from as far away as Wolverhampton (Star 'Cycle runs or holiday outings' 1898) (TB Aug 1 2002 p26). **All-England XI's first visit to Enville** When they came to play against Lord Stamford's Twenty Two at Enville Hall in 1853 and won; the two sides played again at Enville in 1854, 1855 (by then known as the United England XI), 1856; all were wins for the Twenty Two (Staffordshire Cricket. William G Watson. 1924. p19). **'the finest ground in the world', 'the largest and best cricket ground in the world'** Enville cricket ground near Enville Hall. In 1950 upwards of 11 acres in extent (with a space levelled for play at 6.5 acres), when Lord's cricket ground was only 7. It has been described as smooth as a billiard table (TB June 27 2002 p4).

The area...

Enville is the county's 50th largest parish, consisting of 4,986 acres; **13th= farthest parish away from the county town**, 20.6m SSW; **extremist length** 4.5m; **extremist width** 3.9m. **Chief settlement** Enville, a pretty small village in undulating woodland. **Geology** ENVILLE village and W - Permian; E - Bunter. **Highest point** The Sheepwalks at 672 feet. **Lowest point** 200 feet by Mill Brook in the SE corner of the parish. Enville was **66th most-populated Staffordshire parish in 1801** with 799; **75th in 1811** with 746; **77th in 1821** with 842; **83rd in 1831** with 766; **80th in 1841** with 814; **85th in 1851** with 807; **83rd= in 1861** with 850; **85th in 1871** with 793; **85th in 1881** with 773; **88th in 1891** with 715; **92nd in 1901** with 645.

Essington See Bushbury...

Himley
Did you know that...

Himley's top folklore That a boggy area called 'The Swamp' of Himley Plantation is haunted by a phantom horseman who is thought to be the ghost of Gideon Grove, a groom of Stephen Lyttleton, Gun Powder plotter, escaping from Holbeche House on the night of Nov 7 1605. Sightings of the ghost in Wombourne 1955-59 caused a bit of a media frenzy (TB Oct 1980 p12. Feb 1992 pp1,6. Feb 10 2005 p21. July 28 2005 p15). The **name Himley first appears** in Domesday Book, 1086. **What Himley is famous for** Two houses, a leaning brick pub called The Crooked House, and Holbeche House, where the Gunpowder Plotters hid. The former has also been called Glynne Arms, and Siden House. In about the 1920s Fred Lyric and Dan Beno composed a song called 'The Siden House', the first verse of which goes:-
If your footsteps should stray

Down old Himley way
When you're strolling from Dudley Town
There's a pub there you'll find
Of a curious kind
Which lately has won great renown.
No doubt some have seen
This house that I mean,
If so, then I'm sure you'll agree.
Although it stands slanting
It's really enchanting,
And an ideal place for a spree.'

(TB Aug 10 2006 p17p).

'Himley Triangle' Triangular area bounded by Himley, Gornal and Pensnett in which unexplained lights, ghosts, and UFOs have been reported (TB Feb 10 2005 p21. March 3 2005 p15). **One of the AA's 1001 Great Family Pubs** Crooked House Inn, described as **'One of Britain's most aptly-named pubs,'** this really is a crooked house. It was built as a farmhouse in 1765, but when mineshafts beneath collapsed in the mid-19th century, it was condemned, but finally saved by Banks' Brewery.' (book of the above title, 2005).

Himley Hall and the Wards...

The night Charles I slept at the hall May 15 1645 (VB p66). **'one of the best private organs in the kingdom'** An organ installed in the music room at Himley by John Avery in the later C18, an outstanding organ builder who had built or done work on the organs of Carlisle and Winchester Cathedrals (Himley Hall & Park: a History. David F. Radmore. 1996. p21). **First Ward of Dudley Castle** Humble Ward (d1670), who married (1628) Frances daughter of Sir Ferdinando Sutton (d1621), heiress of the barony of Dudley, succeeding (1643) as suo jure Baroness Dudley (6th Baron) (SHC 1912 pp287, 332, 337). **Last to hold the united baronies of Ward and Dudley** William Ward (d1740) brother of Edward Ward (d1704, 8th Baron Dudley and 3rd Baron Ward). 10th Baron Dudley and 5th Baron Ward. JP ?1702-; On his death the Dudley barony passed to Ferdinando Dudley Lea, his nephew, dsp, who became 11th Baron Dudley; after his death the Dudley barony then fell into abeyance, although his sister Anne styled herself as Baroness Dudley. In 1740 the Ward barony, Dudley Castle and estates went to John Ward of Sedgley Park (SHC 1912 p342). **Inherited 'in 1740 potentially the nation's most valuable mineral estate per acre in Staffordshire and Worcestershire'** John Ward (d1774), of Sedgley Park, created 1st Viscount Dudley and Ward, but instead of exploiting the mineral wealth built a new mansion at Himley, and laid out the ornamental grounds in Himley Park (DNB). **'tidied up the (Dudley) castle as a ruin'** William Ward (1750-1823), brother of John (d1788, 7th Baron Ward, see below), 8th Baron Ward and 3rd Viscount Dudley and Ward (VB p48). **First and last Earl of Dudley of the first creation** John William Ward (1781-1833), son of William (d1823), dsp, 9th Baron Ward, politician (liberal Canning Tory), who when in London resided at Dudley House, **'one of the most desirable mansions in Park Lane'**. Brought-up severely by his father he was over-sensitive, and an epitaph by Creevey reads 'Poor Ward, with all his acquirements and talents, made little of it, went mad and died' (DNB) (Himley Hall & Park: a History. David F. Radmore. 1996. p24). **2nd richest nobleman in England** William Humble Dudley, 11th Baron Ward (1817-1885), 1st Earl of Dudley of the second creation 1860 (MR2 p175). **'Duddie'** William Dudley Ward (1877-1946), great grandson of Rev William Humble Ward (d1835); Vice-chamberlain to Royal household 1917-22. **Mistress of Prince of Wales (Edward VIII)** Winifred 'Freda' May (b1894), elder daughter of Col Charles Birkin of Lamcote, Ratcliffe-on-Trent, Notts, who married (1913) 'Duddie' Ward (d1946): She was the Prince's mistress between Feb 1918 to c1931; she divorced in 1931 (Burke's Peerage) (Who Was Who) (Edward, Prince of Wales to Mrs Freda Dudley Ward March 1918 to January 1921: Letters from a Prince. Rupert Godfrey. 1999) (Daily Telegraph June 2 2003 p5p). **Man who impersonated the Earl of Dudley** Neville George Clevely Heath (1917-46), born Ilford, con-man, who resembled and impersonated William Dudley Ward (d1946). Executed for the murder of Margery Gardner (TB Feb 1987). **Only user of a temporary airfield in Himley Park** The Prince of Wales, later Edward VIII (WMA vol 1 p176). **Married 'Gertie' Millar, 4th Governor General of Australia 1908-11, 136th Lord Lieutenant of Ireland 1902** John Humble Ward (1867-1932), 2nd Earl of Dudley and 12th Baron Ward (TB March 7 2002 p13) (Wikipedia). He married Gertrude Millar, widow of Lionel Monckton, the composer, who wrote many songs for the Gaiety plays in which she appeared as one of the best-loved stars of musical comedy in 1924. Her jewels, although sold for £32,630 in 1952, were thought to

Winifred 'Freda' May Ward of Himley Hall, and Edward, the Prince of Wales, later Edward VIII

have been buried with her, and in 1965 vandals desecrated her grave in search of them (VB p66). **'penniless milliner's daughter' killed by drowning 1920** Rachel Gurney, daughter of a self-made Norfolk Quaker banking family (whose fortunes collapsed, reducing Rachel's mother to keep a hat shop, and her daughters into service), became the first wife of John Humble Ward (d1932) on Sept 14 1891, she died in the sea near Screeb Lodge, County Galway on June 26 1920; but they had formally separated in 1918 (VB p66) (TB June 9 2005 p6il). **Killed in a cycling accident 1929** Jeremy Ward, 9 year-old son of William Humble Eric Ward (b1894), 3rd Earl of Dudley and 13th Baron Ward and Lady Rosemary, whilst cycling on Chelsea Embankment, London, on Dec 9 1929 - to him the Garden of Remembrance at Himley was begun (VB p67). **Killed in a plane crash 1930** Lady Rosemary, wife of William Humble Eric Ward (b1894), 3rd Earl of Dudley, travelling on a Junkers aircraft from France when there was a rainstorm and the plane crashed in an orchard at Meopham, Kent. She was the daughter of the 4th Duke of Sutherland of Trentham Hall, and has a memorial in the Memory Garden at Himley Hall (VB p67). This garden opened to the public for the first time in 30 years in summer 1975 (E&S May 7 1975).

People...

Himley's most famous old worthy, 'the butcherly soaker... from Himley ... our graceless Lord' The most illustrious Ward of Himley was John (1725-88), Viscount Dudley and Ward from 1763, industrialist and politician, born Sedgley Park who greatly exploited the coal on his estates in the Black Country, by means of canals, turn-pikes and enclosure acts. He was succeeded by his brother, William (d1823), and was buried at Himley. He was noted for his lack of charm (DNB). **Southern Command Cup winner 1946** Jack Breakwell (1923-2004), 'the Himley cricket legend' along with his other team members in the RAF (captained by Harry Harrison) (TB March 11 2004 p32). **England cricketeer** Jack Flavell (1930-2004), born Wall Heath, as a teenager played for Himley Cricket Club. Whilst playing for Worcestershire (1949-67) he appeared for England in Tests against Australia 1961 (twice), 1964 (twice) (TB March 11 2004 p32). **Benson & Hedges International Open (Golf) winner 1988, Dunhill British Masters (Golf) winner 1993, Scandinavian Masters (Golf) winner 1993** Peter Baker, born 1967 in Shifnal, Shrops, who learned golf at his father's nine hole Himley Hall course and was taught by Sandy Lyle's father Alex. He was as an amateur in the winning team for the Jacques Leglise Trophy 1983, 1984, and the St Andrews Trophy 1986 (Wikipedia 2007). **'the ten-wicket King of Himley!'** Arthur Hale of Gornal, who set a new record with Himley Cricket Club on Sept 3 1955 when he took every one of the wickets in a match against Fordhouses (TB Sept 15 2005 p19p). **Brandt and Grindley Trophy winner 1975** George Birch, Himley parish councillor, of Bridgnorth Road, in his Piper Twin Commanche aircraft at the Malta Air Rally, flying more than 2,000 miles and a total of 12 flying hours (E&S June 27 1975 p). **Himley's kindest** Mrs Lyddyat, mother of Edward Lyddyat £5, John Woodhouse of Chichester £10, Edward Gough of Wolverhampton £10, John Hanson, minister, £20, Silvanus Russell £10 and others gave money with which land was bought the yearly rent to be distributed to the poor of Himley forever, 1681. **Himley's poorest** From 1836 the poor went to Seisdon union workhouse. **First person in the parish register (Bishop's transcript)** John, son of John al Joane Hancox, baptised March 30 1665. **Himley's earliest recorded will** Belongs to Humphrey March, and is dated July 27 1534. **Choicest quote** In 1784 the French Marquis de Bombelles toured the Midlands and kept a diary (Journal de Voyage en Grande Bretagne et en Irlande, published 1989) which mentions visits to The Leasowes, Halesowen, Enville Hall, Hagley Hall (Worcs), Stourbridge; of Himley he wrote 'ce qu'il ya de mieux chez lui c'est la situation de sa maison; quoique dominée par une Colline qui la presse, elle a sufisamment de vue un joli bassin et une piece d'eau dont l'emplacement ainsi que les accessoires sont dignes du fameux Brown, qui les a ordonnés.' Which translated by LE Page, 2000, reads 'The best thing that he (Lord Dudley) has is the situation of his house; although overlooked by a hill that presses on it, there is a good enough view over a pretty ornamental lake, of which the positioning and accessories are worthy of the famous Brown, who ordered them.'

Church...

At Himley is St Michael and All Angels, **one of 12 such county dedications** (of ancient parish churches); **35th last ancient parish county church built** dating from 1764. **Note** The memorial to Thomas Norris (d1790), a musician who was performing at Himley Hall for Lord Dudley when he died on Sept 3 aged 50 (SVS p289) (SHOS vol 2 p225). **In the churchyard** The graves of 'Gertie' Millar (see above), and - near SE wall - that of Sir Gilbert Claughton, Dudley philanthropist (Church Guide. 1979). **Himley's longest-serving vicar** John Hanson, who served for about 36 years, 1633/4-1668/9.

The area...

County's 134th smallest parish, consisting of 1,221 acres; **24th= fartherest parish away from the county town**, 19.5m SSW; **extremist length** 1.9m; **extremist width** 2.2m. **Chief settlement** Himley, a little, Georgian crossroads estate village. **Geology** HIMLEY church, hall and the W - Bunter; HIMLEY Park - Permian; HIMLEY Wood - Upper Coal Measures. **Highest point** 459 feet on the slopes of Lydiates Hill in the far E of the parish. **Lowest point** 203 feet by Smestow Brook at Hinksford. Himley was **125th in 1801** with 267; **121st in 1811** with 341; **120th in 1821** with 379; **118th in 1831** with 421; **113th in 1841** with 409; **116th in 1851** with 400; **120th in 1861** with 367; **117th in 1871** with 389; **122nd in 1881** with 346; **125th in 1891** with 304; **124th in 1901** with 291.

Kingswinford
Did you know that...

Kingswinford's top folklore, Kingswinford's villain Is the story of John Duncalf (b c1655) whose hands and legs rotted off after he stole a bible from Humphrey Babb of the Grangemill at Kingswinford c1677, and believed by the common people to be divine justice. He promptly sold the bible to a maid living near Heath Forge. Mr Babb soon came to hear of the maid's bible and Duncalf was shortly accused. He vehemently denied taking it, stating that if he was lying his hands would rot off. After working for a joiner at Dudley for two weeks his wrists went black and his hands started to rot. He then went to recuperate in a barn at Perton where his condition deteriorated. He was then committed by JPs back to a barn in Stallings Lane, Wall Heath, in his native parish. Here he died on June 21 1677 with both hands and legs rotted and dried hard. The barn became a farm known as Duncalf's Barn, and then an inn called British Oak Inn. **First entry in Staffordshire DB** Kingswinford (Staffordshire County Handbook c1958). **Unique derivation for a surname** Ashwood will be from Ashwood in this parish (PDS). **What Kingswinford is famous for** Sausages, iron-working, glass, and seeds. The **name Kingswinford first appears** in 951-55. **One of the widest high streets in the Midlands** Brierley Hill (Staffordshire County Handbook c1958). **One of the earliest books to be printed in England** A single leaf from 'The Golden Legend', a reprint by Wynkyn de Worde, William Caxton's foreman, of about after 1491 is held by, and on show at, Brierley Hill Library. The leaf has the title 'The lyfe of Saynt Kenelme' (info Brierley Hill Library). **Oldest house in Wordsley** Rose Cottage, Barnett Lane, listed, ? C17 (BCM winter 1999/2000 p69p). **Most beautiful urban flight of canal locks in the country** Delph Locks, a staircase of nine locks on Dudley Canal Line One (SWY p13). In 1858 the staircase was reduced to eight locks. **Black Country's most modernised High Street** Brierley Hill (TB Feb 10 2005 p24). **'Beirut of the West Midlands'** Wordsley village high street shopkeepers on their street in 1992 complaining to executives on the council for improvements (County Express April 30 1992). **County's 4th earliest commutation of tithes when they were dealt with under a parliamentary enclosure act** The great and small tithes of Kingswinford, by allotments of land, 1776. **First meeting of the Brierley Hill Rifle Volunteers** Took place on Nov 22 1859 (SA Jan 14 1860 p5 col 4). **Rare pub name** Blue Ball Inn Quarry Bank; the Blue Ball was the sign of the fortune teller (BCM April 1983 p33p). **Last so-called Black Country Blood Sports** 'Olympics' were held at The Mile Flat, Wall Heath, c1833 (TB Aug 1983 pp1,5. Jan 1984 p29). **First ever Odeon cinema** Oscar Deutsch (d1941) opened his first Odeon cinema at Brierley Hill in 1928; the building has been long demolished (Wikipedia, 2006). **Kingswinford's most famous photographic portrait** Possibly that of John Clarke carrying drinks to the workers in the Bricklaying Department at the Round Oak Steel Works, Round Oak, taken by Frank Power, Dudley photo journalist in Sept 1959 (The Acorn - the journal of Round Oak Steel Works, Dec 1959). **'one of the largest, if not the largest, single-member Borough constituencies in Great Britain'** Dudley in 1907, which then took in the townships of Brierley Hill, Kingswinford (Brockmoor and Pensnett), Quarry

Bank, Rowley Regis (Old Hill and Cradley Heath), with 17,623 voters (Blocksidge's Dudley Almanack 1907) (TB Nov 30 2006 p14). **Home of the Midlands' happiest marriages with least divorces or separations** Kingswinford, according to market researchers Claritas (Daily Telegraph Nov 16 2000 p10) (Midlands Today Nov 15 2000). **Oldest married couple in local authority care in the country 1965** Believed to be Mr & Mrs Arthur Rogers who celebrated their 65th wedding anniversary at New Bradley Hall old people's home on March 5 1965. They retired to Poole from Stourbridge, residing at Wall Heath from 1957 (County Express March 6 1965 p1p). **First Black Country Night Out show** Took place at Citizens' Theatre, Brierley Hill, 1971 (TB Aug 30 2007 p19). **Furthest-travelled balloon by 1971** Winner of the 1970 Alcan Race, Mrs Jean Bridgens, whose balloon was released from Webbs Garden Centre, Wordsley, on Sept 26 1970 and landed 665 miles away near Starnberg-am-See, West Germany (GBR 1971 p169). **Longest stuffed toy** A snake measuring 274 feet and weighing 154.3 lb made in 60 hours by Brettell Lane Day Centre, Feb 1990 (GBR 1992 p218). **Longest coaching marathon** Occurred at Next Generation Club, Brierley Hill, when Butch Heffernan of Australia coached tennis for 52 hours on 23-25 Nov 2001 (GBR 2006 p255). **'Midlands' most famous UFO case'** The Moor Street-Brierley Hill sighting at about 7pm on Nov 19 1987 by Brett Forrest, 27, who saw two stationary white lights in the sky, directly above the old Brierley Crystal Stack. A droning sound was coming from the triangular 'craft' which was also later witnessed by members of his family. Timothy Good, one of the UK's leading experts on UFOs, has no doubts over the authenticity of the case (BBC Black Country website, 2007).

People...

Kingswinford's most famous old worthy, first Englishman to bequeath his private wealth to fund a voluntary hospital John Addenbrooke (1680-1719). Doctor. Born Kingswinford. Student, fellow, and bursar of Catharine's Hall (now St Catharine's College), Cambridge. He bequeathed a collection of rare medical books to the college library. But is principally remembered for his hospital for the poor there, for which he left more than £4,500 in his will. The hospital has expanded significantly since and is now a major teaching hospital becoming the present Addenbrooke's Hospital at Cambridge (Wikipedia 2006) (hospital website, 2006). **Kingswinford's hero** Capt Geoffrey H Piddock R.A. A.O.P. of 'Daviot House' Kingswinford, awarded the D.F.C. in 1945. He was one of the four young pilots of an artillery observation plane squadron hailed nationally for helping avert a major catastrophe in Normandy shortly after D Day landings had been consolidated (County Express April 21 1945 p7). **Wordley's forgotten hero** Pte Joseph Bateman of Wordsley, executed for deserting the army on 30 different occasions, due to some disorder, on Dec 3 1917. In 2008 his name was placed on Wordsley war memorial (BBC Midlands Today. Jan 17 2008). **Kingswinford's bravest** James Bate, Able Seaman and ship's carpenter, born Kingswinford c1824, who lived second longest on the shipwrecked 'Jane Lowden'

Marsh & Baxter's advert, first steam locomotive in the Midlands - the Agenoria, Nine Locks Pit disaster 1869, Delph Locks, Bradley Hall, John Clarke of Round Oak Steel Works, Gunpowder Plotters, John Duncalf, thief who 'rotted to death'

going between Quebec and Falmouth, finally expiring after three weeks adrift on Jan 14 1866; the captain, John Casey, alone survived the ordeal (TB April 3 2003 p10). **Brierley Hill's bravest, its only V.C. recipient** Anthony Booth, awarded the V.C. for gallantry on March 12 1879 during the Zulu attack on the Intombi River, received at Windsor Castle on 14 May 1880. He was born at Carnington, Notts, April 21 1846, and entered the 80th Regt of Foot or 80th Staffs Volunteers. His last posting was to Brierley Hill as Sergeant Instructor to the Brierley Hill 'C' Company 1st Volunteer Batt of S. Staffs Regt. Here, he remained in retirement, died 8 Dec 1899 (County Express April 10 1965 p14p) (BCM Jan 1992 pp48,49p-52). **Brierley Hill's saddest** Timothy Lawley (1849-60), of Quarry Bank, physically ill-treated, often tied up and malnourished at the hands of his brutal parents Thomas and Mary, he died of starvation; the body of the 11 year old at death in August was only three feet tall and weighed just 15 pounds and his intestines were totally empty. Both parents were found guilty of manslaughter, and the father was sentenced to 15 years in prison (TB Dec 23 2004 p12). **Kingswinford's kindest** Rev Francis Ashinhurst by will dated 1701 bequeathed a house at Brierley Hill

built as a school for poor children to his descendants in trust. Elizabeth Hodgetts by will dated 1716 gave 100L for use of the poor at
Kingswinford - but the money had become lost by c1813. **One of the
12 who survived the sinking of HMS Hampshire** Warrant Officer William Bennett of Holbeche. The warship hit a German mine
on June 5 1916 within three hours of its departure from Scapa Flow,
famously claiming the life of the Secretary of State, Lord Kitchener.
Bennett was the officer on watch in the engine room when it struck
the mine, so his survival is all the more miraculous (TB June 8 2006
p23p). **Severest case of ill-treatment by police to a vulnerable**

45

individual ever known The case of 7-month pregnant Mrs Eliza Price of Brierley Hill who on April 16 1845 was chained without bedding or any comfort overnight to an iron fireplace post at the Horseshoes Inn, High St, Brierley Hill, bound over on an unsubstantiated counter charge of assault to appear before a magistrate the next day. She had, understandably, refused to accompany a constable to spend the rest of the night with his wife, as it was late and she did not wish to travel alone at night with a man. She was discharged, and a petition on her behalf was read out to the House of Commons on May 9 1845 which caused one M.P. to exclaim 'a case of greater oppression than that stated in the petition had never occurred. It was a disgrace to the magistrates and the laws of the country'. An investigation was published as a Select Committee Report (The Times May 11 1845) (BCM Winter 2001 pp47-51). **'Brierley Hill's Genial Giant,' 'an unprecedented spectacle'** George Lovatt (1869-1933), originally of Cheshire, a hay and straw dealer in the Brierley Hill area, who weighed at his death between 42-60 stones (TB May 4 2000 pp10-11p). **10th= oldest Staffordshire man ever** 'Poor Old Cookey' allegedly lived to at least the age of 112 (in 1838). Born in Brierley Hill, and removed from Wordsley (where he had been living for a number of years) to London when in his eighties (Doncaster Chronicle Jan 1838) (Broughton's Scrapbook p425). **'England's Oldest Licensee'** John Dutton (1820-1910) landlord of the Old Bush Inn, Hinksford (TB May 1982 p27). **Silver Medalist for metal work 1908** JB Dainty (1883-1972), born Dudley, but worked extensively in Kingswinford. He made three cast bronze panels for Pensnett War Memorial. In Pensnett church he made the chalice and paten, the processional cross in memory of his parents, James & Ellen Dainty, and the WW2 roll of honour tablet. For Kingswinford church he made the altar cross; for Dudley Girls' High School a circular plaque mounted on a shield, a tennis trophy in memory of Dorothy Round, a bronze bowl of lowers in memory of Sarah Benson (1929-1947) who died in a hunting accident (BCM July 1990 pp18,19,20-23). **'one of the first people in Britain to undergo plastic surgery'** Fred Jones (1899-1987), ran an electrical shop in High St, Brierley Hill, underwent plastic surgery in WW1 at Queen Mary Hospital, Sidcup, by pioneering Scottish surgeon Sir Harold Gillies (E&S July 14 1987). **National Canine Defence League Silver Medalist 1933, RSPCA Bronze Medalist 1933** Harold Whittingslow of Tansey Green who rescued a fox terrier called Peter from the bottom of a deep pit shaft in Jan 1933 (TB Dec 2 2004 p15p. Dec 16 2004 p21). **Editor of the first television magazine in England** Charles Hatton (b1905), formerly of Cot Lane, Wordsley, editor of 'Television Weekly', and author of 'No trees in the street' (his most popular novel), 'Black Country Folk' (1945), 'Mr Everyman' (1947, his 1st novel), and 'Radio plays and how to write them' (1948), 'Tax on Marriage' (1953, a novel) died (in Kent) on the same day as his daughter's wedding on Aug 8 1977 (Stourbridge Library newspaper cuttings p674). **Kingswinford's longest prisoner of WW2** Roland Morris (b1917) of Brierley Hill, 2nd Batt of Welsh Guards, taken prisoner at Dunkirk 1940, and not in Allied hands until at least March 1945 (Stan Hill's

Brierley Hill and Life. 1999. p108p). **'Queen of Black Country humour'**, **'Black Country's finest comedienne'** Dolly Allen (1990), born Doris Evelyn Baugh at Stourbridge Union Workhouse at Wordsley on April 9 1906, orphaned just 10 days later. She was brought up with the Parker family of Halesowen. She recited her poetic monologues in the Black Country dialect, capturing the bitter-sweet humour of the region, and was a popular performer in 'Black Country Night Out' shows, only having success as a comedienne from her late 60s. Buried Gornal Wood Crematorium (Hello, my luvvers! The Life and Times of Dolly Allen by her son Ken Allen. 1994) (The Black Country: The Changing Face of the Area & Its People. New Williams. 2002. p16p) (TB Aug 30 2007 p19p). **Junior Miss West Midlands winner 1963, Junior Miss Britain runner-up 1963, Miss Universe Bikini winner 1972, Miss Britain Bikini winner 1973, first 'Britain in a Bikini' winner, 'Britain's Queen of Beauty' winner** Christine (nee Preston) Charles, born Wordsley 1946, former knitwear machinist and funeral director (BCM Spring 2007 pp33-36ps). **Althorpe Award (Painting) 1995, John Goode Prize (Printmaking) 1998, 2001** Paul Bloomer, born Pensnett 1965, artist (BCM Spring 2005 pp43-49ps). **'Mastermind' finalist 1996** Gwendoline Ann (nee Smith) Kingsley (b1943), originally of Brierley Hill, later of Kingswinford, genealogist and 'professional' quiz and competition entrant (BCM Winter 2001 pp9-11p). **First UK drink-drive offence on the school run** A woman at Merry Hill (Daily Telegraph March 16 2006). **'The naked rider'** or **'the pale rider'** Adam of Kingswinford who, aided by friend Boz, posted on the internet a video of Adam naked riding Kingswinford streets on a mini-scooter, 2006/7 (BBC Midlands Today Jan 3 2007). **One of only two in UK to have Familial Mediterranean Fever** Caitlin Turner (b2002) of Bridgend Croft, Pensnett, a condition causing her to have her stomach and half her bowel removed (E&S Sept 4 2003 p32p). **Inland Waterways Personality 2005** Graham Fisher of Kingswinford, chairman of the Staffs and Worcs Canal Society, and Harbourmaster for Dudley Canal Trust's Parkhead Boat gatherings (TB Aug 18 2005 p17p). **Personal Achievement in Local History award holder 2007** Stan Hill (b1929) of Wordsley, retired teacher and Black Country Society stalwart, awarded by the British Association for Local History (BCM Summer 2007 p13). **Dudley Queen of Culture 2008** Pat Wakelam, in her 60s, of Quarry Bank (BBC Midlands Today Jan 15 2008). **Kingswinford's earliest recorded will** Belongs to John Nurthall, and is dated March 28 1533. **Staffordshire's last wills administered by the bishop's consistory court** Belong to Hannah Whitehouse of Pensnett, and others from Stoke-upon-Trent, West Bromwich and Wolverhampton, all proved on Dec 31 1860. This was after the Probate Court Act (1857) became law from Jan 12 1858, replacing ecclesiastical courts with civil District Probate Registries. **'The Quarry Bank Marvel' 'Blind Henry'** Henry Griffiths (d1930), despite blindness was a talented draughts player, weather forecaster, town crier, and general character in his native Quarry Bank (MMBCC pp63-65ps). **'the Brierley Hill tramp'** Harold Thompson (1902-74), well-known figure who wandered the town from the late 1940s, whose nights were spent in the warmth of the brick-kilns of E.J.&J. Pearson's brickyard, Turners Lane, The Delph; buried in Addison Rd Cemetery after the local community clubbed together to give him a proper funeral (Stan Hill's Brierley Hill and Life. 1999. p122p). **the 'Brockmoor rhymer'** Marshall Hadduck, who seems to have penned prize fighting rhymes (TFBC p155). **'Mr Wordsley'** Fred Willetts, born 1919 in Belle Vue road, Wordsley, as dubbed by The Bugle. Wordsley Hospital Head Gardener and long time Chairman and the President of Wordsley Local History Society (founded 1986) (TB Jan 26 2006 p13p). **The Delph's kindest** John Corbett (1817-1901), born Gas St, The Delph, salt producer at Stoke Prior, Worcs, and later politician, who used his vast wealth to benefit many national and Midlands' worthy causes, including large sums to St Michael's, Brierley Hill, Delph Mission Church (1886), the establishment of Corbett Hospital (1892) at The Hill, Amblecote (Stan Hill's Brierley Hill and Life. 1999. p89p). **Brierley Hill's kindest, West Midlander of the Year 2003** Geoff Hill born in Trinity St, Brierley Hill in 1927, he had many occupations until settling on running electrical shops; big fundraiser - founding a chain of charity shops - to pay for the building of the Mary Stevens Hospice, Stourbridge, opened 1992, and set up the Geoff Hill Charitable Trust in 1997; MBE 2004; the other award is run by Central TV (From Riches to Rags: The Life of a Black Country Entrepreneur and Charity Fundraiser. Geoff Hill. 2006). **Kingswinford's poorest** From 1836 the poor went to Stourbridge union workhouse at Wordsley. **First person in the parish register** Nycholas, son of Rychard and Margery Stokes, baptised April 6 1603. **(Brierley Hill)** Samuel son of Ralph and Jane Edge baptised Jan 19 1766. **Choicest quote** Rev Charles Girdlestone, rector of Kingswinford 1847-77 wrote a series of letters to The Times, April 1855, in response to earlier ones by local industrialists on social problems that had led to an outbreak of rioting in Wolverhampton and Bilston about this time. An extract from his which appeared April 18 1855, reads "Few are likely to live by choice where the atmosphere is defiled and the landscape disfigured, as it is here, in every direction; with the din of forge hammers, and the roar of blast furnaces to annoy the ears. Hence there is no resident aristocracy or gentry having leisure, throughout a population amounting to a quarter of a million (Black Country, generally). The clergy are few in number, overworked, and for the most part ill paid; other religious teachers being neither numerous or eminent....In the medical profession there is more practice than profit; great kindness to the poor, but little time to spare for the public. In the law are many upright practitioners, ready to do a good turn to their neighbours in private, but too busy to admit of their undertaking much of the unpaid work of the neighbourhood."

Sport...

The 'Brierley Hill Pet' Charley Hodge, pugilist, fought Jem Hall of Gornal on Kinver Edge, 1836 (TFBC p155). **The 'Wordsley Glassbower', 'Birmingham Pet'** Robert 'Bob' Brettle (1833-72), pugilist and glass blower, who took this appellation at the beginning of his fighting career in 1854. Having beaten one Malpass of Birmingham, he was for some reason adopted by his opponent's fans, and became known as the 'Birmingham Pet'. Tom Sayers, Champion of England, beat him in 1859 (TFBC pp157, 158). **Training gym for the World Bantamweight Champion 1900** The Cross Hotel, Kingswinford, kept by former fighter 'Spider' Webb, where Harry Harris (b1880) of USA prepared for his fight against reigning champion Tom Palmer of UK and went on to take the title (TB Feb 1996 p34). **Olympic Games Participation Medalist** Fred Light (d1963), athlete, ran in the 1928 Amsterdam Olympics 5,000m race. Originally of Shrewsbury, he removed (1926) firstly to Brierley Hill then Pennsett to comply with Birchfield Harriers club rules, that members live within 10 miles of the club (TB Aug 2 2007 p35ps). **Shared his first England appearance with Stanley Matthews** Ray Westwood (1912-82) of Brierley Hill. Footballer for Bolton Wanderers and England; their first international was against Wales on Sept 29 1934 (BCM Summer 2005 p80). **British League of Racing Cyclists' Junior Time Trial Champion 1944** Geoff Hill (see Brierley Hill's kindest, above) (TB Jan 3 2008 p29ps). **England cricketter, Worcestershire C.C.C. captain 1959-67, president 1986** Don Kenyon (1924-96), born Wordsley (Stan Hill's Brierley Hill and Life. 1999. p101p) (Wikipedia 2008). **English Schools' Football Association Trophy finalists 1951** Brierley Hill & Sedgley and District Schools, losing to Liverpool Boys 3-1 (TB Oct 28 2004 p31p). **Most improved rider on British Circuits 1971** Barry Randle, born Wordsley 1942, motor cycle racing driver, awarded by in the Grovewood Awards; in 1971 he came 2nd in the 250cc Isle of Man T.T. at 95.87 mph (BCM Autumn 2003 pp63-65p). **'The biggest, best and brightest swimming pool in the Midlands' 1939** Kingfisher Pool, Wall Heath (advert in The County Advertiser & Herald for Staffs & Worcs May 13 1939 p1). **Bowls team beaten only once at home in 44 years** The Cottage Inn, Kingswinford, between 1921 and 1965 they only lost once at home, to Stourbridge Labour Club in 1959 (County Express June 19 1965 p20p). **Severn (angling) Match weight record champion 1976, 1978** Les Taylor (c 1933) of Quarry Bank, who is the only angler in the history of the competition on the Severn to have held the match weight record twice; his 1978 weight record remains unbeaten, making him the longest record holder in the history of Severn competition (TB Feb 3 2008 p24p). **Field Target Air Rifle Shooting World Champion 2001** Steve Hancox of Brockmoor, despite having only taken up the sport in the late 1990s (BCM Winter 2001 p28).

Wordsley Hospital...

Kingswinford's poorest A parish workhouse at Wordsley continued to be used by Stourbridge Union (the first Poor Law Union formed in the Black Country, formed Oct 13 1836) until a new building was designed by a man named Griffiths. A new workhouse on the same site at Wordsley was built in 1901 (TB Jan 6 2005 pp19-20p). In 1888 there was a proposal to form a new Poor Law Union centred on Brierley Hill consisting of Kinver and Kingswinford parishes (SA March 24 1888 p5 col 5). **Wordsley Hospital's 1st Millennium baby** Benjamin Thomas John Flavell of Cookley, Kidderminster, Worcs, at 1.41am January 1 2000 (E&S Jan 3 2000 p13); **its first test tube baby** Kelly Potter of Stourbridge in April 1987 (E&S April 21 1987); **its last baby** Brandon Clarke of Quarry Bank born at 3.24am on Jan 6 2005; the maternity unit then transferred to Russells Hall Hospital (E&S Jan 7 2005). **Europe's first garden village for the mentally-handicapped** Ridge Hill, in grounds of Wordsley Hospital, built 1975-77 (County Express June 13 1975 p. April 29 1977).

Ashwood Nurseries...

Its first Royal Horticultural Society (RHS) display 1991 at Westminster Show; for which it won a Gold Medal (WP&P p151); and every RHS show since in which it has exhibited it has received a gold medal (quite an achievement given the diversity of the plants shown) (info Philip Baulk, 2008). **Golds at Chelsea Flower Show 1996** (BCM Winter 2003 p44), **2005** for Hydrangeas (Staffordshire Breaks 2006. Staffordshire Tourism). **Gold at Malvern Show** For autumn flowering Cyclamen. **Golds at BBC Gardeners World Live 2004, 2006** For Hydrangeas (info Philip Baulk, 2008). **Williams' Memorial Medal, Farrer Trophy 2000, 2002, RHS Lawrence Medal 2000** Ashwood Nurseries. **RHS Gold Veitch Memorial Medalist** John Massey, proprietor, born Pensnett 1949, awarded 2003 (BCM Winter 2003 pp44-45p) (WP&P p151p). Ashwood Nurseries is situated off Ashwood Lower Lane.

Merry Hill Shopping Centre...

Last working urban farm within the Midlands That that stood on the site of Merry Hill Centre (Wikipedia 2007). **Largest shopping centre in Europe** By 1994 was Merry Hill Centre with approximately 25,000,000 customers (The Guardian Dec 24 1994 p32). **Country's 3rd 10 screen cinema to open** Merry Hill Centre at Easter 1988, after the 1st in Milton Keynes, and 2nd in the NE of England (County Express Dec 3 1987). **Midland Businessman of the Year 1987 (jointly), Black Country's biggest property developers 1987, Developers of the Year 1998** Don and Ray Richardson, twins born 1930 Harts Hill, Brierley Hill; their most famous development in the West Midlands is the Merry Hill Shopping Centre. The 1987 award was run by the Variety Club of Great Britain, and it was the first time the award had gone to two winners (E&S Nov 10 1987) (Birmingham Post Nov 11 1987). **Most pancakes tossed in two minutes** Set by Judith Aldridge at the Merry Hill Centre on Feb 27 1990 when she tossed one 281 times (GBR 1991 p181). **Costa Book prizewinner for first novel 2008** Catherine O' Flynn with 'What Was Lost' (Tindal Street Press) set in Merry Hill Centre. She came a close 2nd overall (BBC Midlands Today. Jan 2 2008).

Work & Commerce...

First 'round hearth' furnace designed and built by John Gibbons of Corbyn's Hall (TB Sept 1977 p13). **'One of the finest seams of Old Mine fireclay in the world'** Nagersfield fireclay mine, plus best equipped and most up-to-date mine in the fireclay industry (Staffordshire Handbook c1966 p49) (TB Jan 1996 p16). **'considered second**

to none in Great Britain' Stourbridge Refraction Co. Ltd firebrick makers, Shut End, according to their own handbook c1950. Its predecessor, Stourbridge Glazed Brick and Fireclay Co. Ltd (formerly Shutend Firebrick Works), was described by The Black Country and its Industries catalogue in 1905 as 'One of the most important firms in the district engaged in the fireclay and brick industry' (TB Feb 9 2006 pp14-15). 'one of the largest private railway systems' The Pensnett Railway, Lord Dudley's mineral line, 1829- (TB May 17 2001 pp1, 18). 'first steam locomotive to work in the Midlands' The Agenoria on the Pensnett Railway (James Foster of Stourbridge etc Roy Peacock 2006 p28). 'one of the oldest Staffordshire marked bar houses' 1897 Messrs Brown & Freer, Leys Ironworks, Brierley Hill. In 1897 the firm converted into a limited liability company for family reasons (SA July 10 1897 p4 col 6). Fastest guns in the world Two oxyacetylene guns in Round Oak's H-Furnace were magnums. They fired the furnace up to a temperature of 1600-1700 degrees Celsius and could turn 75 tons of scrap metal into useable mild steel in just two and half hours, c1973 (TB May 29 2003 p17). Last remaining vestige of Round Oak Steel Works A 90-foot-long 80-tonne footbridge built in the 1960s over the disused Stourbridge to Walsall rail freight line which was removed on April 4 1993 in a 7 hour operation (County Express April 8 1993). 'quite simply the best of its kind in the world' Architectural metal work company Hill & Smith, Bridge and Roof Contractors of Brierley Hill, who produced the steelwork for the dome of Birmingham University, roof of Cheltenham's Winter Gardens and on many railways (TB Aug 28 2003 p16). 2nd largest chain makers of its kind in the world/ largest in district Samuel Taylor & Sons of Brettell Lane, Brierley Hill, founded c1879, by Samuel Taylor, now known as Lloyds of Brierley Hill (TB April 26 2001 p10). First firm in the country to use refrigeration commercially, 'Largest and best known ham and bacon factories in the world', firm that claimed they produced 'The Worlds Best Sausage' Marsh & Baxter Ltd, Brierley Hill. The first claim relates to the mid C19 and is from Q&ABC no. 198. The second claim is from Staffordshire County Handbook c1958. The third claim appeared on their best known advertisement, a picture of pig pulling a cart loaded with a ham with the slogan "Drawing his own conclusion", this was work of copywriter Mary Grealey (1913-75), who later became a nun (Stan Hill's Brierley Hill and Life. 1999. p93p). 'Pig Town' Reference to Brierley Hill because of the presence of Marsh & Baxters (BCM Winter 2002 p21. Spring 2003 p22). They supplied the quadrant davits from which the Titanic lifeboats were suspended Welin Davit & Engineering Co Ltd, an associate company of Samuel Taylor & Sons of Brettell Lane, Brierley Hill (TB March 1997 p20). The 'King's Seedsmen', Royal Seed Establishment Webbs' seed merchants at Wordsley (TB May 3 2007 p4). Last independent brewery in Brierley Hill Batham's Brewery, The Delph (BCM Spring 2002 p66). Only female 'tracer' in the engineering drawing office at Round Oak Steel Works 1965 Marion Dutton, who started work at the Works in 1957 (The Acorn, the journal of Round

Oak Steel Works, Spring 1965).

Glass...

'Father of the Glass Industry', 'one of the most enterprising glassmakers in the world' Benjamin Richardson of Flint Glassworks, Wordsley. Manager of the works from 1827, he is reputed to have invented the method of etching on flint and table glass using acid (E&S Perhaps Dec 2005-Jan 2006). **'Wordsley first glassworks'** Probably the Flint Glassworks, with records dating back to 1725; the works were on the W side of what is now Wordsley High Street. **First glassworks in England to use pressing machines for shaping and decorating flint glass** Flint Glassworks, Wordsley, 1832. **Only intact glassworks cone in region, one of only four in UK,** and **only one open to the public** Red House Works, High St, Wordsley at 87 feet high; others have been truncated. The works opened as a visitor attraction on March 29 2002 (IAS pp162-163) (MR pp396p,397) (BTBC p37p) (TB Sept 1995 p11p) (WFK p23) (BCM Summer 2002 p81) (Black Country Breaks. Black Country Tourism. 2005?). The first craft fayres were held there over the weekend of June 16-17 2007 (TB June 14 2007 p6). **Most expensive glass item in the world** Copy of the Portland Vase reproduced mostly by John Northwood (1836-1902) at Red House Works (leased by Philip Pargeter) in 1873, and shown at the Paris Exhibition in 1878. It eventually went on display at the BM and was sold for a record £30,000 in 1975. On Northwood's tomb in Wordsley churchyard is a stone shape of the vase (County Express Aug 1 1975) (BCM Spring 2001 pp71-73p -? in error by saying in 1979) (additional info Stan Hill). **They supplied glassware to the Titantic** Stuart Crystal of Wordsley (TB March 1997 p20). **'Dudley Moon'** nick-name for the Cone (TB May 16 2002 p21). **First to introduce steam-driven machinery for cutting glass to the area** James Dovey of Brettell Lane, c1790 (VCH vol 2 p228). **World's oldest crystal furnace operating 1968** A First Teison 10-pot crystal melting furnace first fired in Aug 1934 at Stuart & Sons Ltd, Vine Street Glasshouse, Wordsley, switched off in Dec 1968 (County Express Dec 27 1968). **Finest glass training centre in the world** That proposed within 10 years of 1972 for a site in Moor St, Brierley Hill, according to Mayor of Dudley, Alderman EE Morris, to be developed by Dudley Training College; it will be the only one in the country to have full-scale blast furnaces (County Express Dec 15 1972). **'last world-famous glassmaking firm in the Midlands' to close** Stuart Crystal at Wordsley, complete closure in June 2002 (E&S Nov 7 2001). **Last glassmaker in the region to close** Royal Brierley Crystal (a small company which retained the name of the original Royal Brierley Hill at North St, Brierley Hill, and they were formerly Stevens & Williams, founded 1776) operating at other premises near the Black Country Museum; the last piece of glass was completed at the 13th hour (1.00pm) on 13th day of July 2007, it was for Clarence House, London (info Stan Hill) (BBC Midlands Today 13 July 2007).

Churches...

At KINGSWINFORD is St Mary, **one of 23 such county dedications** (most common dedication in the county); **13th= oldest coun-**

ty church dating from 1120. Memorial in the left hand of the porch - Elizabeth Harrison servant of Joseph Scott d1797 (SHOS vol 2 p232). **In the churchyard** The graves of JB Dainty (1883-1972), Silver Medalist for metal work 1908; Stephen Martin Allman died due to road accident on Jan 23 1972 aged 7. At BRIERLEY HILL is St Michael (1765), **'not one of England's most beautiful parish churches'** (County Express June 5 1965 p22p). **In the churchyard** 150 yards SW of the church of C/Sgt Anthony Booth V.C. died 1899, in the section set aside for Catholics. Large grave - George Lovatt, fatman, died March 1933. The R.C. St Mary in the High St (1872-3) is by EW Pugin. At BROCKMOOR is St John (1844-5). At PENSNETT is St Mark; the first stone of which was laid by Mrs Claughton, 1846 (TB Aug 10 2000 p15p); work was completed in 1849. **In the churchyard** The **first grave** (paid by voluntary contributions) was that for Jeremiah Male, 48, of Tansey Green, because as a workman building the church he fell from the tower to his death Oct 2 1849 (TB Aug 10 2000 p15). At QUARRY BANK is Christ Church (1845-6). At WORDSLEY is Holy Trinity (1832-, when continued from St Mary, Kingswinford). **In the churchyard** Grave of Nancy Price, Kinver's heroine (TB Jan 10 2002 p17).

The area...

County's 33rd largest parish, consisting of 7,372 acres; **15th= farthest parish away from the county town**, 20.3m SSW; **extremist length** 4.2m; **extremist width** 6m, making it **15th= widest parish in the county**. **Chief settlement** Kingswinford, a village utterly on the fringes of and in the Black Country residential and industrial conurbation; indeed all the parish's hamlets have expanded to be contiguous with each other. But the industrial town of Brierley Hill has long been the most populated place. **Geology** BARROW HILL - Basalt; BRIERLEY HILL and Quarry Bank - Middle Coal Measures; BROMLEY and Kingswinford village (E) and NE - Upper Coal Measures; BUCKPOOL-Ketley - Permian; WORDSLEY, Kingswinford village (W) and the W - Bunter. **Highest point** St Michael's, Brierley Hill at 535 feet. **Lowest point** 171 feet at the Stour and Smestow confluence. Kingswinford was **7th most-populated Staffordshire parish in 1801** with 6,464; **7th in 1811** with 8,267; **6th in 1821** with 11,022; **5th in 1831** with 15156; **5th in 1841** with 22,221; **5th in 1851** with 27,301; **6th in 1861** with 34,257; **7th in 1871** with 35,041; **7th in 1881** with 35,767; **9th in 1891** with 36,411; **10th in 1901** with 38,490.

Kinver
Did you know that...

Kinver's top folklore The legend of the Kinver and Enville Giants relates there lived a giant in Holy Austin Rock, a rock cottage on Kinver Edge, whilst another giant lived in Samson's Cave, a rock cottage on the edge of the Enville estate. One day whilst the Kinver Giant was out getting water from 'the Giant's Spring' on the west side of the Edge, in 'the Giant's Water Trough,' for water was scarce near his home, the Enville Giant strode across to his neighbour's dwelling and flirted with his wife. The Kinver Giant returned to find the Enville Giant just departing. So furious was he with his rival he hurled a very large stone at him, and this explains why the Boltstone, a glacier bolder lies in a field near Compton. **Only deer park in Kinver Forest** Stourton Park (NSJFS 1968 pp40,47 map). **One of the AA's 1001 Great Family Pubs** The Fox Inn, Bridgnorth Rd, Stourton (book of the above title, 2005). **'one of the oldest place names in the Midlands'** Kinver, probably of Celtic origin (MR2 p190). The **name Kinver first appears** in 736. **Staffordshire's most perplexing modern place name** Stewponey, in itself unique. **'one of Britain's most famous unsolved murder cases'** The murder of Carl Bridgewater, newspaper boy, 13, on Sept 19 1978 at Yew Tree Farm House, Prestwood (E&S Sept 19 2003). **John Giffard's worst moment as Chief Constable** The Carl Bridgewater Case appeal, Feb 1997, when convictions against Jimmy Robinson, Vincent and Michael Hickey, and Pat Molloy were quashed for the murder of Carl Bridgewater (SN March 16 2006 p6). **West Midlands' first pet crematorium** Prestwood Pet Cemetery and Crematorium opened by Derek Lawrence in early 1998 (Stourbridge News Jan 29 1998). **What Kinver is famous for** Kinver Edge. **First winners of the special projects prize in Staffordshire Best Kept Village competition** Kinver in 1978 (E&S Aug 7 1978 p19). **Staffordshire Best Kept Village winner (Large Village category) 1982, 1985, 1986, 1991, 1992** Kinver. **Staffordshire Best Kept Village South Staffordshire District (Large Village) winner 1986, 1987, 1989, 1990, 1991, 1992** Kinver.

People...

Kinver's most famous old worthy, 87th and last Roman Catholic Archbishop of Canterbury, the man 'who almost became pope' Cardinal Reginald Pole (1500/1-58). Famous early reconvert to Roman catholicism, principally responsible for returning England to Catholicism. Born Stourton Castle. After receiving several high posts

The Last Car from Kinver

Daytrippers to Kinver, The Kinver giant, the Boltstone, Holy Austin Rock

in the Church of England he opposed Henry VIII on his divorce. In exile in Italy he was made a cardinal, 1536. In revenge Henry imprisoned his mother (Margaret Plantagenet, niece of Edward IV and Richard III), beheading her in 1541. In Mary I's reign he rose from papal legate in England, 1554, to archbishop of Canterbury, from 22 March 1556 to 17/8 November 1558, dying in office, within hours of the Queen's death (TB March 23 2006 p28p) (Wikipedia 2007). **Kinver's martyr** Margaret Pole, Countess of Salisbury, mother of Reginald Pole, devote Catholic, convicted of treason on the flimsiest of evidence and executed in 1541; she was beatified in 1886 (TB March 23 2006 p28p). **128th, 129th, 138th, 151st Lord Mayor of London** Richard Whittington who served in 1397 (x2), 1406, 1419; he was related to the Whittingtons of Whittington Hall (March Magazine 1823) (SVS pp180-181) (RKE pp20,21) (KRC p24). **'Fiddler Foley'** Richard Foley (1580-1657), forger of nails, most notably at the slitting mill at Hyde, Kinver. Foreign competition was stiff so he wanted to improve his methods of production and increase profitability. His nickname was an allusion to the method of industrial espionage he had used to obtain trade secrets in Sweden. he was said to have gained admission to works by pretending to be a half-witted fiddler. As a result of these efforts he expanded his business and so established the Stour valley forges (BCM Winter 2001 p61). **Staffordshire's most notable survivor of the First Fleet to Australia (1788)** Thomas Tilley (born c1746, dead by 1814) who committed a theft at Kinver, sentenced to transportation at Stafford 1785. Thomas Howell (b c1759) of Tipton, and Joseph Shaw (c1751-91) also survived the journey on the Alexander, but about whom little is known (The Founders of Australia. Mollie Gillen. 1989. p358). **Last gibbeted man in England** (HOWM p155) (RKE p20), or **Midlands** (SCK p8) William Howe for murder, 1813 on Gibbet Wood. **Last burning of a witch in Staffordshire** Was really a re-enactment for the film 'Bladys of Stewponey' (1919), which incidentally was Rev Sabine Baring Gould's only novel made into a film; and got a witchcraft theme woven into the story (TB June 1995 p19). **Kinver's villain** John Poulter, thief who began his criminal career at Lichfield fair in 1749 when he met Mary Brown (already apparently of tarnished reputation). He had a rendezvous with his gang and other criminals at the Rock Tavern, Kinver. The licensees were Edward and Margaret Lyne who were his accomplices and who he informed against in his 'Discoveries of John Poulter' published at Sherborne, 1753. He was hung at Ilchester in 1755 (OP pp4-5). **Kinver's saddest** Ann Edwards (b1843), a simpleton, alias 'Soft Annie', in the care of her aunt and uncle Sarah and Joseph Fletcher (a painting of them by Alfred Rushton c1901 hangs over the fireplace in Kinver Constitutional Club), residing in the Rock House caves. In 1872 Ann gave birth. Her relations were ignorant of her pregnancy. Doubtless, the father of the child had taken advantage of her. In Ann's simplicity she clubbed the baby to death with a shovel, and was charged with wilful murder, but the jury acquitted her on the grounds of insanity (TB Dec 30 2004 p19. Jan 20 2005 p11p). **Kinver's bravest** Jacob Webb, 67, former licensee of the Anchor Inn, who rescued Roy Cox, aged 6, of James Street, from the iced-over canal at Whittington on Feb 8 1945. Mr Webb partially crippled, experienced difficulty getting out of the canal himself, and was awarded the Royal Humane Society's honorary testimonial. In his youth he was an all-round athlete and sportsman, and was a Bisley finalist for the Queen's Prize (County Express Feb 10 1945 p8. Aug 4 1945 p10). **Kinver's kindest, 'Mr Kinver'** Ken Wrigley (d1995), former Kinver sawmill owner and chairman of district and Kinver parish councils, who bequeathed to the village £2 million in his will; this forms the Kinver Trust Fund (E&S Nov 22 2005 p7p). **Kinver's longest prisoner of WW2** Pte Sidney Lane of White Hill, Kinver, who returned home after nearly five years in Germany in April 1945, captured at Dunkirk in 1940 whilst serving with the Oxford and Bucks Light Infantry; his POW camp at Ellring was liberated on Jan 23 1945 (Country Express April 7 1945 p4). **First to swim in the Stewponey Inn Lido** Mary Clarke, daughter of Percy Clarke, its architect, 1936; this famous lido closed in 1968 and remained disused until 2002 when an housing estate was built on its site and that of the adjoining Stewponey Inn (County Express Oct 3 1975 aerial photo) (TB Jan 31 2002 p11) (E&S April 4 2006 photos. Feb 1 2002). **England's No. 1 tennis player, Wimbledon Ladies Singles winner 1934, 1937, Mixed Doubles winner 1934, 1935, 1936** Dorothy (nee Round) Little (1909-82), born Dudley, had retired to Kinver in 1970; entered the Tennis Hall of Fame in 1986 (Q&ABC no. 8) (Stourbridge Chronicle May 6 2004). **First boy bishop elected on the revival of the custom of Boy Bishop at Kinver** Clive Jones, 1956 (County Express July 20 1957 p). **The Black Country dialect authority** Conrad Everson, of Iverley, Kinver, of the Everson Bros, Lye, who had a consuming interest in dialectic origins and etymology (TB Jan 3 2008 p6p). **Wrote for Tommy Cooper, Morecambe and Wise, Frankie Howard, Benny Hill and Charlie Chester, first editor of The Black Countryman** Harold Parsons (d1992) of Kinver from 1965, journalist, editor in 1968-88 (BCM July 1992 p12). **Wrote Cliff Richard's 2nd Christmas No. 1 Single, or 13th UK No. 1 Single** Chris Eaton (b1959) of Kinver with 'Saviour's Day' released Nov 1990, which reached No. 1 in the Hit Parade at Christmas 1990. Chris was a choirboy at St Matthew's church, Tipton, and later he lived with his parents at Woodsetton, Sedgley. By 1981 Cliff Richard was singing his songs (E&S Feb 23 1981) (County Express Jan 3 1991) (Wikipedia 2008). **W.I. Driver of the Year 1990** Kinver W.I. won all first three places in the Stourbridge area heat (County Express May 3 1990). **Worcestershire County Squash champion under 14s 1984, 1985, 1986** Nathan Bailey of Kinver (County Express Jan 2 1986). **Kinver's poorest** By 1758 there was a parish house at Whittington, formed out of three cottages on the S side of Horse Bridge Lane. By 1812 the cottages were five dwellings known as the almshouses, let to poor persons rent free. They continued in some form as poor houses into the C20 (VCH vol 20 p151). From 1836 the poor went to Seisdon union workhouse. **First person in the parish register** Margery daughter of Rob. baptised Sept 8 1560. **Kin-**

ver's earliest recorded will Belongs to Alice Philipps, and is dated June 13 1533. **Choicest quote** Dianne Pye, a reporter for The Bugle, writes "I find living in Kinver during the autumn pure joy, those magical mornings when the Edge is shrouded with a blanket of mist and St Peter's Church is just visible on the hill with its golden weather vane glowing in the sun."

Kinver as a tourist attraction...

'a combination of Jersey, the Lake District, and the Isle of Man' Kinver according to an advert (TB Jan 18 2001 p5). **Most visitors to Kinver on one day** 17,000 on Whit Monday 1905 (TB Jan 18 2001 p5). **First day of Kinver Light Railway** April 5 1901; the official opening was on April 4 1901 (TB Feb 10 2005 p25). **Most passengers transported to Kinver on KLR on one day** Probably when 16,699 people travelled on it on Whit Monday 1905. **KLR's worst accident** In June 1917 when conductor Joseph Compson fell off as the tram neared the Bull's Head and landed on the tracks as another tram approached; Compson died 2 days later (TB Feb 10 2005 p25). **KLR's last day** Feb 8 1930 (TB Feb 10 2005 p25). **Last bits of track removed** 1979 (TB June 17 2004 p13).

Work...

First introduction into England of a mechanical process for converting iron bar into rod Was by Richard Foley at The Hyde mill after 1628 (VCH vol 2 pp114,115. vol 20 p146). **Gold medal awarded** to Webbs of Wordsley for their 'Kinver Chevalier', a barley variety, and mentioned in their catalogues prior to 1941 (BCM July 1971 pp8,10). **Kinver's first glass firm** Kinver Crystal which started production in Summer 1978 in two factory units in Fairfield Drive (County Express July?/ Aug? 25 1978) (Stourbridge Library newspaper cuttings p701).

Church...

At Kinver is St Peter, **one of 15 such county dedications** (of ancient parish churches); **23rd= oldest county church** dating from the C12 or roughly 1150. The gravestone or floor slab to Rev Jonathan Nervey has been brought in from the churchyard (JME part iv p80). **In the churchyard** Grave of Joe Mallen (1890-1970), champion Staffordshire Bull Terrier breeder; he retired from Cradley Heath to Kinver (TB Sept 18 2003 p10).

Kinver Edge...

First National Trust property in Staffordshire In 1917 198 acres of Kinver Edge were given in memorandum of Grosvenor Lee by his children (info NT). **'one of the Midlands' finest beauty spots, and indeed, ranks with anywhere in the country'** Kinver Edge (Staffordshire Quality magazine June 1999 p17). **Last cafe in Kinver Rock Caves** One run for tourists by a cave dweller closed 1967 (info board on site in 1997). **Staffordshire's only cave museum** In Astle's Rock run by Mr Fairbridge for over 20 years in earlier C20 (KRH p18p) (VCH vol 20 p122). **Last occupation of Kinver Rock Caves** 1964 (Staffordshire County Guide 2006/7 p44). **First occupants of the restored Kinver Rock House** Julian Thompson, former soldier and management consultant, and his wife Judith, a shopkeeper, from May 17 1993, tenants/wardens of the National Trust (County Express May 20 1993). **First opening of the restored Holy Austin rock houses to general public** Fortnightly openings began on the weekend before Jan 9 1998, with refurbishment work started in May 1997 (Stourbridge Chronicle Jan 9 1998). **'Battle of Kinver Edge'** Is a reference to a bare-knuckle fight on the Edge on Nov 22 1836 between James 'Jem' Hall of Gornal and Charley Hedge of Brierley Hill; Jem Hall won; there were 38 rounds (TB March 21 2002 p35). **Last occupation of Gibraltar Rockhouses** Mid 1880s; these rockhouses are really by the canal E of Kinver (SPT Nov 2006). **First ever adder spotted by Mark O' Shea** Was on Kinver Edge; Mark (b1956), originally from Wolverhampton, is a T.V. reptile expert, presenting his 'Big Adventure' from 1998 (E&S Aug 1 2003 p9p) (BBC Midlands Today June 4 2007).

Patshull Hall, Colonel William Legge, Katy Cropper, One Man and His Dog winner

The area...

Kinver is the county's 19th largest parish, consisting of 9,011 acres; **8th farthest parish away from the county town**, 21.8m SSW; **extremist length** 5.4m, making it **26th longest parish in the county**; **extremist width** 5.8m, making it **18th widest parish in the county**. **Chief settlement** Kinver, a large linear brick village so attractive it became a resort of Black Countrymen. **Geology** KINVER Edge, village, Compton and all E - Bunter; HERONS Gate-Compton Hall Farm-Brown's Farm - Permian; COMPTON Park Farm and SW corner - Upper Coal Measures. **Highest point** No Man's Green at 663 feet. **Lowest point** 144 feet by the Stour S of Whittington. Kinver was **34th most-populated Staffordshire parish in 1801** with 1,655; **40th in 1811** with 1,668; **42nd in 1821** with 1,735; **43rd in 1831** with 1,831; **42nd in 1841** with 2,207; **33rd in 1851** with 2,872; **32nd in 1861** with 3,551; **37th in 1871** with 3,194; **41st in 1881** with 2,842; **53rd in 1891** with 2,160; **56th in 1901** with 2,176.

Patshull
Did you know that...

Patshull's top folklore That a gipsy girl or her spirit is said to inhabit the body of a large fish and in the pool in the park (GOM p23 p of the pool 3 (c)). **What Patshull is famous for** The Pigots and Legges and their magnificent Patshull Hall. The **name Patshull first appears** in Domesday Book, 1086.

People...

Great grandfather of George Washington, 1st President of U.S.A. Reputedly, John Washington who went to Virginia in c1657 - it was his niece, Elizabeth (daughter of Sir William Washington of Packington, Leics) who married Col Legge of Patshull (WTCEM p77) (P p86). **Patshull's villain** James Pyatt, aged 37, committed Nov 26 1817, convicted Jan 14 1818 for being found in the area of Patshull Hall with intent to commit a felony. He was sentenced to be privately whipped and to be pressed to be resettled (Calendar of Prisoners). **Patshull's hero** William Legge, Viscount Lewisham, Captain in the Staffordshire Yeomanry, only son of William 7th Earl of Dartmouth d1942 at El Alamein (from his memorial in the church). **One Man and His Dog winner 1990, 1st woman to win One Man and His Dog** Katy Cropper of Burnhill Green, sheepdog trainer, and her collie, Trim, who together won this TV sheep dog show (E&S Feb 8 2003 p43pc). **Patshull's kindest** John Nicolls (d1608), Thomas Astley's bailiff, gave £3 as a stock for the poor; nothing else is known about the charity, and no other Patshull benefactors are known (VCH vol 20 p172). **Patshull's poorest** Two houses at Burnhill Green were used by the parish as poorhouses apparently from 1791 (VCH vol 20 p169). From 1836 the poor went to Shifnal union workhouse, from 1894 to Seisdon union workhouse. **Patshull's earliest recorded will** Belongs to John Halel, and is dated April 20 1540. **First person**

in the parish register Margaret Fletcher daughter of Jhon Fletcher and his wife Elizabeth baptised Feb 24 1559. **Choicest quote** The early tourist Celia Fiennes wrote in her diary for 1698 'to Sir Thomas Patsells house, here I went to see his Gardens which are talk'd off as the finest and best kept....and fore right there is a large pitched Court with some open iron gates, that gives the Visto quite across through to other rows of trees which runs up all about the severall avenues.'

Church...

At Patshull is St Mary, **one of 23 such county dedications** (most common dedication in the county); **40th= last ancient parish county church** built, dating from 1743. The **Churches Conservation Trust's only Staffordshire church** St Mary, Patshull. **Earliest Staffordshire funerary monument in the grand C18 manner** That to Sir Richard Astley (d1687) in Patshull church. A huge three-dimensional memorial with figures. Sir Richard rides a horse. Topped with ornamental motifs (BOE pp33,218). **Other memorials of note** Chest tomb with figures to Sir John Astley (d1532); two memorials by PF Chance with a standing female figure by an urn - Lord Pigot (d1795) and Sir Robert Pigot (d1796) (BOE p218). **In the churchyard** A statue said to come from Sandwell Hall (BOE p218).

Patshull Hall & The Astleys, Pigots and Legges...

The family with the coat of arms of Washington in their arms Astley of Patshull Hall (ES Aug 6 1930 p5p. Feb 19 1932 p6); it is six quartered, the second is Washington. Or Legge with the marriage of Col Legge (see below) to Elizabeth, daughter and heiress of Sir William Washington, of Packington, Leics (great-great-great aunt of George Washington) (SLM Winter 1954 p10). **The estate reputedly lost and won back in a day** Patshull; two ornamental gamecocks in ornate gateposts beside the churchyard are said to commemorate the occasion when an Astley lost the estate and won it back all in one day on cockfighting wagers (SLM Autumn 1954 p110) (VB p71). **'one of the bloodiest battles ever witnessed on Shropshire or Staffordshire soil'** Out-of-season cock fighting match between the 'Gentlemen of Staffordshire' and the 'Gentlemen of Birmingham' for 25 guineas a battle - and 500 guineas the main contest, at Patshull Park in Jan 1862 hosted by Lord Dartmouth (TB May 23 2002). **World record for the most holes in golf in a week** Colin Young at Patshull Park Golf Course. Using a buggy for transport, he completed 1260 holes (6412 yards) between July 2-9 1988 (GBR 1995 p259). **'Patshull'** a four year old colt belonging to Sir G Pigot which was ridden in the Bridgnorth July meeting in 1824 by H Arthur (TB July 3 2003 p23). **Staffordshire's 8th earliest commutation of tithes when they were dealt with under a parliamentary enclosure act** The great and small tithes of the manors of Patshull and Pattingham, by allotments of land and money payments, 1799. The **PIGOT** that: was **governor of Madras 1755-63, 1775-77, could be considered Patshull's most famous old worthy** George Pigot, Baron Pigot (1719-77). A nabob, owner of the famous Pigot diamond

- which he reputedly sold for £10,000 to buy Patshull - and Lord of Patshull. In the East India Company, 1736; governor and commander-in-chief of Madras, 1755-63, 1775- (but fell out with his council, and his opponents injudiciously had him imprisoned to his death); baronet 1764; bought Patshull and became M.P. for Wallingford, 1765; created an Irish peer as Baron Pigot in 1766. He was once famously described as 'a man of supreme vanity and vaunt' by a naval officer Samuel Cornish to Lord Anson (DNB) (SLM Autumn 1954 p11); was **first lord of the Admiralty** in 1782 Hugh Pigot (1722-92), brother of George (d1777) (DNB); was the **naval officer killed by his own mutineering crew off the coast of Puerto Rico** Capt Hugh Pigot (1769-97), the son of Hugh (d1792); he supposedly threatened to flog the last man down the mizen-topsail yard, two raced down lost their hold, fell and died. He is supposed to have exclaimed 'Throw the lubbers overboard'. That night the men mutineered. The **LEGGE** that: was **82nd and 88th Lord Mayor of London** Thomas Legge (alias Leggy) in 1347-48, 1354-55 (P p86); **"Honest Will Legge... the faithfullest servant that ever any Prince had"** Charles I said this a little before his death in praise of Col William Legge, to the Duke of Richmond to pass on to the Prince of Wales. Col Legge escaped imprisonment in Coventry gaol after the battle of Worcester (1651) pretending to be a female servant carrying a chamber pot (SLM Winter 1954 p10 il); **plotted against William III and was imprisoned in the Tower of London** George (d1691), formerly he had been Master of the Ordnance, and Master of the Horse and Gentleman of the Bedchamber to James, Duke of York, created Baron Dartmouth of Devon in 1682 (DNB); was **friend of Queen Anne** William (d1750), 2nd Baron, 1st Earl of Dartmouth, Lord Privy Seal 1713, one of the Lords Justices of Great Britain (SLM Winter 1954 p11). **'Brother Dartmouth', "one who wears a coronet and prays", "Twenty-six Letters to a Nobleman", "the good Lord Dartmouth", "the Psalm-singer"** William (d1801), 2nd Earl, so called the first by his fellow Methodists at Wednesbury (HOS 1998 p69), the second by the poet Cowper, the third by John Newton, whom he nominated to the curacy of Olney, the fourth by his admirers, the fifth by his detractors (SLM Winter 1954 p12). He has the finest memorial in Dartmouth College (SLM Winter 1954 p12); was one of **'Fox's Martyrs' 1784** George (d1810) 3rd Earl; was the **last to live at Sandwell Hall** and called **'Billy My Lord'** William (d1853), 4th Earl (WBY p8); was **MP for South Staffordshire 1849-53** William Walter (b1823), 5th Earl; was **1st president of the Staffordshire Parish Register Society** William Heneage (d1936), 6th Earl; was **Lord Great Chamberlain of England** William (d1958), 7th Earl, serving 1928 to 1936 (SLM Winter 1954 p12); was **Chief Constable of Berkshire** Humphry (d1962), 8th Earl, serving 1932-54 (WBY p9).

The area...

County's 124th largest parish, consisting of 1,824 acres; **67th= farthest parish away from the county town**, 14.7m SSW; **extremist length** 1.7m, making it **29th= shortest parish in the county; extremist width** 3m. **Chief settlement** Patshull, a tiny estate hamlet. **Geology** BURNHILL Green - Keuper Sandstones; HIGH PARK - Keuper Sandstones; MIDDLE Ley - Keuper Red Marls; OLD PARK - Bunter; PATSHULL HALL - Keuper Sandstones; SNOWDON - Keuper Red Marls. **Highest Point** 502 feet on Tettenhall boundary in High Park. **Lowest Point** 207 feet on the Shrops border, SW of Lower Snowdon. Patshull was **137th most-populated Staffordshire parish in 1801** with 160; **139th in 1811** with 142; **139th in 1821** with 144; **139th in 1831** with 132; **144th in 1841** with 117; **143rd in 1851** with 112; **141st in 1861** with 194; **136th in 1871** with 208; **139th in 1881** with 193; **134th in 1891** with 234; **134th in 1901** with 222.

Pattingham
Did you know that...

Pattingham's top folklore That there was a lost prehistoric city in Wrottesley Old Park and it stretched southwards to cover common land in Pattingham parish. A flat oval stone about a yard long with a cross moline cut into it in basso relievo ten inches each way has been found near Patshull Park on Westbeech Heath. **Only place in Staffordshire with certain 'ham' (= village) ending in its name** Pattingham (PNSZ p25). **Staffordshire's best treasure trove bargain** A D-shaped gold ingot found in the parish, worth £152, 1780, but the ploughman who discovered it sold it in Birmingham for only 1L.18 shillings (not the same as the torc above) (SHOS vol 2 p279) (SVS p322 note) (THS p188) (NSJFS 1964 p31). The **name Pattingham first appears** in Domesday Book, 1086. **Only Staffordshire possession of the Priory of St John at La Launde, Leics** Land at Pattingham; the priory was founded by Richard and Maud Basset (P p59). **Staffordshire's 8th earliest commutation of tithes**

Patting -ham church, Jack Thomason, strongman, drives a plough,
angel bust from Houses of Parliament in the churchyard

when they were dealt with under a parliamentary enclosure act The great and small tithes of the manors of Patshull and Pattingham, by allotments of land and money payments, 1799. **What Pattingham is famous for** A Middle Bronze Age gold torc found in the village. **Staffordshire Best Kept Village South Staffordshire District (Large Village) winner 1988, 1994** Pattingham.

People...

'The Ploughboy Hercules', 'one of the strongest men in the world', 'The man who challenged 'The Strongest Man on Earth'' Jack Thomason, strongman, members of whose family worked at Clive Farm, Pattingham. In the 1900s he may have taken on Arthur Saxon (who styled himself 'The Strongest Man on Earth'), in a weightlifting contest at a Wolverhampton theatre. In 1908 he was acclaimed 'one of the strongest men in the world' when he lifted a horse and four men on a platform, with the combined weight of 25 cwt, at The Empire Theatre, Dudley. After owning a gymnasium at Merry Hill, Penn, Thomason emigrated to Australia (TB June 1994 p5p. Sept 9 2004 p31p). **The man who conducted an orchestra on the summit of Ben Nevis** Harold W Fones (1901-94), born Pattingham, but his childhood was spent at Old Meeting Road, Coseley. Violinist whose Dudley Youth Orchestra played at the top of Ben Nevis in 1962. The Orchestra were winners at the Blackpool Music Festival on three separate occasions in the late 1950s. In addition he founded the South Staffordshire String Orchestra (TB June 1994 p15p). **Last man known to have been hung at Pattingham** Richard Wygan hung in 1422 for committing diverse felonies, and consequently had his robe and hood confiscated by the lord of the manor. The execution took place probably at the gallows in the Woodhouses area (translation of the Manor Court Rolls by Jim Sutton, 2008) (VCH vol 20 p180). **Pattingham's villains** The Bedhouses of Nurton appear to have been a violent family: Thomas Bedhouse, labourer, violently assaulted and beat the constable William Blakemore at Nurton on July 5 1758; whilst his wife Pen Bedhouse, and three daughters Ester, Mary and Amy on March 19 1764 violently assaulted and beat the constable William Bolton in the road at Nurton. Another occasion the constable was attacked was when Abel Clarke, labourer of Pattingham parish, assaulted William Wheeler on Sept 9 1737 (D21/A/pk/9-11). **Pattingham's hero** Christopher Henry Congreve Dent BA, MB, B.ch (Cantab), MRCS (Eng), LRCP (Lond) Surgeon Lieut. Royal Naval Volunteers Reserve, who was killed in action in HMS Hood in 1941 (from his memorial in the church). **Pattingham's vagabond** Sarah Jones of Pattingham, aged 21, who was committed to the house of correction at Wolverhampton and put to hard labour for seven days from 26 Dec 1800 for 'wandering aboard and lodging in the open air' at Wolverhampton after which she was to be removed to her parish of settlement - Pattingham (D3451/5/407). **Pattingham's saddest** William Doran, labourer on Little Moore farm, occupied by G Faulkner, while driving along the high road in his cart was crushed by a cart heavily laden with manure coming in the opposite direction on June 30 1870: 'The poor fellow soon succumbed to his injuries' (SA July 9 1870 p5 col 1). **Pattingham's kindest** Martha Simmons (d1878) left £200, the interest to be distributed among the poor of Pattingham not receiving parish relief (VCH vol 20 p184). **Pattingham's poorest** A poorhouse was built in 1642-3. A workhouse, erected in the mid 1720s, stood near the vicarage house N of the church; it seems to have gone out of use by 1793 (VCH vol 20 p180). From 1836 the poor went to Seisdon union workhouse. **First persons in the parish register** Rowlande Lawrence and Margerie Dex married Aug 26 1559. **Pattingham's earliest recorded will** Belongs to Elizabeth Cokis, and is dated March 4 1537/8. **Choicest quote** Ellen Thorneycroft Fowler of Tettenhall in her novel 'Place and Power' (1903) evokes the landscape west of Wrottesley Hall (her Baxendale Hall) 'Conrad went out walking, with his gun in his hand, into that far country, belonging to his father, which lay between the Northbridge road and the road to Mattingham.... The ground sloped down in a sudden descent like an emerald waterfall, and then spread itself out into waves and billows of greensward, until it reached the bottom of the valley, where there lay a perfect garden of orchards and meadows and russet-tinted woods. Through this valley a silver thread marked the highway which the river had made for itself; and on the other side, in the far blue distance, were ranged the ramparts of the everlasting hills.'

Church...

At Pattingtham is St Chad, **one of 4 such county dedications** (of ancient parish churches); **5th= oldest county church** dating from 1090. **Note** A reredos by J Oldrid Scott (Scott's son), glass windows by Kempe, and bell ringing notice boards in the belfry which tell of the complete peal of Grandsire Triples consisting of 5,040 changes was rung in 1865 and again by the Yorkshire Association of change ringers in 1892. **In the churchyard** The oldest gravestone is dated 1661, a small stone near the porch (P p56). Against the S wall by the door is the statue of angel bust from Houses of Parliament, presented by Mr Geoffrey H_____? M.P. The grave of **Pattingham's longest-serving vicar** William George Greensheet (d1900), who served for 53 years, between 1847 and 1900.

The area...

County's 105th largest parish, consisting of 2,529 acres; **63rd= farthest parish away from the county town**, 15m SSW; **extremist length** 2.8m; **extremist width** 2.9m. **Chief settlement** Pattingham, a pleasant growing village, because of its proximity to Wolverhampton and Telford. **Geology** PATTINGHAM village, The Clive, Great Moor - Keuper Sandstones; WESTBEECH - Keuper Red Marls; S - Bunter. **Highest point** 525 feet W of Meer Oak. **Lowest point** 187 feet on Shrops border by Nun Brook. Pattingham was **72nd most-populated Staffordshire parish in 1801** with 750; **70th in 1811** with 798; **75th in 1821** with 866; **79th in 1831** with 817; **81st in 1841** with 802; **76th in 1851** with 939; **76th in 1861** with 959; **77th in 1871** with 924; **78th in 1881** with 955; **80th in 1891** with 859; **82nd= in 1901** with 779.

Pelsall

Out-township of Wolverhampton parish, 12.6m SSE of Stafford; **extremist length** 1.9m; **extremist width** 1.8m. The **name Pelsall first appears** in 996. **Chief settlement** Pelsall, a large residential village-cum-town, with an industrial past. **What Pelsall is famous for** An association with the Anglo-Saxon matriarch Lady Wulfrun of Wolverhampton. **Pelsall's earliest recorded wills** Belong to John Holmer, and John Horton, and both date Nov 1 1622.

Penn

Did you know that...

Penn's top folklore There is a story of how the owner of Straw Hall, a brick farmhouse on the Penn Road near the Royal Wolverhampton School, was robbed and murdered by highwaymen just as he was approaching home. His body was thrown into a sandpit opposite the house. Early maps show a number of sand and gravel pits in the area of Straw Hall. There is a local tradition that one pit in front of Goldthorn Terrace, which has never been built on, is a plague burial place (PENOP p49p). **'Penn Nibs'** Affectionate name for local lads (St Bartholomew's (Penn) Trail, Wolverhampton City Council, 2006).

Mock Tudor houses of Finchfield, Penn Common Horse Show and Gymkhana, a 1920s golfer, Tony Butler - creator of football phone-ins

Also The Pen Nib motor bicycle built by HW (Bill) Boulton of Penn Garage, Lloyd Hill, in the early 1920s (Black Country Road Transport. Jim Boulton. 1995. p41ps). **National home (2002) of the Association of Bottled Beer Collectors (1983)** Woodhall Rd, Upper Penn. **What Penn is famous for** A preaching cross erected by Lady Godiva in the churchyard. **First winner of the Earl of Dartmouth Silver Challenge Cup** Mr RH Bailey of South Staffordshire Club at Penn Golf Links, on Aug 25 1894. The Cup, open to members of South Staffordshire, and Staffordshire Golf Clubs, his lordship being president of both, was held at Stafford in 1895, then alternatively at Penn and Stafford. By 1896 the record round at Penn stood at 80 by a player not in a competition (SA Aug 25 1894 p4 col 6. Aug 29 1896 p4 col 6). **Staffordshire's best maintained village hall 'adopted section' 1976, 1978** Victory Hall, built 1953, at Lower Penn, winning the 'adopted section' for a hall converted from an earlier building; the competition is organised by the Community Council of Staffordshire (E&S Nov 25 1976. Nov 23 1978 TN 1). **Staffordshire Best Kept Village winner (Small Village) 1978** Lower Penn, and also it was the first time Lower Penn had entered the competition (E&S Aug 7 1978 p19). It also won the following year 1979 in the same category. **The West Midlands 'Hickstead'** Penn Common Horse Show and Gymkhana, started in 1977, with the intention of becoming the West Midlands 'Hickstead' (Wolverhampton Chronicle Sept 9 1977).

People...

Penn's most famous old worthy, and kindest Dr Raphael Sedgwick (c1679-1747). Philanthropist and "the best known parishioner of Penn" (Prebendary E Hartill in his very erroneous The history of Penn and Her Church, 1974). He came to Penn on his marriage to Ann Bradney (d1728), a Lower Penn heiress, and is remembered for five almshouses (now Penn Hall) in memory of their daughter Anne Bach Sedgwick (d1719), and further instruction in his will that his heirs be charged with the cost of keeping them in repair. **Penn's villain turned hero** Thomas Bradney, heir and kinsman of Dr Sedgwick. When Dr Sedgwick died leaving money for the upkeep of five almshouses at Upper Penn. in 1747 he instructed Bradney in his will to maintain them. But despite a large inheritance from the Doctor, Bradney showed little interest in the almshouses and it was not until a decretal order had been obtained against him in Chancery (in 1760) that he began to comply with the terms of his inheritance. The Black Country Bugle says it was for this reason he became known in the locality as 'Backward' Bradney. 'However, he appears to have had a change of heart for in 1765 he was prominent among several members of the local landed gentry who jointly paid for a new tower to be erected at Penn. Bradney became an influential figure in county circles, serving for a period as High Sheriff of Staffordshire. He died in 1782, leaving his worldly goods to his daughters Esther and Ellen. The latter married William Pershouse Esquire and they were proud enough of their benefactor to have their second son, baptised on November 24th 1787, named Thomas Bradney Pershouse... (TB Dec 1996 p10). The almshouses became a private residence called Penn Hall. **Penn's**

bravest Douglas Morris Henry Harris (1898-1917), born Penn, Royal Naval Volunteer Reservist wireless operator who stayed at his post on a drifter blockading Cattaro port, preventing the Austrian Navy using the Adriatic, continuing to radio for assistance as Austrian destroyers attacked but lost his life, May 14 1917; British and Italian alike mourned his self-sacrifice and he was buried with full military honours at Tarato town cemetery, Italy; in 1919 a bust of him, carved by RAJ Emerson, was unveiled by St Peter's churchyard, Wolverhampton (TB March 17 2005 p13p). **'the most beauteous of women of her time'** Lady Godiva, who possessed the manor of Lower Penn, as described by the chronicler Ingulphus. **Captain of the fastest transatlantic passenger ship** The captain of 'The Mauretainia' (Blue Riband Awardist), may have lived at 'The View' on Church Hill, Upper Penn (St Bartholomew's (Penn) Trail, Wolverhampton City Council, 2006). **British Open runner-up 1925, French Championship runner-up 1929, News of the World Tournament (PGA) winner 1925 and 1927, Gleneagles Tournament winner 1925** Charlie Stowe, born 1893 at No. 11 Turf Cottages, Penn Common, of Penn Artisans Golf Club (PONP pp113-114) (Wolverhampton Chronicle Jan 7 2000 p14). **'The Poet of Penn Fields'** Marjorie Crosbie (1892-1971), born Worcester Lodge, Penn Fields. Her first collection was 'Life's Changes and Other Poems' (1912) (BCM Spring 2007 pp49-50p). **Penn's Pam Ayres** Mrs Edith Bryant, of Springfield Lane, Lower Penn, originally of Tettenhall Road, Wolverhampton, who was a guest speaker addressing her audiences in rhyme at local women's association meetings in the 1970s, a long compiler of poetry. Ayres, of Stanford-in-the-Vale, Berks, made her TV debut on a talent show in 1975, going on to have a successful career as a performer of her own comic verse (Wolverhampton Chronicle April 22 1977 p6p). **Gardener of the Year 1976 runner-up** Mrs AE Simmons of Bhylls Lane, Lower Penn, in a national competition organised by Garden News magazine (E&S Oct 22 1976). **'fast-talking sports king of the local airwaves', creator of football phone-ins** Radio presenter Tony Butler (born Wolverhampton 1935, residing Lower Penn by 1976), on BBC WM; he also fronted the first show for commercial radio station BRMB Feb 1974, where he had developed phone in programmes by 1976 and is famous for his catch phrase 'on yer bike!' and straight talking (Wolverhampton Chronicle June 10 1976 p) (BBC website, 2006). **1978 signet (sailing) class national champions** Graham Burrows, helmsman, of Penn and his crewman Paul Jones of Kingswinford, won all six of their races over a week's sailing in Wales (County Express March 23 1979 p13p). **Penn's poorest** May have been accommodated in a workhouse in Workhouse Lane (St Bartholomew's (Penn) Trail, Wolverhampton City Council, 2006). From 1836 the poor went to Seisdon union workhouse. **Penn's earliest recorded will** Belongs to William Garbott of Nether Penn, and is dated April 9 1543. **First person in the parish register** Thomas son of Harri Wollastone baptised Jan 1 1570. **Choicest quote** The diary of a Penn Fields doctor, for 1863, believed to be Frederick Turton of Ablow House, Dudley Road, was found? on a market stall at Bilston (TB Feb 28 2002 p10). Two concurrent entries well evokes the genteel nature of Penn as an emerging Victorian suburb - 'JULY 17 1863 ...Mrs Hinks (Turton's mother-in-law-to-be from the Isle of Man) came to Mr McMann's last night. Mary (Turton's fiancee) went to stay at Uplands' 'JULY 18 1863 ...went with Mary to Uplands to supper.'

Churches...

At Upper Penn is St Bartholomew, **one of 6 such county dedications** (of ancient parish churches); **48th= oldest AP county church** dating from 1200. **Note** The floorslab memorial to the first owner of Trescott Grange, Richard Chapman (d1645) on the chancel floor (SHOS vol 2 p218). **In the churchyard** Preaching cross base known as Lady Godiva's Cross c1050. Another cross base restored in 1912. The epitaph on the headstone to Edmund Gold d1730 interested historian Stebbing Shaw (SHOS vol 2 p219). **Penn's longest-serving vicar** John Moy (or Monoy), who served 45 years, 1454-99. At **Lower Penn** is St Anne (c1888). At **Penn Fields** is St Philip (1859). At **Finchfield** is St Thomas. At **Muchall** is St Aidan (1962). At **Castlecroft** is The Good Shepherd. At **Merry Hill** is St Joseph of Arimathea (rebuilt 1990).

The area...

Penn is the county's 66th largest parish, consisting of 4,003 acres; **57th= farthest parish away from the county town**, 15.8m SSW; **extremist length** 2.9m; **extremist width** 4.4m. Earliest record of the name Domesday Book, 1086. **Chief settlement** Upper Penn; the rest of the Upper Penn township is also Wolverhampton residential suburb, much of it desirable. Lower Penn township is predominately still rural. **Geology** LOWER PENN - Keuper Sandstones (Lower Penn village, Orton Hills), Bunter (N and rest); UPPER PENN - Bunter (Upper Penn, Bradmore villages, and N), Permian (Penn Common). **Highest point** Colton Hills at 590 feet. **Lowest point** 272 feet on Wombourne boundary by Smestow Brook SW of Furnace Grange. **Southern-most extent of the last Ice Age** About Penn (WJO Nov 1909 p293). Penn was **74th most-populated Staffordshire parish in 1801** with 700; **72nd in 1811** with 780; **82nd in 1821** with 769; **77th in 1831** with 863; **73rd= in 1841** with 942; **68th in 1851** with 1,160; **57th in 1861** with 1,765; **52nd in 1871** with 2,184; **44th in 1881** with 2,804; **40th in 1891** with 2,941; **38th in 1901** with 3,449.

Rowley Regis
Did you know that...

Rowley Regis' top folklore That an Elaine or Eleanor of Hayseech Mill fell in love with a young monk of Halesowen Abbey. The abbot was informed of them and partly went in search of them. They are said to have hidden in one of the secret passages between the abbey and Haden Old Hall and were bricked up in it. Ever since, the monk's ghost is often seen walking and praying, whilst Elaine's ghost is seen crying and with wringing hands. A ghost of a lady in white, seen on

'Cradley Heathens' have the most British National Speedway Knock-out Cup wins, a female nailer in the shadow of the Hailstone rock. The harp represents Rowley Regis' prowess at Jew's Harp-making

the stairs of Haden Old Hall and drifting across the surface of a pond in the south part of Haden Hill Park, has been identified with Elaine. **What Rowley Regis is famous for** Chain making, Staffordshire Bull terriers, hills, rag stone, Jews' harps. The **name Rowley first appears** in 1173; Kings Rowley appears in c1564. **14th building society ever** Rowley Building Society, which had their inaugural meeting on April 9 1794, with the founding members - John Mackmillan, Anthony Miller, William Bridgewater, Benjamin Bolton, John Auden - agreeing to establish a society in Oct 1792. Thirteen houses were built on a site which is now Stanford Drive, opposite where the Rowley Regis Grammar School used to stand (TB Aug 24 2006 p15p of the cottage built by the Society, which were demolished c1970). **Staffordshire's 6th earliest commutation of tithes when they were dealt with under a parliamentary enclosure act** The impropriate and vicarial tithes of Rowley Regis, by allotments of land, 1799. **'one of the most extraordinary civil cases ever tried before any tribunal whatever'** The 'Rhinoceros Case' which tried to prove British Iron Co. had unlawfully taken possession of the Corngreaves estate since they had rescinded on the original contract. After 14 trials 1826-38 the House of Lords ruled in favour of the estate's owner. **'one of the poorest parishes in the Black Country'** Rowley Regis, according to its Parish Church Magazine of May 1923 (TB March 2 2006 p23). **First street lights in Cradley Heath High Street** Sept 14 1880 (TB Jan 18 2007 p6). **The Christmas carol tune called 'Rowley**

Regis' A tune composed in c1880s by Joseph 'Singer Joe' Parkes of the old Causeway Chapel, Blackheath, for the carol 'Brightest and Best' by Rev Reginald Heber, 1811 (TB Dec 22 2005 p13). **Last tram from Cradley Heath to Dudley** Ran on Dec 31 1929 (TB March 1 2007 p21). **'one of the worst ever Black Country blazes'** A fire on Aug 23 1932 at the works of T.W. Lench Ltd at Blackheath, beginning at 10.00am, because of over-filling an fuel-oil tank, flames reached a height of more than 75 feet. Fifty men from from eight fire brigades attended (TB Feb 12 2004 p2ops). **'Rowley Salmon'** Is cheese (Q&ABC no. 193). **First films in Cradley Heath** Shown at the old Workers' Institute in Lomey Town, corner of Whitehall Road (TB April 19 2001 p6). **England's first Christie console organ with an all-electric action and the largest of its kind produced** Installed in the new Majestic cinema, Cradley Heath, opened March 27 1933. The first film shown was 'The Flag Lieutenant' (TB Nov 1997 p16. March 1 2007 p21). **The ship Rowley Regis adopted in WW2** HMS Tumult; it captured a German flag which was then shown round the borough (RRAH p120). **First of the four Rowley Hall (Blackheath) flats** Moorlands Court, 15 story high, opened on June 12 1965 (County Express June 19 1965 p20p). **Climate extremes for the Rowley Hills** Coldest March in recent times - 1975 with 3.1c average; warmest March in recent times - 1990 with 7.7c average; longest surviving snow - Turner's Hill still had snow in July 1947 (TB April 5 2001 p23. Sept 6 2001 p25). **One of the first schools to be elevated to Selective Central School status** Upper Standard Council School, Wright's Lane, Old Hill, in Jan 1925; it became Rowley Regis Grammar School in Sept 1946, and moved to Hawes Lane, 1962 (TB Dec 19 2002 p20p). **The Real Curry Restaurant Guide Best in Britain Award 1998** Rowley Village Tandoori, Portway Road (TB June 1998 p20).

People...

Rowley Regis' most famous old worthy James Woodhouse (1735-1820). 'Cobbler Poet' of the Woodhouse family of Portway Hall. Became a shoemaker as a boy. William Shenstone was an early patron and his 'Poems on Sunday Occasions' (1764) earned him celebrity. Johnson, who did not think too highly of him, told him to "Give days and nights, Sir, to the study of Addison." He was later a bailiff in the north of England; returned to Rowley c1778; and resident of London where he died in a curious street accident. He is buried in the churchyard of St George's chapel, near Marble Arch. **Rowley Regis' villain** A man also known by the alias Jack the Ripper, who was active at Hawes Hill fields; his chief crime was the hamstringing of horses (BCWJ p107). **Rowley Regis' kindest** Lady Elizabeth Monnins of Tividale Hall who was the first person to give money for education in the parish, 1703. **Rowley Regis' poorest** Rowley Regis workhouse stood on the S side of Dudley Road, near the present St James Ave, at Tippity Green. It existed some years prior to 1800 (RRAH p21). In 1849 there was a proposal to vacate it in favour of a new Union workhouse to be built at Dudley (SA Oct 20 1849 p5 col 1). Of one workhouse governor, Joseph Windsor (d1800), it was said he 'lived

like an infidel' (RRAH p44). **Rowley Regis' saddest** Perhaps Sarah Bennett, whose burial on April 7 1813 at the age of 20 is recorded in the parish register, which notes she was "A dwarf and dumb idiot and a dwarf of not much above three feet high" (TB March 1 2007 p5). **Last-known sale of a wife in Staffordshire** Lydia Green sold by her husband Job Green of Cherry Orchard at Old Hill in 1840s. Theophilus Dunn 'The Dudley Devil' had advised Job of this old custom to get rid of an unwanted wife. Lydia was 'knocked-down' to a local bachelor for sixpence, but purchaser's mother refused to let the her into their house. Happily, for Lydia her family took her in, with whom she lived for the rest of her life (TB June 1993 p1. Oct 1996 p5). **Staffordshire's most famous female impostor** Lillias Lima Valerie Barber (b1895) who posed as her husband on his death, or reconstructed herself as Col Sir Leslie Victor Gauntlet Bligh Barker DSO, Bt, obtaining many short term positions; including groom to a baronet of Hall Street, Dudley, and perhaps as Col Barker or Baker, the manager of a colliery at Oakham in the 1920s; she married two women at different times, and went to prison for deception and indecency. She died reputedly in Suffolk in 1960. Her last identity was as a Geoffrey Norton (News of the World) (TB Feb 1994 p5. March

1994 p13. April 1994 p17). **Woman with over-productive breasts** Leah Aynsworth, who lived in C16, is said to have produced as much milk from her breasts as the Mary Eagle of Little Wyrley Dr Plot noted in the C17; she reputedly could produce two quarts of milk from her breasts per day, besides what her child sucked (NHS p285) (BCWJ pp107-108). **Strange but true!** The wife of Daniel Johnson, who lived at Portway, was a 'thoughtless woman' who made a boast that she would outlive her son, William Eagles Johnson. She was then suddenly taken ill and died within 12 hours, late 1800 (RRAH p45). **'one of the great Black Country characters of the 19th century'** County Express on Benjamin Billingham (1811-95) alias 'Benny Fiddler', who weighed some 29 stones and was unable to climb the stairs of his pub, Bell Inn, Five Ways, Cradley Heath, where he was publican in 1841. Benny got his nickname because of his skill with the fiddle. Buried St Luke's churchyard (County Express Sept 25 1970 photo) (TB April 12 2001 p25. May 10 2001 p25p). **First charter mayor of Rowley Regis** Ben Hobbs of Blackheath, when Rowley Regis became a borough on Charter Day Sept 28 1933 (TB Feb 3 2005 p37. March 3 2005 p18p. Feb 14 2008 pp20-21ps). **First female mayor of Rowley Regis** Polly Pritchard (b1888) of Cradley Heath, mayor 1959-60. She was the first lady in the borough to hold the two offices of alderman (1957-) and mayor (TB Jan 24 2008 p19p). **Rowley Regis's 1st soldier killed in WW1** Gunner William Hughes, 13th Battery, Royal Field Artillery, of Powke Lane, Blackheath, killed Sept 15 1914, aged 19. His name is recorded on the La Ferre-Sous-Jouarre memorial in France. It's **last soldier to die in WW1** was Sergt TJE Price, 14th Light Armoured Motor Battalion, of Hollybush St, Cradley Heath, who died in Russia on May 25 1919, and is buried in Baghdad North Gate Cemetery, Iraq (TB April 19 2007 p25). **'Oldest Scout in the world'** Joseph Jaquiss died 1943 aged 87, district scoutmaster at Old Hill, and headmaster of Cradley C of E school. He had formed possibly the first troop (known as Lone Scouts) in Worcs in Jan 1908, only months after the launch of Scouts in 1907 (TB Aug 17 2000 p11). **'one of the youngest women in the country' appointed headteacher 1947** Miss Maud Westwood, born Old Hill, appointed head of Rowley Regis Secondary School for Girls (popularly known as Siviters Lane) in 1947; retired 1972 (Rowley: Britain in Old Photographs. Anthony Page. 2001. p37p). **'World's Champion Ox Roaster'** As Harry Johnson of Cradley Heath styled himself (TB July 6 2000 p13p. Aug 2 2007 p15p). **One of the Black Country's greatest church organ exponents** Thomas Cartwright (1893-1985) born Meredith St, Cradley Heath. He was deputy organist at St Luke, Cradley Heath 1908-16, and organist 1939-55; organist at:- St John, Dudley Wood 1919-39, Lye parish church 1955-60, St Luke, Dudley 1967-8, St Augustine, Holly Hall 1968-, and at St Peter, Darby End (TB Feb 8 2001 p14p). **'One of the Black Country's best known sopranos'** Nora Pegg (nee Bennett) (1911-2007), born Blackheath, former office clerk at TW Lench Ltd; later resided at Cradley and Hagley (TB Oct 4 2007 p13p). **Daily Mail Literary Competition winner 1971** Susan Price (b1955/6), native of Tividale (BCM July

1975 pp61-62) (VFC p109). **The girl who asked the Prime Minister if he would like to be Manager of the England football team** Helena Cobb, aged 11, a WBA supporter of Rowley Regis in Oct 1999. She also asked if so, what team would he pick. Tony Blair replied he would leave the job to the then England manager Kevin Keegan, adding "I've got enough on my plate as it is" (BBC news Oct 7 1999). **Turner Prize nominee 2001** Richard Billingham of Cradley Heath, 31, photographer (Daily Telegraph Magazine Nov 17 2001 pp60-67pc). **First person in the parish register** Thomas son of Richard Lyddiate baptised Jan 1539. **Choicest quote** Francis Brett Young in his novel 'The Iron Age' (1916) evokes the New British Ironworks and the Hall at Corngreaves in this extract: "For the next thirty years the new stony continents had never ceased clamouring for iron; and round the centre of the little thudding Gunbarrels and the old brick mansion with had been bought for the sake of the veins of coal beneath it, the little world of Mawne pushed out along the valley, burning into the hem of the green fringe."

Sport...

The Black Country's 'Greatest ever' footballing product Perhaps Steve Bloomer, born Lyde Green, Cradley, Worcs, but played briefly for Cradley Heath 'Lukes'; scored 28 times in 23 games for England, 1897-; setting a record not beaten for almost half a century (TB April 1996 p35p). **Rowley Regis' pugilist** Ned Round alias Ned Brade, the 'Rowley Bruiser', acknowledged champion of Rowley village and the area, winner of many fights (TFBC p163). **Amateur Boxing Association Light-Welterweight Champion 1964** and **Midland Counties Light-Welterweight Champion 1961-4** Robert 'Tag' Taylor of Blackheath (TB July 20 2000 p18). **Hottest forward of the future in English soccer** James Hunt (b1993) of Tividale; played for Kingswinford Boys; 78 goals in 14 matches (BBC Midlands Today Jan 19 2001). **'one of the finest bowlers in cricket of his generation', 'Peter Pan of Cricket', record holder for most wickets in a career with Warwickshire CC** William Eric Hollies (1912-81) grew up in Old Hill. He played for England c1935-, and Warws 1932-57 achieving 2,201 wickets (ORR p124p) (TB Sept 12 2002 p25p). He is one of only a handful of bowlers to have dismissed the great Australian batsman Don Bradman for a duck - breaking his wicket in the 5th test at The Oval in Aug 1948, which was Bradman's last appearance for Australia (TB Aug 25 2005 p30). **Most British National Speedway Knock-out Cup wins** Cradley Heath, alias the 'Cradley Heathens', winners 8 times by 1992. Speedway Provincial League winners 1961, 1963 Cradley Heath (GBR 1990 p283. 1992 p297). **Masters World Champion Over 70's Squash player 2004-5** John Cox, born Old Hill, retired doctor of Hereford (TB June 16 2005 p31p).

Staffordshire Bull Terriers...

First reference to the breed as Staffordshire Bull Terrier c1928, before which it was known as the Fighting Terrier, or Bull and Terrier and the Pit-Dog, or 'miner's dog'. Even in the Black Country the name commonly used was only the Stafford (by 1866), or Bull and Terrier (TB Nov 28 2002 p13p. July 29 2004 p16). **Original home of the Staffordshire Bull Terrier** The breed was first reared at Cradley Heath (SGS p90). **First recognition as a pedigree breed by the Kennel Club** 1935. **First meeting of the Staffordshire Bull Terrier Club** The Old Cross Guns, Cradley Heath, July 16 1935 (TB Dec 19 2002 p15. Sept 18 2003 p10). **Their first show** Cradley Heath, Aug 17 1935 (TB Aug 28 2003 p18). **Dog on which the original standard was based** Shaw's 'Jim' or later renamed 'Jim the Dandy' (TB Dec 19 2002 p15). **First showing at Crufts and first award there for Best of Breed** Cross Guns Johnson reared by Joe Mallen in 1936 (TB Aug 28 2003 p18). **Most famous 'Stafford' terrier, Crufts best Stafford pup in show 1938, Staffordshire Bull Terrier Supreme Champion 1939** Gentleman Jim (d1947), born May 25 1937, champion of many battles, owned by Joe Mallen of Cradley Heath (The Staffordshire Bull Terrier Handbook. John F Gordon. 1951) (TB Aug 28 2003 p18). **Britain's best living breeder of 'Staffords'** Harry Rogers, born Brickiln Street, Wolverhampton 1926, former boxer, though he has never bred a champion under English K.C. rules, he has given some of his finest stock away (TB May 6 2004 p31p). **Most Staffordshire internet sites** Staffordshire Bull Terrier with 1,252,569 hits in Nov 2006.

Work...

One of the largest producing centres in the Midlands Rowley Regis (Staffordshire County Handbook c1958). **First deep mine in Rowley Regis** Perhaps that opened at Tividale in 1794 by James Keir (RRAH p40). **Last working colliery in Rowley Regis** Bell End Colliery, which closed 1919 (TB Jan 25 2001 p31). **'inferior to none in the kingdom'** Hayseech Mill, a claim in SA March 1807 announcing the sale of the property by auction on March 19 1807, the announcement goes on 'and the machinery is all upon the newest and most approved principles.' (TB Feb 5 2004 p6). **Oldest quarry in the Rowley Rag stone** Cox's Rough near Darby's Hill (NSFCT 1876 p9). **'Superior to any other in Staffordshire for paving and Macadamising purposes... in any quantities'** Frost Brothers of Tividale (Rowley Rag) Stone Quarry as claimed by their own advertising in 1860 (RRAH p65). **'Queen of Commerce', 'The Black Widow'** Eliza Tinsley (1813/4-1882), business woman and nail factor mainly at Old Hill and Cradley Heath, whose chain works produced the longest mine-chain ever made. As the most important employer in the area c1871, employing some 4,000 people (though many of were out-workers), she had the largest business of its kind in Staffordshire, with seven warehouses (BCM July 1982 pp43p-46) (TB July/ Aug 1973 p25p. Dec 17 1998 p21p. Oct 4 2001 p7p. March 16 2006 p20p). **'White slaves of England'** What Robert Sherand dubbed the women chainmakers of Cradley Heath in Pearson's Magazine 1896 (TB May 22 2003 p7. Sept 27 2007 p7). **'The Chainmaker's Friend'** Benjamin Billingham (1811-95), publican, brewer, and landowner who ran The Bell Inn on Scholding Green Road (now St Anne's Road) 1840-90; the pub was the base of the local chainmakers' union, in addition Billingham lent the union money during a strike (TB Aug 21 2003 p5p). **First to forge calibrated pulley block chains** Apparently Emmanuel Woodhouse of Premier Works, Newtown Lane, Cradley Heath, in c1860s. These chains being used on the original Weston type pulley blocks (Rowley Regis Official Handbook 1952 p65). **First to manufacture electrically welded chains in England** Samuel Woodhouse & Sons Ltd of Eagle Chain Works, Cradley Heath, c1900; if they were not the first in the country then they were the first in the Cradley Heath district (Rowley Regis Official Handbook 1952 p67). **Last woman chainmaker in England to make chain by hand** Lucy Woodall, born 1899 in Old Hill. Employed at Harry Stevens in Oak St, Old Hill from 1920s; she retired in 1973, due to arthritis, after working for 60 years and one month (E&S Feb 21 2008 Black Country People p21ps). **Cradley Heath's last saddler** Joseph Coles in Graingers Lane; the only traditional saddler left in Rowley Regis borough by 1954 (TB Aug 19 2004 p22ps). **Rowley Regis' largest employer 1952, 'Britain's Best Hollow-ware' 1952** 'Judge' holloware of Ernest Stevens Ltd of Cradley Heath, with 2,000 employees (Rowley Regis Official Handbook 1952 p61, advertising slogan). **First to build and have occupied a post-WW2 private enterprise house in the district** John Harris & Son (Builders) Ltd, of New John St, Blackheaths (Rowley Regis Official Handbook 1952 p61).

Churches & temples...

At **ROWLEY REGIS** village is St Giles and St Michael, **Staffordshire's only such duel dedication** (for ancient parish churches); **2nd last ancient parish county church built** dating from 1922. **'most spectacular (fire) ever seen in the Black Country'** Reputedly when Rowley Regis church was destroyed by fire in 1913 (Q&ABC no. 138). **Rowley Regis' longest-serving vicar (also vicar of Clent)** Thomas Walker, who served for 50 years, 1669-1719. **Rowley Regis' most reforming curate** Rev George Barrs, the reforming curate of Rowley Regis, appointed 1800, who 'was to be one of the major forces for change in the parish for next 40 years'. He was born near Nuneaton. In the parish he married the widow of John Haden of Haden Hill. It was from this house he as much administered the parish as from the vestry (RRAH p44 il). **In Powke Hillock graveyard** Is the grave of Abel Gentry which has a life-size portrait in Rowley Ragstone of this prize fighter and keeper of The Champion Inn on Pennant Hill (TB Aug 1998 p36il). **'a cradle of Christianity' CRADLEY HEATH** on account of its numerous places of worship (TB March 31 2005 p12ps): ie- St Luke (1847), St James' (1876), alias **The 'rhubarb' chapel** as it was perhaps built on fields formerly used for growing rhubarb (RRAH p101), Reddal Hill Methodist church (1871, dem 1984), New Connexion Methodist Christ Church (1885) at Five Ways, Corngreaves Road Baptist church (1904), Graingers Lane Methodist church (1906, closed 2004, dem 2006) (TB Oct 12 2006 p22), Newtown Lane Salvation Army Citadel (dem 2005). **In St Luke's churchyard** The epitaph on the grave of fatman Benjamin Billington reads 'The sweet remembrance of the just, shall flourish when they sleep in dust' (County Express Sept 25 1970). The grave of an extended family who died by suffocation at Cradley Heath within a few days of each other in 1873 Edward Whitehouse aged 29, Jan 20, son of James and Roshannah Whitehouse; also Phoebe Whitehouse, his wife, Jan 22; and Edward Whitehouse, aged 27, Jan 22; also Joseph Edmonds, aged 29, Jan 21; also George Edward Edmonds, aged 11 months, Jan 20; the last three were daughter, son and grandson of Joseph and Hannah Edmonds (TB July 11 2002 p5p). At **BLACKHEATH** is St Paul (1869), Long Lane, and is 100 yards inside Worcs (County Express June 5 1965 p14p). At **TIVIDALE** is Saint Michael the Archangel (1984, rebuilt 1996), Tividale Road; St Augustine (1883), Dudley Road East; Holy Cross (1966), Ashleigh Road. Also the Ebenezer Chapel (Methodist). **Europe's first Hindu temple in the Southern Indian architectural style, and first for the deity Shri Venkateswara (Balaji)** The Shri Venkateswara (Balaji) Temple, at SO 980906, on N side of Dudley Rd East, Brades Village. It was designed to replicate the Tirupati Venkateswara temple in Tirupati, India, opened in 2006 (info Wikipedia 2007, Doug Parish, Dr VPN Rao, David Mawson and others).

The area...

Rowley Regis is the **county's 72th largest parish**, consisting of 3,828 acres; **22st= farthest parish away from the county town**, 19.8m due S; **extremist length** 4.7m; **extremist width** 4.2m. **Chief settlement** Rowley village has long been superseded in size by Black Country towns of Blackheath and Cradley Heath. **Geology** Upper Coal Measures (most), Dolerite (Rowley Regis Hills). **Highest point** Turner's Hill at 890 feet, and therefore is the **highest peak of the Rowley Regis range and in the south of Staffordshire** (SHOS vol 2 p240) (GNHS p183). **Lowest point** 269 feet by the Stour at Cradley Heath. Rowley Regis was **11th most-populated Staffordshire parish in 1801** with 5,027; **16th in 1811** with 4,974; **16th in 1821** with 6,062; **15th in 1831** with 7,438; **12th in 1841** with 1,1111; **11th in 1851** with 14,249; **11th in 1861** with 19,785; **11th in 1871** with 23,534; **12th in 1881** with 27,385; **12th in 1891** with 30,791; **12th in 1901** with 34,670.

Sedgley
Did you know that...

Sedgley's top folklore That people from the two Gornals are dimwits. Hence they are known as Gornal Donkeys. A Gornal man will play a coal shuttle as a musical instrument. A local butcher? had an advertisement showing a pig pulling a trolley loaded with pork with the caption 'Drawing his own conclusion'. A Gornal man could also put a pig on a wall to let it see the village brass band go by. An old picture postcard proves this once happened, although, in fact, it never did. However, this story has become Black Country folklore. Another story tells that the brass band drummer was so small and his drum so big he once lost his way trying to follow the band and arrived

A 'Dudley Locust' fossil as found in Wren's Nest, a Gornal man with a pig on a wall, Sedgley Beacon, a Gornal donkey, Ruiton windmill, bear baiting

at Ruiton beating the drum by himself. As a real instance of this in 1853 a married woman aged 48 who had lived from birth at Gornal appeared before a court but she neither knew the name of the present month, nor those of the first or last months of the year; the case in which she was a witness was adjoined for better testimony than she could give (SA May 21 1853 p5 col 3). **What Sedgley is famous for** Nail making and iron working. The **name Sedgley first appears** in 985. The **last Sedgley manorial court** Took place at Court House Inn (the former manorial court house), by All Saints church, 1925 (SDOP p10p). **First Roman Catholic college established after the Reformation** Sedgley Park School, at Sedgley from 1763 (VCH vol 6 pp156-157). **Most unruly place in the Black Country C18-early C20** Hell Lane. **2nd largest urban district in the country 1867** Lower Sedgley civil parish, later Coseley urban district (CWBT p21). **First order served under the Act empowering the Local Government Board to penalise Boards of Health if they fail to cleanse and deal with refuge** Upper Sedgley LB, described as notorious, served Jan 11 1876 (SA Jan 15 1876 p4 col 6). **First school erected by Sedgley School Board** Daisy Bank School, which opened May 1878 (SA May 4 1878 p7 col 7). **Chavviest school in England** Would be Dormston Secondary School in Sedgley town centre if it wasn't for the school uniform, according to ChavTowns website 2007. **Sedgley's most famous photograph** Probably the one of a dancing bear performing in the Bull Ring, in front of Hilton's, c1901 (Sedgley & District. Trevor Genge. 1995 p114p). **Gornal Cuckoo** Is a donkey (Q&ABC no. 110). **Coseley fan** Is a type of leek (Q&ABC no. 109).

People...

Sedgley's most famous old worthy, first man to produce iron commercially using coke Abraham Darby of Coalbrookdale, born at Old Farm Lodge (just off Wrens Nest Hill) in 1678 (Q&ABC no. 5) (TB June 30 2005 pp22-23). **Sedgley's villains** Rev William Lewis, greedy vicar of Sedgley 1837-70. He rigorously enforced tithe collection, even confiscating goods in lieu of payment. John Cornfield Jnr wrote 'A Round Unvarnished Tale of the Exploits of the Vicar of Sedgley' (1862) condemning him (TB May 1994 pp12-13). Mr W Addenbrooke of Ruiton, treasurer and secretary of the £25 Money Society, who allegedly forged a number of bills which he had discounted by a loan company in a neighbouring town, absconded in 1864 leaving his wife and five children (SA March 19 1864 p5). **Sedgley's poorest** There was a workhouse in Vicar Street by 1777. In 1849 there was a proposal to vocate it in favour of a new Union workhouse to be built at Dudley. About 1858 the poor were removed to Dudley Union workhouse. In Feb 1856 Sarah Wilkes was admitted to Sedgley workhouse with a bad leg, but she bound the wound with a copper coin (a penny) so as to prevent it healing, in order to prolong her visit; she denied it; but was ordered to leave. The old building was sold c1870, and site became the police station (SA Oct 20 1849 p5 col 1) (AMS pp168,178-179). **'one of the best working class composers of the period'** Joseph Nicholds (c1784-1860), in the opinion of HW Small in 'Radio Times' Nov 23 1934 (WBY p64). Landlord of the Hop and Barleycorn Inn, West Coseley, composer of 'Babylon', and 'The Monmouthshire Melodist' (c1812), he ended his days in Dudley workhouse and is buried in the Old Vicar Street cemetery, Sedgley. **Staffordshire's last surviving out-door Parish relief office** Perhaps a brick building in Groucutt Street, Coseley, which stood to at least 1976, in a wall a plaque read 'Sedgley Relieving Officer'; but the word 'Sedgley' had been defaced, probably when Coseley became an urban district in 1895 (Sedgley & District. Trevor Genge. 1995 p85ps). **Coseley's most famous old worthy** John Cornfield Jnr (1820/7-90). Brickmaker, pawnbroker and **'Coseley's Poet'** of Hurst Hill. Radical in local politics, his 'A Round Unvarnished Tale of the Exploits of the Vicar of Sedgley' appeared in 1862, and he was involved in a dispute about tithes with Rev William Lewis, vicar of Sedgley. His **best-known work** is perhaps the long narrative poem 'Allan Chace and other poems' (1877). He drowned in a pond on his Coseley estate on December 6th. **Coseley's villain** Abel Hill, notorious rogue and engineer at Princes End colliery, born in Abigail Lane, Sedgley parish, but much frequented Bilston, where he got into a relationship with a Mary (or Maria) Martin. On Feb 23 1820 he murdered her and their 16-month old son, Thomas, by either drowning them in the canal at

*SEDGLEY PEOPLE -Abraham Darby,
Rev Charles Girdlestone, Reanne Evans*

Glasshouse Bridge, or, and near the Seven Stars Inn, close by Capponfield and Highfield furnaces near Moses Hill, or disposed of their bodies in the canal at this spot. Many folk tales also abound how he reacted at his victims' funeral; that he showed no remorse at the gallows on July 27 1820; that his body was displayed in public in Bilston; that his ghost has been seen in local pits. **Coseley's hero** Thomas Barratt of Coseley who won a V.C. in 1917 while on patrol as a scout and twice came under heavy fire from snipers whom he stalked and killed. When the Germans began to outflank his unit he volunteered to cover the withdrawal but was killed by a shell before he reached friendly lines (TB Feb 8 2007 p15). **Coseley's bravest** Stanley Bertram (Tony) Smith and Teddy Bennett, both aged 15 when they tried to save four children between the ages of 8 and 13 who had fallen into the openwork pool at Brampits on Jan 5 1940; sadly despite the attempt all four died (E&S Jan 6 1940) (TB Oct 27 2005 p18p). **The man who claimed he was "Five feet and an inch/ Five stone and a pound/ D____n such another man"** John Turton Fereday of Ellowes Hall (alias Ellers Hall), near Lower Gornal, who suffered a severe reversal in fortune and died in London 1849, aged 62 (SSUN pp11-12). **The famous scientist who made Wrens Nest famous** Sir Roderik Murchison by his visits with the British Association for the Advancement of Science in 1839 and 1849 (info Dudley Archives). **'The Deepfields Tragedy'** The case of Mrs Mary Davies of Deepfields, accidentally shot dead by her son-in-law John Wise after discovering his wife, Martha, was having an affair with their lodger James Davies, 1890; Wise was convicted of manslaughter (TB Jan 17 2002 pp10-11). **'Most elegant wedding solemnized in Sedgley for a number of years'** When Miss SE Whitehouse, eldest daughter HB Whitehouse of Hurst Hill House married Mr CS Hudson of Wick House, Pershore; the church and principal gates were beautifully decorated with flowers, and the procession was composed of upwards of eight carriages (SSUN p88). **Sedgley girl who worked as a maid for Rudyard Kipling** Betty Thelma (Bess) Williams of Louise Street, Lower Gornal, removed from the Black Country because of suffering from tuberculosis to Sussex where she eventually got a position as housemaid in Kipling's household at Bateman's, Burwash, Sussex in 1930s (TB Dec 15 2005 p23). **The Sedgley man who went down on the Titantic** James Lester, an ironworker travelling with his brother-in-laws, the Davies brothers of West Bromwich, moving jobs to Michigan (TB March 1997 p20). **Distinguished Conduct Medalist** Harry Rollinson (1889-1950), born in Sedgley, award for gallantry and devotion to duty in the field, April 1918. He was a Sergeant in the South Staffordshire Reg (Bilston) (TB May 13 2004 p11). **16th Lieutenant Governor of Saskatchewan** Frederick William Johnson (d1993), born Sedgley, his family emigrated to Canada when he was a child. He served as Lieutenant Governor July 6 1983 to Sept 7 1988. He was given a state funeral (TB Nov 1 2007 p5). **School Technician of the Year 2006** John Burfoot, a design technology technician at Willingsworth High School, this is the top award in the annual National Awards for School Support Staff (TB Dec 14 2006 p6p). **Strange but true!** Dormston School, Sedgley, made the national headlines in March 1999 after 21 female pupils aged from 11 to 16 were suspended and a number of others removed from lessons because their skirts were deemed too short (Wikipedia 2007). **Sedgley's kindest** Mrs Anne Webb of Lichfield, widow, who gave 50L in her lifetime for yearly distribution to poor 'housekeepers' of Sedgley parish, each to get 1 shilling on Thursday before Middle Lent Sunday. **Sedgley's earliest recorded will** Belongs to Henry Cross, and is dated April 13 1518. **First person in the parish register** Thomas Walton baptised Nov 20 1558. **Choicest quote (for the Sedgley side of the parish)** JB Priestley in his English Journey, 1934, reflects on perhaps the **most 'Black Country' of villages**, Lower and Upper Gornal, "I remember arriving at the very end of the earth, where the land appeared to have been uprooted by a giant pig and where there were cottages so small and odd that they must have been built for gnomes, and this end of the earth was called Gornal, and there the women, returning home from the brickworks, wore caps and shawls." **Choicest quote (for the Coseley side of the parish)** The author of 'Towns of South Staffordshire' series in the Staffordshire Advertiser wrote in 1849 "It is difficult for strangers to such districts as these to conceive of a grouped yet scattered community like Coseley, comprising in all about 10,000 souls, broken up into thick parenthetical turfs of population in three or four separate faubourgs of about 3,000 souls each, baffling the visitor as he emerges from suburb after suburb, to discover which of them is "the town", till he finds there is 'no town in particular', and no suburb above another, but that the suburbs are like their inhabitants, all of a class, and all of a piece, with none above another..." (SA Nov 24 1849 p7 col 1).

Pubs...

One of the AA's 1001 Great Family Pubs Beacon Hotel & Sarah Hughes Brewery, 129 Bilston St, Sedgley 'Little has changed in 150 years at this traditional brewery tap, which still retains its Victorian atmosphere. The rare snob-screened island bar serves a taproom, sung large smoke-room and veranda. Proprietor John Hughes reopened the adjoining Sarah Hughes Brewery in 1987, 66 years after his grandmother became licensee.' (book of the above title, 2005). **Oldest pub in Gornal** Reputedly, The Bush Inn, Summit Place, Gornalwood; dates from the C18. But The Jolly Chispin also vies for the title. The Bush Inn is said to be haunted by the paranormal activity of a former customer (TB June 26 2003 p11p. Aug 14 2003 p6p). **'Rosie'** A well known stuffed whippet long displayed at Peartree Inn, Lower Gornal, by 1979 (Q&ABC no.196).

Sport...

Gornal pugilists John Bate, the 'One-eyed Wonder', Gornal champion 1835. Jem Hall, a collier, Gornal champion 1836, who famously defeated Charley Hodge of Brierley Hill on Kinver Edge, Nov 1836 (TFBC p155). Jem Scunner, Gornal Champion. In 1837 he took on the Tipton Slasher and lost in an hour (Birmingham Post June 24 1967). Another, probably mythical, version of this fight is it was the Tipton Slasher's first fight, and that his opponent was 'Skim Skinny (or Skummy)' and it was fought over two days near Park's Hall Pool, the prize being a donkey and a bag of sand (AMS p455), or all the donkeys and lily white sand in Gornal. **Furthest ever distance run by members of one family in 24 hours** Gordon Bentley (1938-2003) of Hurst Hill, Coseley, and his brother Ron of the Tipton Harriers, 1973; Gordon ran 119 miles. In 1971 the brothers achieved the fastest ever 100 miles by two brothers in a race, at Uxbridge, with Gordon making the 5th fastest time in the world. Gordon retired to Gornalwood (TB Dec 30 2003 p23p). **IBSF World Ladies Snooker Champion 2004, 2007, World Ladies Snooker Championship Roll of Honour winner 2005, 2006, 2007** Reanne Evans (b1986), of Lower Gornal (WLBSA website, 2008) (BCM Summer 2005 p41).

Work...

Earliest documentation of coal mining in South Staffordshire Sedgley 1273 (HOS 1998 p15). **One of the largest coke furnaces in the Midlands 1718** At Deepfields, set up by the Penn brothers (HC p53 il of Deepfields). **'perhaps unequalled in another coalfield in the world'** Earl of Dudley's seam of coal lying only a few yards deep at Wren's Nest with a thickness of 13 yards instead of 10. It was being exploited in 1897 by the 'open work' method (SA Aug 21 1897 p4 col 5). **Last deep mine to work the South Staffordshire Thick Coal seam, last Black Country colliery to close** Baggeridge Colliery, closed 1968 (Staffordshire Handbook c1966 p73) (SL p265). **'Saltman's Village'** Reference to Ruiton, being the home of saltmen hawkers (BCM Spring 2007 pp12,17. Summer 2007 p21). **Originator of the steel pen** Daniel Fellows, a journeyman blacksmith of Sedgley, who issued a pamphlet on June 20 1805 confirming his claim to be the originator of the steel pen; this would be a hand-filed product; however, the first record of the manufacture of a steel pen in Britain is credited to Samuel Harrison who made a steel pen for Dr Priestley, c1780 (AMS p158) (SARA Feb 25 1955. March 4 1955) (BCM Spring 2006 pp31-32p). **Most extensive manufactory in Sedgley 1850** The Wednesbury Oak, established 1814 by Messrs Williams Brothers (SA Jan 12 1850 p7 col 1). **Best known firm in Coseley** Cannon Industries, Deepfields, founded in 1826. **Britain's best cooker 1950s** Cannon Gas Cooker A125 (Cannon advert). **Best-selling package boiler in Britain** 'Multipac' by The John Thompson Group, Ettingshall. **World's largest aircraft refueller** Built by The John Thompson Group, Ettingshall (Staffordshire Handbook c1966 p87). **Heaviest load ever carried by British Rail** A 122-foot long boiler drum weighing 240 tons. It was made in Ettingshall and taken to Eggborough, Yorks, 1965. **Maker of segments for first Harwell Cyclotron particle accelerator** Joseph Sankey & Sons Ltd, Manor Works, Spring Rd, Ettingshall (TB Sept 6 2007 p20). **Final giant magnet for Harwell** There were 365 magnets in all for Joseph Sankey & Sons Ltd/ GKN of Manor Works, Ettingshall (TB April 26 2001 p25p). **Lower Gornal's last nailer** James Marsh (1825-1922), who had a nailshop in Hopyard Lane (Sedgley & District. Trevor Genge. 1995 p35p).

Churches & Chapels...

At **SEDGLEY** is All Saints, **one of 19 such county dedications** (of ancient parish churches); **25th= last ancient parish county church built** dating from 1826. **In the church note** The curious tablets made of iron to Elizabeth Bradley (d1627), and her daughter Elizabeth Parkshouse (d1650) (SR pp54,55). Old Vicar Street Cemetery in Sedgley has the grave of Joseph Nicholds of Hurst Hill (1784-1860), composer of hymn tumes for the Methodists, and died in Dudley Union Workhouse. **Sedgley's most energetic vicar, vicar said to be descended from Charlemagne** Rev Charles Girdlestone, vicar of Sedgley 1826-37. He rebuilt the parish church, built Christ Church, Coseley, and Holy Trinity, Ettingshall. From 1847 he was rector of Kingswinford (see); he regarded his time in the two incumbencies as "the best and happiest years of his life" (BCM summer 1992 p42,43il). Congregational church in Bilston St (1856-7). Hope Baptist Chapel (1927), a 'tin tabernacle' Arcal St (TB June 16 2005 p13). At the junction of Catholic Lane and High Holborn is the RC St Chad and All Saints (1823). At **COSELEY** is Christ Church (1829-30). At **ETTINGSHALL PARK** is Holy Trinity (1961), Farrington Rd. At **LOWER GORNAL** is St James the Great (1822). At **UPPER GORNAL** is St Peter (1844). Rehaboth Chapel, Upper Gornal (TB June 16 2005 p13). Ruiton Independent Chapel (1830) (TB June 16 2005 p13). At **HURST HILL** is St Mary the Virgin (1872), Gorge Rd. At **LADY MOOR** is St Oswald (1888). **Unique as a church structure** Because it was made of cinder. It closed in the mid 1970s (BCM April 1982 p50il). At **ROSEVILLE/ WEST COSELEY** is St Chad. The Old Providence Baptist Chapel (dem 1991), Coseley (TB June 9 2005 p16p) (alias? Ebenezer Baptist Chapel (1856), Birmingham New Road, S of Ivyhouse Lane).

The area...

Sedgley is the **county's 28th largest parish**, consisting of 7,743 acres; **51st= farthest parish away from the county town**, 16.5m due S; **extremist length** 5.3m, making it **27th= longest parish in the county; extremist width** 5.6m, making it **19th= widest parish in the county**. **Chief settlement** Sedgley, a hilltop Black Country town; Coseley, is a smaller industrial town in the valley below; Black Country conurbation has merged the two and all the intervening former higgledy-piggledy villages. **Geology** BRIERLEY, COSELEY and the GORNALS - entirely Middle Coal Measures; COTWALL END - Middle Coal Measures (S and Sedgley village (W)), Permian (N); ETTINGSHALL - Middle Coal Measures (E), Upper Coal Measures (NW fringe), Silurian (Ludlow) Limestone (Sedgley village (E), Ettingshall Park), Silurian (Wenlock) Limestone (Hurst Hill), Permain (W fringe); GOSPEL OAK - entirely Permian; WOODSETTON - Silurian (Wren's Nest escarpment; the escarpment is Ludlow limestone; Wren's Nest Hill is Wenlock limestone; the heart of the hill is composed of the **oldest of the Silurian rocks**, the Wenlock Shales), Middle Coal Measures (most). **Highest point** Sedgley Beacon at 781 feet. It is the **highest cultivated land in England** (WJO

Aug 1906 p211), or rather the highest inhabited tableland in England (AMS p2), or reputedly the **highest point of land between Sedgley and Russia's Ural Mountains** (TB July 21 2005 p7), and is the **second-highest point in the West Midlands** (Wikipedia). **Lowest point** 344 feet by Wodehouse Mill Pool. **Most fascinating cavern of Wren's Nest Hill** The infamous 'Devil's Mouth' (TB March 1990 p5). **Most famous visitor to Wren's Nest Hill caverns** Perhaps Henri Charles Ferdinand Marie Dieudonne, Comte de Chambord, alias Duc de Bordeaux, uncrowned Henri V of France, born 1820, when in exile in 1844 (TB Feb 17 2005 p18). **The best sort of lime** Could be found at Hurstfield in Sedgley parish, according to Dr Plot (SHOS vol 2 p221). **First registered nature reserve in UK** Wren's Nest 1956 (info Peter Nichols). **'Largest earthquake to hit the UK for nearly 10 years'** The Dudley earthquake which registering 5.0 on the Richter scale on 23 September 2002 00:54 UTC (01:54 local time) and lasted approximately 20 seconds. The epicentre was located at the junction of High Arcal Road and Himley Road (grid reference SO 898913). The tremor was felt in many distant parts of the United Kingdom, including Wales, Liverpool, Derby, North Yorkshire, West Yorkshire, Wiltshire and London (Wikipedia 2007). Sedgley was **3rd most-populated Staffordshire parish in 1801** with 9,874; **3rd in 1811** with 13,937; **3rd in 1821** with 17,195; **3rd in 1831** with 20,577; **4th in 1841** with 24,819; **4th in 1851** with 29,447; **5th in 1861** with 36,637; **6th in 1871** with 37,355; **6th in 1881** with 36,574; **8th in 1891** with 36,860; **11th in 1901** with 38,179.

Smethwick & Harborne
Did you know that...

Smethwick's top folklore That the ghost of Thomas 'Tommy' Chandler haunts Old Rolfe Street Station. He was captain of Smethwick Fire Brigade and committed suicide by gassing himself in July 1923. In 1979 Rolfe Street Station was moved to Stoney Lane, where his plaque had been re-erected (TB May 1993 p31). **Harborne's top folkore** That courting couples met under the boughs of a certain oak in the north west of Harborne township in the C17 and C18 Court Oak. By 1951 the three-dimensional sign of the Court Oak Inn showed a man and a woman in C18 dress on either side of an oak. But it is as likely the oak may have had its name from the meeting place of a manor court. **Most easterly of the Black Country towns** Smethwick. **How Black Country people pronounce Smethwick** 'Smerrick' (TB June 5 2003 p26). **Smethwick's oldest pub and 2nd oldest building** The Old Chapel Inn, near the Old Church (TB April 25 2002 p23p. Jan 10 2008 p27p). **Smethwick's last farm** Greenfield Farm, bounded by Taylors and Hales Lanes, Uplands, which was demolished c1939-40 (TB July 1995 p21p). **'Greatest storm ever witnessed by anyone' at Smethwick** Lasted two hours (5.20 to 7.30) on July 11 1927; Smethwick power station suffered severely; a big landslide occurred on the LMS at Galton Bridge fill-

*Memorial plaque to Thomas 'Tommy' Chandler,
Court Oak inn sign, Harborne, the Guru Nanak
Gurdwara - Europe's largest Sikh temple*

ing the canal full of sand and stopping the trains (TB April 4 2002 p17). **'One of the largest provincial theatres in the country'** Theatre Royal, Rolfe Street, opened 1897, closed 1932 (blue plaque on site of theatre) (TB Oct 23 2003 pp10-11). **'Smethwick's greatest fire tragedy'** The Theatre Royal fire lasting 2 hours from 5.30am Sept 2 1929, according to W. Ellery Jephcott (STELE SARA Nov 6 1953). **'one of the largest and finest such buildings in the land'** Smethwick Baths in Thimblemill Rd, Bearwood, opened 1933 (TB Oct 19 2000 p14). **'The greatest gift bestowed upon the people of Smethwick'** Smethwick West Park, the gift of Sir James Timmins Chance in 1895 (TB Sept 14 2006 p21). **What Smethwick is famous for** It's national engineering prowess. **World's first Girl Guides** Originated out of a group of about six girls from Harborne formed by Miss GN Commander, aged 15, their patrol was called the Ravens. In 1909 they went to a scout rally in Warley Woods attended by Lord Baden Powell who, on seeing them, suggested to his wife that she form a separate movement (HOHE p32). **First UK service to use the 'Heli Telly'** West Midlands Fire Service, which has its HQ at Smethwick. This is a remote controlled model helicopter used for surveillance, produced by MW Power Systems of Stoke-on-Trent (BBC Midlands Today July 9 2007).

People...

Smethwick's most famous old worthy Sir James Timmis Chance (1814-1902). Glass manufacturer and lighthouse engineer. Born Birmingham. Joined his uncle and father at their Spon Lane glassworks,

Smethwick, 1836, devoting himself to manufacturing and to scientific developments. He invented a process for polishing sheet glass so as to produce 'Patent Plate'. But is remembered for the perfection of lighthouse lenses; a product the Chances started making c1850. He was sheriff of Staffordshire 1868, and resided at Brown's Green, Handsworth 1845-69; later at Sutton Coldfield and London. Although he died at Hove, Sussex, his ashes were buried at the Cemetery in

SMETHWICK
& HARBORNE
PEOPLE -
Dorothy Parkes, William Caldow, Julie Walters, Elihu Burritt (American consul in Birmingham, resident at Victoria Road, Harborne from 1865 - see Clent choicest quote), Arthur Keen, Sir James Timmins Chance, Sydney Francis Barnes, Frank Skinner, Henry Mitchell III

Warstone Lane. He gave West Smethwick Park to the public, 1895. **Harborne's biggest man** Job Freeth, 40 stone farmer, who lived at Tennel Hall in 1750s (OHOPP p24). **Birmingham's first MP** Thomas Attwood (1783-1856) who lived at The Grove 1811-45 (now Grove Park, Harborne) (HOHE p16). **'Father of Forestry' in the Midlands** William Caldow (d1892), a Scot who moved to Smethwick in 1841. He was known as this for his work on behalf of the Order of Foresters in south Staffordshire and north Worcestershire (VCH vol 17 p136). **'the maker of modern Smethwick'** Arthur Keen (1835-1915), chairman of Smethwick Local Board of Health 1871-89, founder of the firm of Guest, Keen and Nettlefolds, president of Smethwick Cricket Club 1880 (STELE OSm Aug 26 1950, SARA May 8 1953). **'one of the few women newspaper proprietors in the country'** Kathleen MJ Billingsley, owner of Smethwick Telephone on the death of her father 1943 to her own death 1962 (VCH vol 17 p135). **Smethwick's hero** Able Seaman William Alfred Savage born Raglan Ave, Raglan Rd, Smethwick, Oct 30 1912; later employed in Mitchells and Butlers bottle dept. In 1939 he was resident at Durban Road. On March 28 1942 he displayed great gallantry, skill and devotion to duty as gunlayer of the pompom in a Motor Gun Boat which guarded a British destroyer used to destroy the docks at St Nazaire, France, in the successful Operation Chariot, but lost his life as he kept up fire as his boat exited the harbour. He has a memorial tablet in the vestibule of Smethwick Council House (TB Sept 29 2005 p21il. Feb 8 2007 p23p). **Smethwick's bravest** Sgt Harold Colley of Smethwick, and of the 10th Lancashire Fusiliers and later 52nd Brigade 17th Division in V Corps. His courage earned him a Military Medal in 1917, and his conspicuous bravery and initiative commanding a platoon in the battle of Martinpuichs on Aug 25 1918 preventing the enemy from breaking through the defence line earnt him a posthumous V.C. (TB Jan 12 2006 p23p. Jan 26 2006 p17). Flt Sgt Allan Cox and Flt Sgt Gordon Preston who whilst on a routine mission over the Black Country when their RAF Miles Marston training aeroplane developed engine trouble and crash-landed in West Smethwick Park, sparing residential areas, July 31 1944; a memorial was erected to their memory on Nov 21 2004 (TB Nov 25 2004 p15). **'singing postman poet'** Edward Capern (1819-1894) of Moor Pool Lane (Ravenhurst Rd), later of Heath Rd (High St), Harborne, formerly of Devon (Birmingham Post Feb 18 1933) (GMH p27). **'Oyster Jack'** Christopher Purnell (1813-1914), orginally from Cladon, Somerset, centurian and character. Railway and tram construction navvy who came to live at West Smethwick 1867. When too old to labour he used to go round the pubs selling sea food - he also earnt a little giving children rides on his pony and float in Sutton Park. Buried old Holly Lane cemetery (STELE OSm Dec 4 1948). **Staffordshire's 2nd oldest man ever** James Sands of Harborne who lived to the age of 140. **Smethwick man who went down on the Titantic** William Edward Hipkins, managing director of Avery's Scale Company, Smethwick, although his residence was at Edgbaston (TB March 1997 p20). **Inventor of the mass spectrograph** Francis W Aston (d1945) who was born in a house at Camomile Green 1877 (GMH pp18-19). **Nobel Prize award winner for Chemistry 1922** Francis W Aston (d1945) (HOHE p29). **Unique derivation for a surname** Harborn(e) will be from Harborne in this parish (PDS). **Strange but true!** The bride and groom were left waiting at Baptist Chapel, Regent St, Smethwick unable to marry because the registrar failed to turn up. Embarrassingly, when they emerged from the vestry after being told this by the vicar the wedding party showered them with the traditional rice believing they had just been married. They were married the next day; the registrar disclaimed any responsibility for the mistake (SA Jan 11 1890 p5 col 2). **Staffordshire pub with most WW1 conscripts** Perhaps The Grapes Inn, Oldbury Rd, West Smethwick, which has 78 names on its own WW1 Roll of Honour; 11 lost their lives in the War (TB June 14 2001 p5). **JB Priestley's grimmest street he'd ever seen** Grice Street on the W side of Spon Lane, alias Rusty Street in his 'English Journey' (1933). He visited it with his brother-in-law, Harry N Siddens of Dunsley Manor, Kinver, who was the proprietor of a firm of steel stockholders with a warehouse there, and with whom he was staying (STELE OSm Aug 12 1950) (VCH vol 17 p10). **First British man to die on D-Day** Lieutenant Herbert Denham Brotheridge, born Smethwick 1915, 2nd (Airborne) Battlion The Oxford and Bucks. Light Infantry, in the capture of Pegasus Bridge, in the early hours of June 6 1944 (TB Aug 26 2004 p25ps) (memorial plaque on Smethwick Council House). **'King of the Black Patch'** Esau Smith (1809-1901), headman (though not crowned) of the Smith-Clayton tribe of gypsies, occupying the common land at Black Patch. His wife was 'Queen' Sentinia alias Henty (1809-1907) (STELE SARA Sept 3 1954. Sept 10 1954. Sept 17 1954). **'one of the youngest war brides'** Yvonne 'Bonnie' Sadler (d2004) from Smethwick, aged 17 when she married Canadian serviceman Neil Gillies at St Hilda's church, Warley in 1945; widowed in 1949 she remarried in Canada (TB Sept 21 2006 p3p). **Malcolm X's last TV interview** In front of Smethwick Council House on Feb 2 1965 (9 days later he was assassinated) with Conservative MP for Smethwick Peter Griffiths, amid rumours Griffiths' supports had covertly circulated the slogan 'If you want a nigger for a neighbour, vote Liberal or Labour'; the interview was not then shown (Wikipedia, 2006). **First turban-wearing Sikh employed on the buses by West Bromwich Transport Dept** Turlochan Singh, aged 27, of St Paul's Road, Smethwick, on Monday after March 5 1968, taking advantage of the Dept's decision to allow Sikh's to wear turbans on buses (E&S March 5 1968 photo). **Perrier Award winner (stand-up comedy) 1991** Frank Skinner of Smethwick. **9th least pleasant voice (for a celebrity)** Frank Skinner, as voted in a BBC survey, 2005 (BBC website). **Exceptional Work Guide Dog of the Year 2006** Logan, belonging to Carl Griggs of Harborne (BBC Midlands Today Sept 13 2006). **Smethwick's earliest recorded will** Belongs to Samuel Jervase, and is dated Sept 20 1675: Harborne's belongs to Richard Mason, and is dated April 3 1662. **First baptism in the parish register (Parkes' Chapel)** Henrietta Anna Maria, daughter of James and Bridget Turner Oct 15 1732; **first marriage** William Colesby and Sarah Renolds, by banns, Oct 9 1732; **first burials** Joseph and Mary, children of Samuel and Annie Kettle, Nov 18 1732 (STELE OSm Jan 20 1951). **Smethwick's kindest** Dorothy Parkes (d1728). She not only founded Smethwick Old Church, but instructed additional income from her lands support Harborne and Smethwick poor. In Smethwick there was a weekly penny-loaf dole for 12 poor inhabitants, annual clothes for three poor women, and bibles for the poor; she also bequeathed £200 for a school building at Smethwick, which opened in 1734 (VCH vol 17 p142). Also Sarah Hadley (1850-1936), spinster. She had an eccentric manner of endowing beds at Birmingham Children's Hospital, left considerable sums to charities for the blind, and her house, Bell House, Smethwick to the Corporation (STELE OSm Jan 27 1951). **Smethwick and Harborne's poorest** A parish workhouse existed by 1796 at the junction of Lordswood and Gillhurst Roads, Harborne. From 1836 the poor went to King's Norton Union workhouse at Selly Oak, and the building became known as 'High Harborne' (VCH vol 17 p119) (HAHEC p46p). **Choicest quote (Smethwick)** bearing in mind the area is now very multi-ethnic. In 1965 shortly before his assassination Malcolm X, the American civil rights activist, came to Smethwick to speak against racism 'I have come here because I am disturbed by reports that coloured people in Smethwick are being treated badly. I have heard they are being treated as the Jews under Hitler. I would not wait for the fascist element in Smethwick to erect gas ovens.' **Choicest quote (Harborne)** Thomas Priest (pen name Tom Presterne), whose father was a spectacle maker on the corner of Ravenhurst Road and High Street. Thomas was author of 'Harborne Once upon a time' in which he is showing an illusionary friend, Charles Undertone, the delights of Harborne:- 'The little belt, including the Vicarage, the Church and Harborne Hall is, I should say, unequalled in any part of the Midlands.'

Societies...

First Penny Club on record Perhaps that established at Harborne, 1799, by a man named Green (Aris's Birmingham Gazette. April 27 1801) (S&W pp153-154) (Century of Birmingham Life. Langford. vol 2 pp109-110) (HOHH p9). **Longest running gooseberry society in the country by 1900** Harborne Gooseberry Growers' Society, founded 1815 (SARA May 18 1956). **The Society's heaviest gooseberry to 1956, largest gooseberry in England 1875** The 'Bobby' of James Barton grown 1875, weighing 34 dwt, 20 gr (STELE SARA May 11 1956). **Heaviest dozen gooseberries ever grown record holder 1901** Emmanuel Withers of Harborne, producing one dozen 'Bobby' weighing 15 and three quarters ozs in 1901 (STELE SARA May 11 1956). **'Concrete jungle'** Reference to failed 1960s housing estate called 'Galton Village' which was redeveloped in early 1990s.

Sport...

'the Leviathan', most effective 'cutting' batsman in England 1880s, 1st Smethwick native and Warwickshire player selected for a team that toured Australia Ludford Charles Docke, born

1860 South Street, Smethwick, cricketter noted for his unprecedented batting feats. When playing for Smethwick C.C. and Derbyshire C.C. in 1880s he was ranked 10th amongst the amateurs in the first-class cricket averages. His Australian tour with Warwickshire was in 1888; he played for that county to 1895. In later life he was chairman of H.P. Sauce Ltd (STELE SARA April 24 1953. May 1 1953). **First century scored by a Smethwick C.C. batsman** Philip Perrott in 1874 on the Broomfield ground (SARA May 29 1953). **Birmingham and District Cricket Association Challenge Cup winners 1882-84, 1886-88** Smethwick C.C. In 1884 it was decided that the club could keep the cup (STELE SARA May 15 1953). **'one of the greatest bowlers in English cricket', 'the peerless incomparable master of the art of bowling', only man to have been selected for England while a minor counties and league player** Sydney Francis Barnes (1873-1967), native of Smethwick (HOS 1998 p22) (Staffordshire Handbook c1966 p26) (Stafford: A History & Celebration. Roger Butters & Nick Thomas. 2005. p97). **Staffordshire Water Polo champions 1898, 1899, Birmingham & District Water Polo League winners 1899, 1900, 1901, 1903** Smethwick Swimming Club, founded 1888 (STELE SARA Aug 19 1955). **'hardest kid in the Black Country', 6st 7lb Junior Schoolboy Champion of the Midlands 1927, 6st 7lb Schoolboy Boxing Champion of Great Britain 1928** Herbert 'Spud' Baker a pupil of Crocketts Lane School, Smethwick, was crowned this by the Amateur Boxing Association (TB Jan 20 2005 p31p). **Midland Featherweight champion 1928** Tommy Gardner (b1896) of Smethwick, originally of Stroud, Glous (TB June 5 2003 p35). **Hill Climb Championship (motor racing) 1951** Ken Wharton of Hume St, Smethwick (SME-OP p145p). **World's Games for Women's Championships 1930 800m winner** Gladys (Sally) Lunn of Smethwick (TB April 1983 p7p). **'one of the finest fullbacks in the country'** Bobby Thomson, footballer, born Dec 5 1943 in Smethwick, called this when a member of Alf Ramsey's England squad; remembered as the 'classy right-back' who went on to play for his country at both Under-23 and senior levels, winning a total of eight full caps Nov 1963-Dec 1964. In retirement he ran a sports shop in Sedgley (TB Jan 29 2004 p31p). **British National Team Championship winners 1952, 1953, 1954, 'Smethwick Cycling Twins'** Stan and Bernard Higginson, born Sept 20 1931, attended Crocketts Lane and Smethwick Junior Technical School; Halesowen Athletic & Cycling Club from 1950; the third member of the Championship team was Ken Sparks of Merrivale Road, Smethwick. In 1954 the twins set the 30 mile British Tandem record (TB March 2 2006 p35p). **Inventor of the World Cup game** Arthur Workman, born Smethwick 1928, former Chad Valley toy maker employee, who conceived this flick of a finger ball board game on a visit to a park in the Black Country in 1966, and called his game after the current Football World Cup championships (TB July 21 2005 p19p). **World mini tramp (Trampolining) champion 1973** Lesley Pallett, aged 19, of 63 Roebuck Lane, West Smethwick (E&S May 13 1974). **John O'Groats-Land's End triple walk record**

breaker Ben Haywood, born 1916, retired sailor of Smethwick, who walked back and forth thrice between John O'Groats and Land's End in 153 days in 1982. In 1984 he walked 15,000 circuits rounds Smethwick Hall Park pool for charity (TB April 7 2005 p27p).

Municipal Life...

Most densely populated county borough in England Smethwick when it comprised 2,496 acres; outside London it was exceeded only by Salford in 1951 (Staffs County Guide c1958 p125) (VCH vol 17 p88). **Smethwick's first freeman** Henry Mitchell III (1837-1914), chairman of Mitchells and Butlers, in July 1902 in recognition of his eminent services to the borough over the 20 year period (STELE OSm Nov 4 1950). **Smethwick's first mayor** Jabez Lones of Paxton House, South Rd, Smethwick, who served 1899-1902 (TB May 31 2001 p10). **Smethwick's youngest mayor** Leslie Llewellyn Morris 1960-61, aged 36 (TB April 13 2006 p18p). **Smethwick first town clerk** William Shakespeare (1833-1912), born Wollaston, Stourbridge, later of The Hollies, South Road, Smethwick. He was clerk of the Urban Council 1895-99, prior to his becoming the first clerk of the borough in 1899, and served until his death (STELE OSm Feb 3 1951 photo).

Churches...

At **HARBORNE** is the ancient parish church, St Peter, **one of 15 such county dedications** (of ancient parish churches); **52nd= last ancient parish county church built** dating from 1450. In the church - was a memorial now (2004) lost to Thomas and Sarah Birch:

> A greeable couple could not be,
> Whatever pleased he, always pleased she.

(HAHEC p38). According to legend an apparent opening at the east end of the church is the start of a tunnel leading to Metchley Abbey (HAHEC p39). **In the churchyard** - The graves of Job Freeth, the 'big man' of Tennall Hall; David Cox (d1859), the famous artist; Thomas Baker 'Leamington Baker' famous painter of pastoral cattle scenes, of Leamington, Warws; Rebecca Robinson, servant at the vicarage, and was burnt there so badly that she died (HA pp5,6). A sad grave commemorating many infant deaths: Mary, daughter of Thomas and Hannah Green d1761 aged 3, Thomas Green, son Theodore and Ann Price d1782 an infant, also Thomas Green their 2nd son d1782 aged 2, also Ann, wife of Theodore Price d1786 aged 26, also Theodore Price their 3rd son d1787 aged 2. In addition, against the S wall the three daughters of Hezekiah and Phebe Green - Mary d1771 aged 3, Martha d1772 aged 4 months, Diana d1785 aged 19 at Bristol Wells (SHOS vol 2 p125). One grave which has now (2004) disappeared recorded the deaths of three successive husbands of one woman:

> This turf has drunk a window's tear,
> Three of her husbands slumber here.

(HAHEC p39). At **HARBORNE HEATH** is St John the Baptist. At **BEARWOOD** is St Mary the Virgin (1892), corner of Bearwood Road and St Mary's Road. At **BEECH LANES** is St Faith and St

Lawrence. At **CAPE HILL** was St Chad (1901), corner of Shireland and Edith Roads, until demolished 1971 (VCH vol 17 p127). At **SMETHWICK** is Parkes' Chapel (1732), The Uplands; Holy Trinity (1838), Trinity St; St Matthew (1855), Windmill Lane. At **SMETH-WICK (NORTH)** St Stephen (1902), Sydenham and Cambridge Roads. At **WEST SMETHWICK** are St Paul (1858), St Paul's Rd; St Alban's (1906), Silverton Rd. **Staffordshire's first Sikh temple, largest Sikh temple in Europe 1962** Guru Nanak Gurdwara, High St (formerly New Street), Smethwick, 1961 (HOS 1998 p70p) (The Times July 31 1962) (VCH vol 17 p134). This was formerly the Congregational church, built by John Harley, a Wesleyan, in 1856. It closed 1931 and became a sweet factory (STELE SARA Oct 19 1956).

Engineering & Work...

Oldest condensing engine in existence 1959 A Boulton & Watt engine of 1779 for the Birmingham Canal Old Cut Old Main Line to pump water from one canal level to another at Smethwick; from 1890s it was at Ocker Hill, and from 1959 at Birmingham Museum of Science and Industry (now Thinktank) (HOS 1998 p100) (OH pp63-65) (SMEOP p6p). **'the first factory in the engineering industry in the world'** Soho Foundry, W of Soho Park, opened 1795/6 (HOS p45). **First Smethwick ironworks** Appears to have been that belonging to Joseph Hadley, soap maker, in Brasshouse Lane, first mentioned in 1829 (STELE SARA July 10 1953). **Earliest steamship engines** (notably that for the Great Eastern) were made at Soho Foundry (Staffs County Handbook c1951 p124). **World's longest single span bridge over world's largest man-made cutting** The iron Galton Bridge, 1826-9, carrying Roebuck Lane over Telford's New Main Line of the Birmingham Canal and is 50 feet above the navigation. **First 'Patent Plate' a polished sheet glass, largest crown and sheet glass works in England 1851, world's/country's only works dedicated to lighthouse machinery 1851, world's largest manufacturers and pioneers in spectacle lens by 1860s** Chance glass manufacturers, Spon Lane, Smethwick. Sir James Timmis Chance (d1902) was producer of the first 'Patent Plate'; in 1851 the company was employing 1,200 people (DNB) (W p704) (VCH vol 2 p229. vol 17 pp115-116) (BCM Spring 2002 p62). (LGS p21) (SHCB p7). **'the finest and most compact range of (industrial) buildings in South Staffordshire'** London Works Cranford Street, Smethwick, built by Charles Fox (d1874), which produced iron work for the Crystal Palace in Hyde Park for the Great Exhibition of 1851. **First to manufacture two cycle compression gas engines** Tangyes Ltd of the Cornwall Works, of Smethwick in 1880. It was invented by James Robson (1833-1913) of North Shields in 1877 (STELE SARA April 9 1954). **First manufacture of tin oxide in Great Britain** Henry Wiggin & Co. Ltd (formerly Adkins & Co.) of Merry Hill, Smethwick, 1896 (VCH vol 17 p117). **Country's principal makers of glassmakers red lead, 'one of the largest manufacturers of soap in the country'** Adkins & Nock of Smethwick, sometime in the C19 (STELE SARA Dec 29 1951). **Smethwick's most important business** Mitchells & Butlers Ltd at Cape Hill Brewery (TB Feb 8 2001 p20). **First provincial student to gain a City and Guilds of London silver medal for brewing** William Walters Butler (d1935) in 1890, chairman of Mitchells & Butlers Ltd from 1914, Bart from 1926 (STELE OSm Nov 25 1950 photo). **One of the best-known British toy manufacturers** Chad Valley Toys, Rose Rd, Harborne, 1897-1972 (HOHE p31p). **World's largest manufacturers of machines for weighing, counting, measuring, and testing** Avery Weigh-Tronix, Foundry Road, Black Patch (Wikipedia, 2006). **First all aluminium tennis racket** The 'Birmal' racket made by Birmingham Aluminium Casting (1903) Co. Ltd at Dartmouth Rd, Smethwick, from 1922 (TB Feb 24 2000 p10). **Asian Business of the Year Excellence Award winner 2003** Ninder Johal, managing director of Nachural Records in Smethwick, in the 2nd Black Country Asian Business Association Business Awards (E&S Sept 6 2003 p17p).

The area...

County's 79th largest parish, consisting of 3,420 acres; **10th farthest parish away from the county town**, 21.4m SSE; **extremist length** 4.3m; **extremist width** 4m. The **name Harborne first appears** in Domesday Book, 1086. **Chief settlement** Harborne, a large, once quaint, satellite village of Birmingham. Smethwick, the other township, is a massive industrial centre. The former was removed to Birmingham in 1891, the latter in 1966. **Geology** SMETHWICK - Permian (West Smethwick and NW), Bunter (Rolfe St-Smethwick town-Lightwoods Park; HARBORNE - Bunter (Harborne village and most), Upper Coal Measures and Permian (extreme SW fringe). **Highest point** 600 feet on Harborne Smethwick boundary at Lightwood. **Lowest point** 423 feet by Bourn Brook on Worcs border. **'a rich jewel in an Ethiop's ear'** (Romeo and Juliet) Reference to the shape of Harborne parish by Edward Capern (GMH p28). **Staffordshire parish furthest from the sea** Harborne, about 80 miles to the Point of Aire, North Wales, or 90 miles to The Wash. Harborne was **26th= most-populated Staffordshire parish in 1801** with 2,275; **26th in 1811** with 2,612; **24th in 1821** with 3,350; **22nd in 1831** with 4,227; **18th in 1841** with 6,657; **14th in 1851** with 10,729; **12th in 1861** with 16,996; **13th in 1871** with 22,263; **9th in 1881** with 31,517; **6th in 1891** with 44,105; **5th in 1901** with 64,713.

Tettenhall
Did you know that...

Tettenhall's top folklore That a battle took place at Tettenhall in 910 on the 8th of the Ides of August in which the Danes failed to invade Saxon England and were defeated under Edward the Elder. The battle is folklore because it has never been established that for sure that it did take place at Tettenhall, or exactly on that date. Some of the suggested sites have included Wednesfield, Stowheath, Old Fallings, Wombourne Common. According to further legend three

Northumbrian (or Danish) kings were killed. **What Tettenhall is famous for** All sorts of things:- its greens, its villas, its eccentrics, and the old county family of Wrottesley. The **name Tettenhall first appears** in 910. **'Tettenhall is one of the prettiest villages in England'** Star 'Cycle runs or holiday outings' (guide) 1898 (TB July 25 2002 p20). **Unique pear** The Tettenhall Dick, only found in Tettenhall parish (HOPTT p103) (DUIGNAN); although they are said to have grown in neighbouring parishes, for example Brewood (TB March 1 2007 p3). **Last wallpapers designed by William Morris** Are called 'Compton' (1895-6) at Compton Hall. **The night Tettenhall was defended in a mock attack** On the evening of April 10 1897 Tettenhall Volunteer Company had to defend Tettenhall in a night manoeuvre exercise with other Wolverhampton companies connected with the 3rd Volunteer Battalion South Staffordshire Regt playing the assault parties: 'The plan was to endeavour to gain possession of Tettenhall'. The Wolverhampton men were divided into

Danes at the battle of Tettenhall, John Wilkes Booth assassinates Abraham Lincoln, the arms of Wrottesley
TETTENHALL PEOPLE
- Ellen Thorneycroft Fowler, Rachel Heyhoe Flint

two sections. One marched via Stafford Street and Whitmore Reans into Lower Road, Tettenhall, where they ascended the hill by the church. The other section proceeded by way of Compton Road to Upper Green. The Tettenhall defenders were eventually outflanked (SA April 17 1897 p3). **First community venture for Perton 'new' village** The 1976 November 5th bonfire event. The village continued to expand on the old Perton airfield (Wolverhampton Chronicle June 23 1978 p18). **National HQ of Birmingham Midshires** Pendeford Business Park from the mid 1990s (Wikipedia 2007).

People...

Tettenhall's most famous old worthies Judge John Pearson (1771-1841), famous advocate, born at Tettenhall Wood; attended Wolverhampton Grammar School, Christ Church, Oxon; was Advocate-General of Bengal 1824 (HOPTT p269). Francis Smith (1672-1738), architect and builder, was born at Wergs, the son of a bricklayer (VCH vol 20 p5). **Worst dean of Tettenhall College** Ingelard Warley, dean 1314-18, at least in the eyes of those who opposed Edward II; Warley was one of the most hated of Edward II's household officers. He had been expelled from royal service by the Lords Ordainers at the end of 1314. On his return from a timely pilgrimage overseas in 1315 the manner of his executing his duties at Tettenhall was attacked by the Chancellor of the Exchequer, John Sandall, whom the Ordainers had put in office. Edward II then forbid the Chancellor to meddle with Tettenhall's spiritual affairs (VCH vol 3 p316). **'Dark Lady of the Sonnets'** Mary Fitton (d1641), cousin and mistress of Vice-Admiral Leveson, lived at Perton Hall, possibly the 'dark lady' of Shakespeare's sonnets (VCH vol 20 pp5,25). **'the earliest Australian factor'** Thomas Elwell of Compton Hall (1781-1856), first to trade from Britain with enterprising Sydney traders who were the emancipated convicts of Botany Bay (WOb Jan 7 1888 p7). **Tettenhall's villain, 'The Aldersley Assassin'** John Wilkes Booth (1839-65), President Abraham Lincoln's assassin, whose family came from Aldersley (TB Nov 1993 pp18-19p). Another, more recent, villain, is Maurice Dean (b1943), of St Michael's Court, Tettenhall, who stole £36,000 from parish funds in Wolverhampton 1999-2002 (E&S Feb 11 2003 p1pc). The **'Roving Ranter', 'one of the most original characters of his day'** Henry Higginson (1806-71) born Pendeford Mills, a Primitive Methodist of the Brierley Hill Circuit 1850,57,58, and what Rupert Simms thought of him (TB Dec 21 2000 p17p) (BS p224). **First to install electric lighting underground, first motorist in Wolverhampton, inventor of Coalite, 'Honest Tom Parker'** Thomas Parker (1843-1915), born Coalbrookdale, pioneer in electrical engineering, resided at Tettenhall. He was in partnership with Bedford Elwell by 1882, forming the first company in the Black Country to manufacture electrical equipment. He had an electrically-powered vehicle running as early as 1884. Elwell-Parker Ltd installed the first electric lighting underground in the country for the Trafalgar Collieries in the Forest of Dean; constructed the first significant electric tramway in England, at Blackpool - its first tram - the first electric tram to run along an English street - ran on

July 2 1885. In 1905 Parker invented Coalite, smokeless fuel, and also made developments in storage batteries. The Elwell-Parker Dynamo was a big advance on its predecessor. His work led to the development of the tramcar and the London Underground. During political electioneering for the Kingswinford seat 1892 he became known as 'Honest Tom Parker' (VCH vol 2 pp155,156) (WF p45) (BCM Summer 2005 pp19-24. Spring 2006 pp56-57). **First Wesleyan Methodist to hold government office and be created a peer** Henry Hartley Fowler (d1911), 1st Viscount Wolverhampton of Woodthorne, Wergs Rd (VCH vol 20 p5). **Authoress whose first novel sold over a million copies** Ellen Thorneycroft Fowler (1860-1929), daughter of above, with 'Concerning Isabel Carnaby' (1898); her last novel appeared in 1923 (TB Feb 12 2004 p7). She lived with her family at Woodthorne, a house on the south side of Wergs Road in Tettenhall, c1867-1903. Of her many novels Fuel of Fire (1902) and Place and Power (1903) have Tettenhall and Wolverhampton settings. She is buried at All Saints, Branksome Park, Bournemouth. **Most eccentric Staffordshirian** Probably Col Thomas Thorneycroft (d1903), crack-pot inventor of Tettenhall Towers, who used his butlers as test pilots for his flying machines (VCH vol 20 pp21-22) (take a brain sip website, 2006). **Local historian who signed himself 'Staffordiensis'** James P Jones who wrote the History of the parish of Tettenhall (HOPTT), 1894 (N&Q 2 series vi p247) (WA vol 1 No. 10 p298) (SH p134). **386th lord mayor of London** Sir John Wollaston (1595-1658), in 1643-4, son of Edward Wollaston of Perton (VCH vol 20 p5). **Only mayor of Wolverhampton knighted** Sir John Morris of Elmslie Bank, Wightwick, 1866 (Commemorative Plaques by the Wolverhampton Civic Society). **Tettenhall's bravest** Sgt TM Garner, South Staffs Regt, of 80 Aldersley Road, killed in 1917. His commanding officer writing to his wife Mrs Garner, said he was 'my bravest sergeant and did not know what fear was. He repeatedly did acts of bravery, and was a grand example to his platoon.' He was the third Tettenhall man to win the M.M. in WW1 (ELSONSS p181). William Booth Mycock, a boatman in the employ of the Shrops Union Canal Co. rescued a boy from drowning in the canal at Autherley Junction. He was presented with the Royal Humane Society's testimonial in recognition of his bravery on July 26 1888 by the Mayor, Alderman J Jones, at Wolverhampton Borough Police Court (SA July 28 1888 p7 col 6). **'one of the C20 leading British mathematicians'** Herbert Western Turnbull (1885-1961), born Tettenhall. Regius Professor of Mathematics St Andrews University 1921-50, and author of eminent books on mathematics (TB Feb 2 2006 p17p). **Best After Dinner Speaker 1973** Rachel Heyhoe Flint, cricketer of Tettenhall, as awarded by the Guild of Professional Toastmasters (TB Aug 11 2005 p30). **Tettenhall's kindest** Members of key local families - Wrottesley, Wightwick, Wollaston, Smith, Fowler and Thorneycroft - have been parish benefactors. Richard Cresswell (d1708) of Barnhurst, provided an almshouse for his retired servants (VCH vol 20 pp46-7). **Tettenhall's poorest** Brych House, Wrottesley Rd, W of the junction with Redhouse Road, was the parish poorhouse from

1714. By 1746 it had been turned into a workhouse. From 1836 it was the Seisdon Union workhouse until 1860, thereafter Union inmates were sent to Trysull (VCH vol 20 p37). **First person in the parish register** Marie daughter Richard Phippes baptised March 27 1602. **Tettenhall's earliest recorded will** Belongs to Henry Southwick, and is dated 1634/5. **Choicest quote** Rev William Fernyhough wrote, 1789,

'Here Hampton's sons in vacant hours repair,
Taste rural joys, and breathe a purer air.'

Sport...

Strange but true Wakes! Tettenhall Wakes of 1812 which included blind men recruited into two teams to play ninepins; the ugliest men in the village taking part in the competition at "grinning through a horse's collar"; competitors jumping in sacks from the Old Rose and Crown down the hill to the turnpike; men and women trying to earn the distinction of having the least sensitive mouth in a 'hot and hasty pudding-eating' competition, and women racing round the green for prizes which were (1) three balloon tuckers, (2) two flannel dickies, and (3) a black velvet reticule (E&S Nov 25 1937 - 100 years ago recalled by Quaestor). **First Women's World Cricket Cup winners** England, captained by Rachel Heyhoe Flint of Tettenhall, 1972 (TB Dec 7 2000 p7), **'Most famous woman cricketter ever'** arguably, Rachel Heyhoe Flint of Tettenhall (BBC Midlands Today June 4 2007). **First lady to hit a six in Test Cricket** Rachel Heyhoe Flint, England Women's Cricket Captain (1966-77) of Tettenhall, in 1963 (TB Aug 11 2005 p30). **Prix du Jockey Club (the French derby) winner 1995, champion flat race jockey 2000, St Leger winner 2005** Kevin Darley, born Tettenhall 1960, champion apprentice jockey 1978 (TB June 15 2006 p34p). **Most step-ups in an hour** 1,873 by Gareth Morris of Perton on Jan 30 1993 using a 15 inch high exercise board (GBR 1995 p210). **'fastest pensioner in the world'** Allan Meddings (b1928), sprinter of Tettenhall, after winning the 100m (13.76 seconds) and the 200m (22.38 seconds) at the 15th World Masters Championships in July 2003. Earlier in 2003 he set new British records for the over-75s in 100m (12.8 seconds), and 200m (28.98 seconds), both in 2003 (E&S June 13 2003 p21p. July 30 2008 p11p). **'world's most demanding one day survival ordeal'** Tough Guy competition, an 8-mile assault course event at Tettenhall Horse Sanctuary (formerly South Perton Farm), in late January and late July, since c1986, organised by former British Army Officer Billy Wilson, who claims nobody has ever finished all the course according to his extremely demanding rules (Wikipedia, 2007).

Wightwick Manor...

One of the most representative late C19 houses in the country Wightwick Manor (SLM Oct 2005 p26). **'Among the stateliest'** great houses of the county Wightwick Manor (Staffordshire Handbook c1966 p15). **Best stained glass in a Staffordshire house** Wightwick Manor; much of it by CE Kempe (BOE p38).

Wrottesley Hall and the Wrottesleys...

'one of the most complete sets of ancient English Chronicles in existence' Was housed at Wrottesley Hall, until destroyed by fire on Dec 15 1897. 'only family living who can trace a direct male lineal descent from one of the original Knights' the Wrottesleys in 1894 (HOPTT p236). The **WROTTESLEY** who:- **Fought in the Black Prince's retinue at Crecy, an original Knight of the Garter** Sir Hugh de Wrottesley (1314-81) (SHC 1898 p299. 1912 p311) (NHS p273) (LGS p233) (SOSH p135); **Governor of Calais** Sir Walter Wrottesley (d1473), a post he held from 1470 (HOPTT p205) (LGS p233); **acquired Tettenhall College at the Dissolution** Walter Wrottesley (c1486-1563); was **created a baronet** Sir Walter Wrottesley (d1659), created in 1642 (SHC 1912 pp330, 331, 332); **pulled down the old moated hall and built a new hall** Sir Walter Wrottesley (d1712), in 1693; **Page to George II** General Sir John Wrottesley (1744-87), 8th Baronet. He was equerry to the Duke of York to 1767, and served with the Guards in America 1775-78, becoming critical of the Government and opposed to the war. In parliament he was a critical member of the Gower party, which called itself Whig and was in effect Tory (SHC 1922 pp288-9. 1933 p13); **erected a monument to Lady Mary Wortley (d1762) in Lichfield Cathedral** Henrietta Wrottesley (d1790), daughter of Sir John Wrottesley (d1726), who married Theodore William Inge (d1753); the monument was erected in 1789 (Three Spires: Friends of Lichfield Cathedral Newsletter. Spring 2003); **contested the Staffordshire seat 1747 but lost!** Rev Sir Richard Wrottesley (1721-69), 7th Baronet. In politics he was a Bedford Whig (SHC 1922 p257n); **raised to the peerage** Sir John Wrottesley (1771-1841), 9th Baronet, in 1838, politician and soldier, serving with the 16th Lancers in Holland and France under the Duke of York; **28th President of the Royal Society** John Wrottesley (1798-1867), who served between 1854-58. He was 2nd Baron Wrottesley and 10th Baronet; he helped found the Royal Astronomical Society 1820; was president of the British Association 1860; **lord-in-waiting to Queen Victoria 1869-74, 1880-85, 22nd in direct male descent from Simon de Verdon, Lord of Wrottesley in 1167** Arthur (b1824), 3rd Baron Wrottesley; **'the Nestor of genealogists'** Major-General George Wrottesley (1827-1909), 3rd brother of Arthur, 3rd Baron, so called by JH Round (VCH vol 20 p5), his greatest achievement, according to James P Jones, in the line of genealogy was the transcribing and translation of the priceless Chartulary of Burton Abbey (HOPTT p233); **killed in the Kaffir War** Hon Henry Wrottesley (d1852), 4th brother of the 3rd Baron, Lieut in the 43rd Regt (SA Oct 28 1899 p5 col 5); **died on a P&O steamer at Marseilles** Capt Hon W Wrottesley eldest son of 3rd Baron, in the 4th (Royal Irish) Dragoon Guards, on Oct 7 1899 (SA Oct 28 1899 p5 col 5); **drowned at sea on way to South Africa** Lieut-Col AE Wrottesley, aged 44, son of Hon EB Wrottesley, DL, brother of 2nd Baron, in Oct 1899 (SA Oct 28 1899 p5 col 5); **had Queen Victoria as his Sponsor** Victor Alexander Wrottesley (b1873), 3rd son of the 3rd Baron.

Airfields...

Oldest military aerodrome in Staffordshire Perton airfield in WWI on the N side of Pattingham Road at SO 860995. **Pendeford Airfield's worst disaster** When a De Havilland Dove flew in to pick up the Dowty Boulton Paul directors, April 9 1970 and crashed in Redhouse Drive killing the two pilots and the occupant of the house, and led to the closure of the airport (WMA vol 1 pp119-128) (BCM April 1971 p69) (VCH vol 20 p14) (Wolverhampton Chronicle March 19 1999 p17).

Churches...

At **TETTENHALL** is St Michael and All Angels, **one of 12 such county dedications** (of ancient parish churches); **98th= oldest ancient parish county church** dating from 1390, although most - save the porch and west tower - was destroyed in a fire 1950. **In the church** was a monument to William Smith (d1724), the architect, erected by his brother Francis Smith (SHOS vol 2 p197). **In the churchyard** - Grave of Hugh Moore (d1839) of Compton - **Staffordshire's 16th= oldest man ever** - who lived to aged of 107, and was wagered to walk one mile for £50 aged 105 on condition he beat a man of the age of 80 in the feat (TB May 1992 p17. Dec 1992 p21). Allegedly the grave of Mary Fitton (Mrs John Lougher) of Perton Hall - possibly the dark lady of Shakespeare's sonnets (SA&C May 19 1955 p6). The graves of William Pitt (1749-1823), author of 'Agriculture of Staffordshire' 1794, and 'Topographic History of Staffordshire', 1817 (W p91) (OPB p9) (SH p121), and Harriet Segar, shot dead by her insane and immature lover, Christopher Robinson in 1865 (TB Dec 1981 p5). **Tettenhall's longest-serving vicar** Christopher Tyrer, who served for 37 years, 1708-45. At **ALDERSLEY** is Christ the King (1956), Pendeford Ave. At **CASTLE CROFT** is the Good Shepherd (1954-5), Windmill Lane, and the R.C. St Pius X (1956), Castlecroft Ave. At **COMPTON** is St Thomas (1875), Oak Hill, and the St Thomas's United Reformed Church (1966), Castlecroft Rd. At **PENDEFORD** is St Paul (1981), Whitburn Close. The Ecumenical Church at **PERTON** (1982-3), Anders Square, serves the new village of Perton. At **TETTENHALL WOOD** is Christ Church (1865-6), Church Rd. At **TRESCOTT** was a mission church 1931-72 (VCH vol 20 p43).

The area...

Tettenhall is the **county's 26th largest parish**, consisting of 7,965 acres; **66th closest parish to the county town**, 11m SSW; **extremist length** 7m, **making it 9th longest parish in the county**; **extremist width** 5.6m, making it **19th= widest parish in the county. Chief settlement** Tettenhall, a very desirable suburban village. **Geology** CRANMOOR-The Hollies - Keuper Marls; PERTON-Wightwick-Tettenhall villages, Wrottesley Hall, Lodge, and Pendeford - Keuper Sandstones; TRESCOTT - Bunter. **Highest point** 545 feet in Wrottesley Old Park. **Lowest point** 272 feet on Wombourne boundary by Smestow Brook. Tettenhall was **37th most-populated Staffordshire parish in 1801** with 1,570; **35th in 1811** with 1814; **33rd in 1821** with 2,234; **32nd in 1831** with 2,618;

29th in 1841 with 3,143; 29th in 1851 with 3,396; 31st in 1861 with 3,716; 32nd in 1871 with 4,416; 29th in 1881 with 5,474; 30th in 1891 with 5,982; 29th in 1901 with 6,459.

Aynuck and Ayli, The Aaron Manby, a worker with a Joseph Wright & Co. sling, a model of the Thunderbolt car

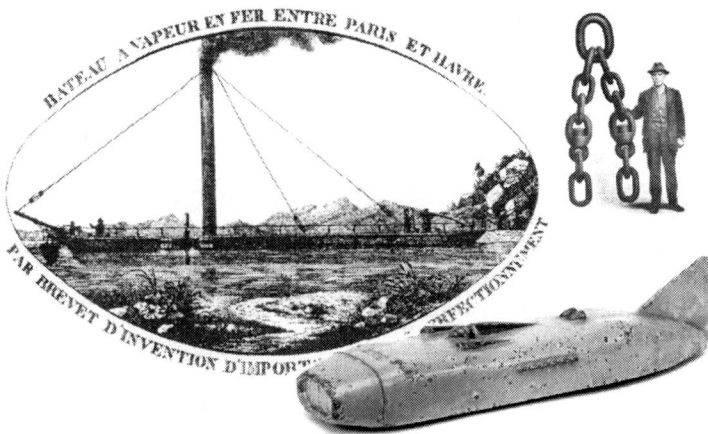

Tipton
Did you know that...

Tipton's top folklore The Staffordshire Advertiser author of the Towns of South Staffordshire column noted about Tipton - 'There is an old jeu d' espirit which the inhabitants, with a grave legendary humour relate of their immediate ancestors, which is worth a chronicle. They say "The old Tipton folk were a sad lot, for they sold their church, and put the parson into the workhouse". All this was indeed true in a sense, but the real truth was in c1800 the church had become unfit for use by mining subsidence and needed to be sold; a new church was built with the money raised, whilst the parson at that time needed a residence, and nothing suitable being found, a wing of the workhouse was fitted up to the standards befitting a parson (SA Dec 29 1849 p7 col 1). **What Tipton is famous for** Iron working. **The name Tipton first appears** in Domesday Book, 1086. **Unique derivation for a surname** Tipton (chiefly a Shropshire surname) will be from Tipton in this parish (PDS). **'Tippon'** How Black Country people pronounce Tipton (Where I live: The Black Country BBC website). **Oldest parish register in the country** Tipton, dating from 1513 (Staffordshire County Handbook c1958); **first person in the parish register** Joane daughter of Thomas Whitehouse baptised Dec 20 1513. **Oldest surviving Freemason lodge in Staffordshire by 1917** Noah's Ark Lodge, Tipton, No. 347, founded by at least 1817; the only other oldest lodge by 1917 was St Martin's, Burslem (SA Dec 29 1917 p7 col 7). **Tipton's 'Lost City'** Former pub name for what was The Drayton Inn in 1971, on the Moat Farm Estate (Evening Mail April 14 1971). **First town in England to introduce street lamps** Reputedly, Tipton (OH p11). **First Black Country town in which cholera broke out with force** Tipton in 1832 with 404 deaths, raging so severely that out of one family of 14, 12 died (TEBC2). **'Champion of Champions' bonfire in the Black Country** Ocker Hill for the coronation of George V, 1911, made of 260 tons of wood; the barrels at the corners were filled with tar to further feed the blaze (TB Feb 10 2005 p13p). **'Tipton's most terrible tragedy'** The explosion on March 6 1922, which claimed the lives of 19 young girls (see Tipton's heroines, below) at a factory in Groveland Road, Dudley Port. They were engaged on very low wages breaking-up 'live' cartridges. The factory was owned by Mrs LK Knowles of Stourton near Kinver, and run by her husband John Walter Knowles. He was found guilty of manslaughter and sentenced to 5 years in prison. 'Lucky' Gladys Williams, 14, alone miraculously escaped, being the only girl working in the shop at the time (TB Sept 15 2005 pp14-15ps). **First Methodist Boys' Club in the world** Founded at Bloomfield Methodist Church in Nov 1925, conceived by the then Minister, Rev Ran Holtom. In 1933 it became the Comradeship Club, in 1950 the Youth Club, and in 1965 the Boys' Club (Midland Chronicle etc. Oct 16 1975 p16ps). **The ape who stood trial for manslaughter** Bonzo, pet ape (from 1901) of Jack Jevons of Cottage Spring, Alexandra Rd, Tipton, who was pitted in a barefist fight with the pretended 'New Tipton Slasher' Josiah Smith in 1905 and so maimed him he died a few days later. Bonzo was arrested and tried at Wednesbury, where he was sentenced to have 'his teeth drawn'. In addition, Smith's brother set his bulldog onto him, but Bonzo only dragged it to the canal and drowned it (TB May 1994 p11). **World Champion Pickled Onion Eater 1970** Joe Williams, a moulder, of 97 Ivy Road, Tipton, who ate 106 pickled onions in half an hour at the Brewer and Baker Inn, Tipton, beating Bill Morris's record of 67 set at the Sportsman Inn, Tipton. This was perhaps the last Pickled Onion Eating championship (Evening Mail April 9 1970). **Poorest area of the Black Country 1974** Tipton, according to a report published in Oct 1974; figures should Tipton had a higher proportion of unskilled workers than other area of the Black Country, and more older people (E&S Oct 22 1974).

Buildings...

Most railway stations in a Staffordshire borough Tipton, with six (Staffordshire County Handbook c1958). **'one of the first victims of the Beeching Axe'** Tipton 'Five Ways' Station, S side of Sedgley Road which operated between 1850-1962, and the line (between Dudley and Bilston) closed in 1968 (Wikipedia 2007) (TB Aug 14 2003 p9p). **'probably the most famous baths in the Black Country'** Tipton Baths, Queens Road, opened 1933. Closed on July 31 2002. After a campaign apparently later reopened (TB Oct 30 2003 p19p). **'the largest electric power installation in England'** Ocker Hill power station (TSSOP p72) (TWDOP p21p) (BCM Autumn 1999 p24). **UK's first health park development** Neptune Health Park, Neptune Street with Sedgley Road West, 1998. **2nd best-known Black Country crooked pub** The Tilted Barrel, Princes End (Q&ABC no. 183). **Best Pub in Britain 2000** The Rising Sun Inn, 116 Horsley Road, Horseley Heath by the Campaign For Real Ale (BBC Midlands Today. Jan 26 2000).

Canals...

'Venice of the Black Country' 'Venice of Midlands' References to Tipton because it is dominated by canals; more specifically Ocker Hill has been called 'Venice of the Midlands'; more generally the Black Country has been called 'Black Venice' (Observer magazine Jan 17 1971). **'the finest packets of its kind ever built'** 'Euphrates' a very swift flyboat famed for its record passages to and from Wolverhampton and Birmingham, built by Thomas Monk (1765-1843) at Monk's Dock, Tipton. **Widest canal tunnel in Britain** Reputedly, Netherton Tunnel (1858), the N entrance is at Dudley Port (MR2 p223).

Churches...

The parish church, St Martin (originally at Tibbington, from 1797 at Horseley Heath). It is the **only such county dedication** (for ancient parish churches); **27th last ancient parish county church built** dating from 1795. Locally, known as **'Pepper Box Church'** in view of the shape of the top of its tower, it was made redundant in 1988, and converted into a dwelling 2005 (BCM Winter 2005 p62). **The churchyard** Closed in 1856 (BCM Winter 2005 p62). **DUDLEY PORT** The **Methodist Cathedral of the Midlands** Chapel in Park Lane, Tipton. By 1979 it had been replaced by a smaller modern building (Q&ABC no. 40). The Park Methodist chapel, Victoria Rd, Tipton, built 1903, replacing a small cottage in Coneygre near to the Brown Lion beerhouse, used from 1863 (TB March 8 2001 p23). At **TIBBINGTON** is St John the Evangelist (1857), Upper Church Lane (formerly the ancient parish St Martin), winner of the 1979 Best Kept churchyard competition in Lichfield Diocese (E&S Sept 24 1979). At **TIPTON GREEN** is St Paul (1839), Owen St; St Matthew (1876), Dudley Rd, described by Christopher Robinson in The Bugle as **'the quart in a pint plot!'** (TB July 27 2006 p23p). **Staffordshire's first Wesleyan 'preaching house'** Tipton Green, opened 1750 (HODW p132). At **OCKER HILL** is St Mark (1849), St Mark's Rd. Another church was St Luke.

Courage & service...

'The welfare of the people is the highest law' 'Salus populi suprema lex' Motto of Tipton Borough (CH pp336,337il). **First Zeppelin raid over the Black Country** Aircraft L21 over Union St,

Tipton, on Jan 31 1916 killing 14 persons: **Survivor who lost the most** Thomas Morris, the boy soldier of the S. Staffs Regt, who lost most of his family: **Last survivor** Violet Butter, Tipton native, later of Tividale, aged 92 in 2002 (TB Jan 17 2002 p26. Feb 7 2002 p23p. Feb 21 2002 p15). **Only place in Staffordshire to annually award one of its citizens for good works** Tipton with the Tiptonian of the Year Award, run by Tipton Civic Society, sponsored by Tipton & Coseley Building Society; the recipient has to be from Tipton and their efforts confined to the Tipton area; the **first winner** was Ray Brothwood, 1992 (TB Nov 8 2001 p6). The founder and first chairman of the Society was John Brimble, MBE (1940-2006) (BCM Autumn 2006 p40).

Engineering & work...

First steam engine erected in England, Thomas Newcomen's first engine 'Dudley Castle' erected on Lady Meadow (on what became Coneygree Colliery, 1712; reports of two slightly earlier engines erected in Cornwall are inconclusive - SL p207) (SHOS vol 2 pp119-120) (SOSH p296). A rival theory claims the site was behind Moore Street off Willenhall Road, Wolverhampton (E&S March 22 2008 p13). **First commercial beam engine in the country, first to embody the separate condenser invented by James Watt** A Boulton and Watt pumping engine set up at Bloomfield Colliery, 1776 (VCH vol 2 p165) (IAS p87) (TSSOP p8p). **World's first iron steamship, first iron ship to cross the Channel** The Aaron Manby, made by Mr Manby and Capt Charles Napier at the Horseley Iron Company at Great Bridge 1821/2; departing from London, continuing on from Le Havre up the Seine she arrived in Paris on June 10 1822 (Evening Mail May 11 1972). **'one of the largest chain and anchor works in England'** Neptune Forge, Owen St, Tipton (Griffith's Guide to the Iron Trade. 1873) (TB Nov 29 2001 p19p). **'the largest anchor in the world'** That for the Great Eastern, made by Messrs HP Parkes, 1866, according to Wolverhampton Chronicle, 1867. The iron used was made by Barrows & Sons of Bloomfield. It was the patented invention of Joseph Beterley of Liverpool, and weighed 8 tons, the length of the shank was 20 feet 6 inches, the length of the wood stock was 19 feet 6 inches, the tread of arms 7 feet 4 inches (Wolverhampton Chronicle Jan 2 1867) (BCM Oct 1978 pp47-50. Autumn 1996 pp19-22). **First railway engine made with a solid plate frame, the first with its reversing motion controlled directly by a reversing lever**, the **first incorporating arc or link motion with fixed centres**, and the **first with a boiler free to expand on its frame** The Star, made by a Tyneside engineer at Tipton, 1833 (Story of Railway Pioneers. S Snell. 1921. pp21,24) (VCH vol 2 p162). **First to refine iron using a process known as 'pig boiling'** Joseph Hall (1798-1862), born probably at Kingswinford, but lived at Tipton for 60 years. His discovery was made c1816 - the secret lay in 'boiling' the metal instead of 'dry' puddling and revolutionised the iron trade of South Staffordshire (The Iron Question. Joseph Hall. 1858) (HOTIP p7) (STELE SARA Feb 3 1956 photo). **First to introduce sand bottom puddling furnaces** Joseph Hall of Tipton, 1825

(OH p69). **Horseley Coal and Iron Company's most famous achievement** Galton Bridge in Smethwick, designed by Thomas Telford, 1829, used to 1970 (TB Feb 5 2004 p20): **Their first engine built** Was for a vessel, the Prince of Coburg, 1817 (BCM Spring 2006 p22). **World's only central Mond gas plant** Built at Dudley Port and in operation by 1905 to 1964. This was the only gas station (serving a region (the north Black Country area) and not individual works) in the world. It was authorised under the South Staffordshire Mond Gas Bill 1899. The plant produced a form of cheap gaseous fuel for industrial purposes, and was developed by Ludwig Mond (BCM Summer 2004 pp77-81). **First testing house of Lloyds British Testing Company** Set up in 1864 at Tipton, set up to undertake chain, cable and anchor testing to the trade, following the Act of Parliament 1864 which laid down regulations (TEBC2). **Largest sausage maker in the world 1892** Palethorpes, Dudley Port, founded 1850; the business acquired Park Lane Brewery premises in 1890, and moved to Market Drayton in 1967 and the factory was demolished in 1968 (TB April 13 2006 p13) (West Bromwich Local History Fair 2008). **'one of the largest makers of Iron and Steel Colliery Tubs in the country'** W.G. Allen & Sons Ltd of Bradley's Lane, Prince's End as claimed in the company's own literature in the 1920s (BCM Autumn 2004 p72). **Largest dome in the world** The Dome of Discovery for the 1951 Festival of Britain made by Horseley Bridge and Thomas Piggott of Tipton, requiring some 232 tons of aluminium, 133 tons of steel, and was 365 feet in diameter at the base (BCM Summer 2000 p14). **'One of the oldest working foundrymen in the Black Country' 1975** Charlie Sargeant (b1895), of Roberts Road, Tipton, still working a full day at Ashmore Foundries Ltd, Lewis St, Great Bridge, aged 80 (E&S May 20 1975). **First Bean car of Tipton** Appeared in 1920. **British Safety Council award 1974** Conex-Sandra Ltd (part of the Delta Group), Whitehall Rd, Great Bridge, winning for the seventh year in succession (West Bromwich Midland Chronicle (Dudley ed) July 11 1974 p3). **Last Black Country bellow maker** Syd Royall (b1921) of Wheatsheaf Rd, Tividale. Worked at Vaughans (Hope Works) Ltd, Hope St, Dudley, 1935-90 (BCM Autumn 2003 pp67-70p). **Britain's largest steel bending firm by 1980** The Angle Ring, Tipton, founded in 1951 at a site in Bloomfield Road. It has since expanded to become one of the most prominent benders/curvers of metal and alloys in its region (Wikipedia 2007).

People...

'The Dudley Poet and Rhymist', 'the best of Poets - the worst of men' Ben Boucher born at Horseley Heath in 1769; former miner who moved to Dudley maintaining himself there by selling his own poems at one penny each (TB June 1978 p18il). **First mayor of Wolverhampton** George Benjamin Thorneycroft (1791-1851), born in Tipton, 1848 (TB Oct 1977 p4 il) (VB p53). **'more 'Aynucks & Aylis' than anywhere else in the Black Country'** The Tipton district according to The Bugle (TB Sept 1997 p17). **Strange but true!** A collier Samuel Tinley of Great Bridge was killed in a pit by a fall of rock strata. But during the previous night he awoke, saying he had a ton of rock on his head, though he had no headache. He was convinced this was a bad omen and was reluctant to go to work the following day, but his wife persuaded him to go. Leaving home he went to his child and said "Let me have my last kiss" (SA Nov 23 1872 p3 col 2). **'Orator Bayley'** What Edward Bayley, local ironmaster, was always referred to. He was elected to Tipton Local Board of Health in 1882; chairman of it from 1885. There is a portrait in Tipton library (BCM April 1990 p20). **The woman who had 'the biggest feet on earth'** Miss Fanny Mills, a (non-existent?) showwoman, who appears on a billposter in a publicity stunt by The Marriage Speciality Company c1890. The poster claims she is the daughter of a farming, coal

TIPTON PEOPLE - Jack Holden, Muriel Hopkins, William Perry, Joseph Hall, Sir John Chalstrey, Ben Boucher

and iron magnate of Tipton and is soliciting marriage suitors. She is very pretty, refined, highly accomplished; eight and half stone; has been noticed by every newspaper in the land; she wears No. 30 size shoes - the largest shoe ever worn - for 19-inch long and 7-inches wide feet, requiring three goatskins to make. Such a poster, enamelled and framed, once hung in The Crooked House Inn, Himley (TB June 1998 p17il). **'Emma Sweep'** A well known old Tipton character who conceived a child with a black man (then a rarity in the Black Country) but placated locals by insisting the child was black as in pregnancy she was frightened by a chimney-sweep, hence her nickname (MMB-CC p103). **First senior registrar and research fellow in transplantation surgery at the Royal Free Hospital, 1967; establisher of the first fibre-optic endoscopy unit in the independent health care sector, 1975;** one of the **first British surgeons to perform minimally invasive 'keyhole' surgery for gall bladder and other abdominal problems, 1990; 743th Lord Mayor of London 1995-6** Sir John Chalstrey, native of Tipton (57 Black Country People. Stan Hill. 2002 pp142-3); the Wikipedia ranking makes Chalstrey 745th Lord Mayor of London. **Heaviest woman in Great Britain and Ireland 1979, Britain's heaviest woman ever by 1979** Muriel Hopkins of Tipton (b1931) who weighed 47 stone 7lb at her death in April 1979; for the former claim she weighed 43 stone 11 lbs (Sandwell Evening Mail Aug 18 1979 photo) (GBR 1995 p56). **Where Frank Skinner made his debut** The comedian performed some of his first gigs at Mad O'Rourke's famous 'Pie Factory' pub on the corner of Sedgley Road West and Hurst Lane. Formerly the Doughty Arms Inn becoming The Pie Factory in 1987 (Wikipedia 2007). **'The Mario Lanza' ghostwriter or scribbler** An illusive person who draws cartoons of the Italian singer Mario Lanza to his memory on beer mats in Black Country pubs since perhaps Lanza's death in 1959, and certainly since the 1970s when a concentration of them appeared at the Old Cat Inn, Wordsley. 'AJW', as he signs himself, appears to have attended Park Lane Boys school, Tipton, and his mats have turned up for instance at The Nags Head Inn, Tipton (E&S April 3 2006) (TB Sept 28 2006 pp22ils,23. Oct 12 2006 p19 - he is also sometimes known as 'Picasso of the Black Country'. April 5 2007 p25) (BBC Midlands Today Jan 3 2007). **First mayor of Tipton** Arthur Frederick Welch from Sept 10 1938. The first mayoress was his wife Minnie. When the borough of Tipton was abolished in 1974 its mayoral regalia was put on display at West Bromwich Town Hall, but unfortunately the mayoral chains were stolen in a smash-and-grab robbery in 1981 (TB Jan 3 2008 p22ps). **'King of the (Dudley Canal) Tunnel'** Jack Wheeler, a legger through the tunnel who retired in his 70s in 1952 (VB p45). **Black Country's most phenomenal memory** Harry Harrison (1922-2007), poet, entertainer and journalist, Tipton native and resident, best remembered for his Black Country Bugle 'Off the Cuff Black Country Stuff' column, written from c1983. He could remember all his 1,000 or so poems and local knowledge off by heart (info Stan Hill, 2006) (TB Aug 30 2007 p5). **Tipton's hero** Cpl Joseph Davies

(1889-1976), Royal Welsh Fusiliers, born Nock St, Toll End, awarded a VC for bravery at Delville Wood on the Somme, July 20 1916. He was also awarded the Order of St George; his V.C. is displayed at the Fusiliers Museum at Caernarfon Castle; a garden opened to his memory at Alexandra High School in July 2005; a plaque to his memory was erected by Tipton Civic Society in Great Bridge. He was the only Tipton-born man to be so awarded in WW1 (TB Feb 1991 p21p. Nov 1 2001 p17. July 7 2005 p13. July 13 2006 p17. April 26 2007 p25). **Tipton's heroines** The 19 girls killed in the Dudley Port cartridge factory explosion on March 6 1922 to whom there is a monument in Horseley Heath Cemetery:- Laura Dalloway 14, Nellie Kay 15, Mabel Weaver 14, Annie Freeth 15, Violet May Franklin 15, Annie Elizabeth Florence Edwards 15, Priscilla Longmore 13, Annie Naylor 14, Elizabeth Williams 13, Edith Drew 15, Edith Richards 14, Elsie Fellows 15, Gladys May Bryant 14, Lizzie Griffiths 15, Margaret Burns 15, Hannah Hubbard 16, Elizabeth Aston 14, Edith Jukes 15, and Lucy Edwards 14 (TB Sept 15 2005 pp14-15). **Tipton's kindest** Rev Angelo Solari, MA, vicar of St Mark's, Ocker Hill 1854-88. He was instrumental in getting the National Schools at Ocker Hill open in 1854 'from the first he interested himself in benevolent objects'... 'It was by his efforts for the relief of the poor and unfortunate in the districts around him that Mr Solari chiefly distinguished himself, assisting them in obtaining admission to hospitals, convalescent homes, blind asylums, and other institutions'. During the great distress in the district in 1885 he was 'indefatigable' in raising funds for distribution of necessities for the starving poor, 'and it is well known he gave a considerable portion of his own income from the living in works of charity'. He may have had financial troubles, frequently expressing in letters to his London relatives great concern for the poor of his district. This may have led him to take his own life, aged 64, by cutting his throat on March 8 1888 (SA March 10 1888 p5 col 4). **Tipton's saddest** Sarah Louisa Lawley, mistress of the infant dept of Ocker Hill Church Schools, who took her own life in the canal on Dec 21 1901 to free herself from her alcoholic husband, James, out of work for a year and kept by her; the family were descending into poverty. A suicide note was left for her sister, and there was a suspicion Sarah had taken £50 from the School's penny bank over which she had charge (SA Dec 28 1901 p5 col 3). **Tipton's poorest** A squat, brick, C18-looking building of two storeys, at the junction of Alexandra Road (formerly Workhouse Lane) and Lower Church Lane, served as the parish workhouse. In 1849 there was a proposal to vocate it in favour of a new Union workhouse to be built at Dudley. The old building at Tipton was demolished in 1912 (SA Oct 20 1849 p5 col 1) (TB June 1995 p10p). **First official visit to Tipton by a reigning monarch** When Elizabeth II visited Tipton on June 24 1994 (BCM Spring 2002 p45). **Tipton Three** Collective name for former Tipton residents - Shafiq Rasul (b1977 in Dudley), Ruhal Ahmed (b1981), Asif Iqbal (b1981, in West Bromwich) held c2002-04 in extrajudicial detention at Guantanamo Bay detainment camp, Cuba, on suspicion of involvement in international Islamic terrorism. The three were repatriated to the UK in

March 2004, and released, without charge, the next day (Wikipedia, 2008). **Tipton's earliest recorded will** Belongs to Edward Round, and is dated Sept 24 1662. **Last Staffordshire will proved in a Peculiar ecclesiastical court** Belongs to Samuel Hickinbottom of Tipton, and is dated Jan 5 1858. **Choicest quote** Princess Victoria (later Queen) passing through the Black Country, in her journal, 2nd August 1832, wrote 'The country is very desolate every where; there are coals about, and the grass is quite blasted and black. I just now see an extraordinary building flaming with fire. The country continues black, engines flaming, coals, in abundance, every where, smoking and burning coal heaps, intermingled with wretched huts and carts and little ragged children.' (from Lines and Letters: Queen Victoria in her Letters and Journals. Christopher Hibbet. 1984).

Sport & gambling...

'only man in recorded history to gain championship honours in pugilism and also ride his own horse in The Grand National' John Broome (b1818), employee of Walkers Cannon Works, Tipton, for whom he invented a piece of heavy artillery decades ahead of its time, but not taken up by the company; for his equestrian skills he was billed as 'The Young Ducrow' (TB Nov 1993 p31il). **'The Little Elephant'** James Stone, Tipton wrestler, and fist-fighter who stood only just over 5 feet high but weighed over 200 lbs. Most memorably he took on and lost to Devon's Abraham Cann in 1835 (TB Oct 1995 p31). **Another Tipton pugilist** Tommy Cartwright (E&S March 12 2008 p9). **Imperial Services middleweight champion** Abe Naylor, 11th Hussars, of Tipton, when in the Egyptian Expeditionary Force took on Haig Assadourian, Lightweight Champion of Egypt in Cairo, 1921, and won. He was later a councillor in Tipton (TB April 1996 p10p). **'The Tipton Tornado'** Tom Whitehouse, Bantamweight, Welterweight boxer. Born Eve Hill, Dudley, but schooled at Burnt Tree, and later ran The Doughty Arms Inn, Tipton. His career spans 1913 to late 1920s (TB Dec 1995 p36p). **AAA ten-miler champion 1934, AAA six-miler champion 1933-35, International Cross Country Gold medalist 1933-35, English Cross Country winner 1938, 1939, 1946, Midland Marathon champion 1946-48, CN Jackson Memorial Cup winner (awarded by AAA Championships Committee) 1950, Commonwealth Games and European Games (there being the oldest runner ever to win) marathons winner 1950, Sportsman of the Year 1950 runner-up** Jack Holden, born 1907 in Bradley, but was the Tipton Harriers' most famous athlete, died at Papcastle, Cumbria in 2004 (TB Sept 18 2003 p12. March 11 2004 p27ps). **'One of the first international cross-country runners for Tipton Harriers'** Thomas Kay (d1976) of West Bromwich, running twice for his country; he and his team mate, Jack Holden, were picked to run for England in 1929 (West Bromwich Midland Chronicle Sept 9 1976 p9). **Cross Country Champion 1972** Malcolm Thomas of the Tipton Harriers. **Road Relay Midland Champions 1974** Tipton Harriers, winning by 4 mins 53 seconds (Evening Mail April 3 1974). **Cross

Country Champion 1978 Bernard Ford of the Tipton Harriers (TB Sept 18 2003 p12). **First double crossing of Australia** A Bean car of Tipton, 1924. **First West Bromwich Albion player to reach 100 goals** Fred Morris (1893-1962), born Tipton, playing his early football at Great Bridge primary school, Tipton Victoria, and Redditch. Albion player from 1911, and scoring a 100 goals for them in 1922 (TB Dec 11 2003). **World speed record** 357 mph by the Thunderbolt car, made in Tipton, 1938; the driver was Capt George Eyston. **World record for a pools win** Eight Tipton workmates with £1.5 million Littlewoods pools, Aug 1990 (WF p54). **Triple jackpot lottery winners, defying odds of 350 million to one** A Tipton family, by Oct 1999, on the British National Lottery, winning a total of £3.25 million (The Sunday Telegraph Magazine. Oct 31 1999 p22).

The Tipton Slasher...

'Tipton's most famous son', Bare-knuckle champion of England 1850-57, first Staffordshire man to hold the title, 'one of the greatest pugilists that the Black Country has ever produced' William Perry (1819/20-80), alias 'Tipton Slasher' born Park Lane (Lea Brook), Tipton. He obtained the nickname 'Tipton Slasher' aged 17 by thrashing a Birmingham rival. He was known as 'K-legs' by some contemporary fight writers because a bout of rickets, during infancy, weakened his right knee, which ben inwards. In his fighting prime he was six feet high and weighed 13st 4lbs. Lord Dudley was a patron. On the proceeds of his winnings he opened The Champion of England Inn, Spon Lane, West Bromwich. After failing with it he returned to work on the canals and died poor. Buried St John's churchyard, Kate's Hill, Dudley (BCM Spring 2002 p45. Spring 2003 p12) (TB July 1998 p36il). **His first fight** Aged 16 against a man named Dogherty at Chelsea (Birmingham Post June 24 1967). **His most difficult opponent** Charles Freeman, the 'Amercian Giant', who dwarfed Perry, Dec 1842 (BCM Spring 2003 p9). **His first serious bid for the Championship of England** Was against Tom Paddock in Dec 1850; Perry won on a foul (Birmingham Post June 24 1967). **His last fight as champion** Against Tom Sayers, June 16 1857 (TB May 30 2002 p34il). **His name used in a Mummers play** The Netley Abbey Mummers Play (possibly dating to c1893) who had a 'Tipton Slasher' as the Valiant Soldier character, who was in any case sometimes otherwise called Capt Slasher, Valient Slasher or Bold Slasher (BCM Spring 2003 p9). **His biggest modern critic** Perhaps A Fellows of Bilston whose myth-denting rant against Perry appeared in E&S March 12 2008 p9 claiming he was perhaps born in Darlaston, hardly lived at Tipton, only shone in the world of pugilism because the prize ring was then on its last legs, and deserved to lose against Sayers. **The T.V. play which portrayed him** 'Gie it some 'ommer' a series about life and times of the Black Country for Central Television 1984 (E&S Nov 30 2005 p8). **Self-styled 'The New Tipton Slasher'** Josiah Smith, who challenged a pet ape to a bareknuckle fight but the ape won and Smith died 1905 (TB May 1994 p1). **'The New Tipton Slasher'** Kid Plested (1886-1945) of Tipton, born Great Bridge, light-welter boxer, in days before there was such a category. He was being billed this by 1911. Frank Butler, the old 'News of the World' sporting writer once dubbed him 'The 10st 2lb Champion of Great Britain'. He was a 'top liner' until 1921, and was still boxing in the early 1930s (TB March 1993 p34p. May 1994 p34p). **The 'New Tipton Slasher'** Brian Huckfield of Tipton who emerged as a heavyweight boxer in the mid 1970s (TB March 1 2001 p34p). **The Tipton Slasher footballer** Billy 'Bullet' Jones, alias 'Little Bloodhound', who began his football career with native Prince's End in the late 1890s, went on to play for Smethwick, Halesowen, Small Heath, Brighton & Hove Albion (TB Aug 12 2004 p30).

The area...

Tipton is the **county's 115th largest parish**, consisting of 2,171 acres; **38th farthest parish away from the county town**, 18.1m due S; **extremist length** 2.8m; **extremist width** 3.8m. **Chief settlement** Tipton, a large Black Country town with several centres. **Geology** S and E - Upper Coal Measures; N and W fringes - Middle Coal Measures. **Highest point** 558 feet on the Rowley Regis boundary at Burnt Tree. **Lowest point** 394 feet on Wednesbury boundary on Leabrook Road. Tipton was **16th most-populated Staffordshire parish in 1801** with 4,280; **6th in 1811** with 8,407; **4th in 1821** with 11,546; **7th in 1831** with 14,951; **7th in 1841** with 18,891; **7th in 1851** with 24,872; **8th in 1861** with 28,870; **8th in 1871** with 29,445; **10th in 1881** with 30,013; **13th in 1891** with 29,314; **13th in 1901** with 30,543.

Tinker's Castle, near Abbot's Castle Hill

Trysull & Woodford Grange
Did you know that...

Trysull's top folklore A number of traditions relate to Tinker's Castle, a C18-looking colour-washed house near Abbot's Castle Hill. It may have received its name from a tinker having once inhabited its sandstone rock-hewn cellar; that Charles II took refuge here after escaping the battle of Worcester (1651). **What Trysull is famous for** Abbot's Castle Hill escarpment. The **name Trysull first appears** in Domesday Book, 1086. **Unique name in England** Trysull

(DUIGNAN). **Only Staffordshire Hundred of sufficient importance listed as a vill in its own right in DB** Seisdon (PNSZ p44). **Staffordshire's most affected Rural District under the Local Government Act 1966** Seisdon, from April 1 1966; it lost some land to Wolverhampton CB, and gained from Sedgley and Tettenhall UDs (Staffordshire Handbook c1966 p57). **Staffordshire's 3rd earliest commutation of tithes when they were dealt with under a parliamentary enclosure act** The vicarial tithes of Trysull, by allotments of land, 1773. **Wombourne places that wanted to join Trysull and Seisdon parish** Awbridge and Ebstree who petitioned the council to be included in their parish, claiming they had no recognition from Wombourne PC, and wanting the parish boundary changed (E&S March 10 1978). **Staffordshire Best Kept (Small Village category) winner 1968, 1995** Trysull. **Staffordshire Best Kept South Staffordshire District winner (Small Village) 1991, 1994, 1995, 1998, 2004, 2005** Trysull. **Staffordshire's biggest tomato grown** Perhaps that grown by the Huszak family at their nursery in Trysull in 1978, measuring in circumference 18 inches, weighing 2lb 2oz (E&S Aug 20 1978 p5p).

People...

Trysull's most famous old worthy Elizabeth Harriotts (d1728). Kind-hearted kinswoman who brought her second cousin the young Samuel Johnson to her home, Trysull Manor House, in 1711 to be seen for eye and ear trouble by occultist physician Dr Thomas Attwood. In her will she left him £40, which partly founded his time at Oxford. **First agriculturist in Staffordshire to use guano, pioneer of the steam-driven thresher** Daniel Banton, who owned and occupied farms in Trysull in the mid C19 (W p209) (TB June 1986 p11). **'One of Britain's leading sheep farmers'** John Farquharson (d1976) of Wolmere Farm, Seisdon, who bred pedigree Suffolk sheep and won practically every championship including the Royal Show, and the Royal Smithfield Show. In addition he won many championships with the Aberdeen Angus beef cattle that he bred (E&S March 1 1976 p). **Seisdon's oldest man** George Brayne (1878-1980), lived to the age of 102 and served in the Boer War. In 1977 he had to quit Meadow Farm, Post Office Road, Seisdon, after renting it since 1932, as the farm sold to a new owner, Ronald Goldie of Wombourne, in July 1976, but could continue to live in his cottage, but was finally moved to a council bungalow in Trysull in summer 1980 (E&S March 7 1977 p. March 12 1977. March 29 1977. March 3 1981 pT1). **Observer Young Driver of the Year 1978** Paul Baker, aged 16, of Trysull, in the first Cup for this category sponsored by The Observer, held at Donington Park racing circuit (The Observer Nov 19 1978) (E&S Nov 20 1978 p20p). **Trysull's kindest** Thomas Rudge of Westminster who helped found the local school, 1707 (VCH vol 20 p195). **Trysull's poorest** By 1773 there was a poorhouse on Trysull Green, still in use in 1835, it had been pulled down by 1843, when a school was built on the site. From 1836 the poor were sent to Seisdon Union workhouse at Tettenhall until a new union workhouse was opened at Trysull in 1860 (VCH vol 20 p193). It could accommodate

120 inmates, and was referred to by children as 'The Haunted House' (TB July 1998 p13p. Aug 1998 p17). **Trysull/Seisdon's earliest recorded will** Belongs to Richard Shenton, and is dated 1529. **First persons in the parish register** Margerie _____? buried, baptised, married? Aug 10 1558. T_____? buried, baptised, married? Aug 12 1558. **Choicest quote** William Scott in his Stourbridge and Its Vicinity, 1832, includes notes on several adjoining parishes. And about Abbots Castle Hill he writes "From Chesterton to the minor station of Ashwood, the road had been described as entering Staffordshire at Rudge heath, thence passing by New Inn. In taking this course, it must necessarily have approached near to Abbots' Castle. The entire steep from Ape-wood promontory to Clasp-hill, (a mile in length) having the two hills for bastions, is considered by Dr. Plot, as a continued fortification of British construction....The modern aspect of this crescent-shaped hill, presents a bold ridge, discernible at considerable distance, having numerous rock cottages, with appendant gardens scattered over it."

Church...

At Trysull is All Saints, **one of 19 such county dedications** (of ancient parish churches); **84th= oldest ancient parish county church** dating from 1310. **2nd earliest stone figure/ effigy in the county** A figure of a bishop in Trysull church, c1200 (BAST vols 69-71 p27). In the bell tower is a charity board listing the charity of John Rudge of Seisdon who gave 20 shillings a year to a grave person to keep people awake in sermon time, and to clean the church windows, 1722 (SHOS vol 2 p210) (FCRE p163). **Trysull's longest-serving vicar** John Kendall, who served for 43 years, 1449-92.

The area...

Trysull is the **county's 92nd largest parish**, consisting of 2,951 acres; **44th= farthest parish away from the county town**, 17.3m SSW; **extremist length** 3.1m; **extremist width** 3.1m. **Chief settlement** The villages/ townships of Seisdon and Trysull are about the same size. **Geology** Bunter (all). **Highest point** 456 feet at the north point of Abbot's Castle Hill. **Lowest point** 243 feet by Smestow Bridge. **TRYSULL** was **91st most-populated Staffordshire parish in 1801** with 529; **100th in 1811** with 491; **103rd in 1821** with 539; **100th in 1831** with 562; **104th in 1841** with 541; **101st in 1851** with 559; **97th in 1861** with 610; **98th in 1871** with 583; **99th in 1881** with 567; **99th in 1891** with 554; **97th in 1901** with 553. **WOODFORD GRANGE** was **160th= most-populated Staffordshire parish in 1801** with 14; **161st= in 1811** with 14; **161st= in 1821** with 14; **159th in 1831** with 18; **164th in 1841** with 14; **164th in 1851** with 8; **163rd in 1861** with 13; **163rd in 1871** with 11; **164th in 1881** with 8; **164th in 1891** with 8; **162nd in 1901** with 15.

Upper Arley
Did you know that...
Upper Arley's top folklore There is said to have been a chapel at

Hextons called Hextan's Chapel; the name 'Chapel Leasowe' is a field adjoining the farmyard. The Crusader's Tomb (now in Upper Arley church) is said to have been placed in this chapel (AOA p29). **What Upper Arley is famous for** Arley Castle Arboretum. The **name Arley first appears** in 963. **First excavation of a particular freestone excellent for grindlestones** Probably the quarries S of Hextons Farm c1680 (History of Worcs. Nash. vol 2 App. 1) (DUIGNAN) (VCHW vol 3 p7). **'One of the country's oldest and most spectacular arboretums'** Arley House Arboretum, originally founded in 1820. It was officially opened to the public on Monday May 13 2002 by Lord Lichfield (Kidderminster Times May 16 2002. Kidderminster Chronicle May 16 2002). **'One of the prettiest villages in England'** Arley (Kidderminster Shuttle Sept 28 1984). **First ride of the Clarion Cycling Club** Wolverhampton to Bewdley through Arley in 1894 (BBC Radio 4 April 20 2004). **Best parish magazine in Worcestershire 1977** The Arley Grapevine, edited by Arley vicar Rev William Mowll (Kidderminster June 17 1977). **Best Restored Station Award 1983** Arley Station on the Severn Valley Railway. On Sept 22 1984 a plaque commemorating this award was unveiled on the station by Bernard Kaukas, BR's Director of Environment - it was his last public duty (Kidderminster Shuttle Sept 28 1984). **Most southerly point of Staffordshire** Hawkbatch.

Ferry...

'One of the oldest public services in Worcestershire' Running Upper Arley ferry, operating since C14. But the ferry was in the possession of the lords of Upper Arley manor to May 2 1931 when Alfred Chad Woodward (later Sir Chad Woodward) give it to Worcs CC (Kidderminster Times Feb 25 1959). **Record passengers in one day** 4,500 on Easter Monday 1953; the ferry day was 16 and half hours (Kidderminster Times Feb 25 1959). **Last chain ferry over River Severn** At Upper Arley (Companion into Worcestershire. Maxwell Fraser. 1949 p3). **Last ferry** Built at Bathhurst's, Tewkesbury, and came into commission on June 24 1952. After decommission in 1972 it was sold to Louise and Benjamin Eginton of Bewdley. By 1984 it was owned by Barry Branhill and kept at Shatterford (Kidderminster Shuttle Jan 14 1972. March 2 1984). **Last ferrymen** Robert Evans (1909-1990) of Frenchmans Street, working the ferry since 1939, and Edwin Merchant (b1930), employed on the ferry since 1969 (Kidderminster Shuttle Jan 28 1972. March 2 1984. Aug 2 1990). **Last day of the ferry** Saturday Jan 22 1972, the footbridge was opened by Sir Tatton Brinton at 2pm later that day (Kidderminster Times Jan 28 1972).

Churches...

The parish church, St Peter, Apostle and Martyr, **one of 15 such county dedications** (of ancient parish churches), on a hill to the NW of Upper Arley village and overlooking the village, is perhaps of Saxon origin, but the present church was built in c1100, which makes it **8th= oldest county church**. It was restored in 1885 and 1886 (AOA pp110-116). **Most interesting things** Memorial to Hon.

Henry Arthur Annesley 6th son of Arthur Earl of Mountnorris d1818 aged 27 two weeks after his marriage whilst bathing at Blackpool. Also note the effigy to Sir Walter de Balun, who died in 1220 on his wedding day; it was believed to be to a member of the Heckstan/Hexton family of Hexton (SHOS vol 2 p261) (GNHS p182) (GNHSS p32). Brass to Sir Henry Lyttleton, who as a prisoner at the battle of Worcester, 1651. A stain glass window to the memory of a past vicar who had served 41 years, painted by his wife (Kidderminster Shuttle Sept 28 1984). St Andrew's served the Button Oak, Pound Green area (Kidderminster Times June 16 1967).

People...

The man 'who restored England to the English' Hubert de Burgh (d1243), Statesman, soldier and lord of Arley 1227-43 (with periods of forfeiture). He urged King John to sign the Magna Carta; defended the castles of Chinion and Dover; defeated the French in the Straits of Dover 1217 which forced Louis of France to accept the treaty of Lambeth and renounce claims to the English crown. He was Justicular in Henry III's minority, but later fell from his favour. The King even tried to have him shackled, though the smith declined saying, "I will die any death before I put iron on the man who freed England from the stranger and saved Dover from France." De Burgh was granted Arley in 1227, and subsequently forfeited and regained it several times. Maxwell Fraser in his 'Companion into Worcestershire' (1949) writes "Many great lords have held Arley, but the lord of the manor whom Arley is most proud to remember is the great Hubert de Burgh, immortalised by Shakespeare in King John for his refusal to blind the unhappy young Prince, Arthur of Brittany." **Upper Arley's**

The last ferryman, Robert Evans, with his wife Florence, by the former Upper Arley ferry, 1984

hero Robert Evans (1909-90), of Frenchmans Street, last ferryman to work Upper Arley ferry, chimney sweep, grave digger, verger and bell ringer at St Peter's for 25 years. In 1957 he received a Royal Humane Society Award for saving the life of the Hampton Loade ferryman after his boat broke loose in high water, pulling him to safety even though he was a non-swimmer. In 1980 he received Maundy Money from the Queen at Worcester Cathedral (Kidderminster Shuttle Aug 2 1990). **Upper Arley's villainess** Margaret Mousole of Arley by the later C17 had been convicted of killing her bastard child and hung by the neck at Stafford, but she came to life again (NHS p291) (SD p35). **Forestry Authority Certificate of Excellence Award winner, Upper Arley's kindest** Roger Turner, Black Country industrialist, owner of Arley Castle estate, of 1,600 acres, since 1959, died in April 1999 leaving £15 million to charity (BCM Autumn 1999 p31). In 1962 Mr Turner demolished Arley Castle, retaining the barbican, and in 1963 built the modern Arley House approximately on the site. Mr Turner received the Forestry award in 1996 for dedication to Wymore Wood in Wyre Forest, on his estate. The estate is still held by his trustees who have opened the grounds of Arley House (the Arboretum) to the public (info Nigel Goodman) (Kidderminster Shuttle Sept 26 1996 photo). **Played for Kidderminster Harriers FC when they won their first Birmingham Senior Cup 1933-34** Frederick Perkins, Arley village school headmaster 1935-67 (Kidderminster Times June 16 1967). **Upper Arley's earliest recorded will** Belongs to Richard Hackfote of Over Arley, and is dated 1564. **Choicest quote** Marc de Bombelles, the French nobleman who toured Britain, wrote in his Journal de Voyage en Grande Bretagne et en Irlande, 1784 (1989), 'le lieu ou j'ai rendu mes premiers homages `a cette riviere, se nomme over areley. Milord Valencia pair d' Irlande ya une maniere de Chateau qui domine sur les bords encaissé de la Severn.' In 2000 it was translated by LE Page as 'The place where I paid my first respects to this river is called Over Areley. Lord Valencia, peer of Ireland, has a sort of country house which overlooks the embankmented Severn.'

The area...

Upper Arley is the **county's 69th largest parish**, consisting of 3,969 acres; **3rd= farthest parish away from the county town**, 25.3m SW; **extremist length** 5m, making it **31st= longest parish in the county**; **extremist width** 5.25m, **making it 25th widest parish in the county. Chief settlement** Upper Arley, a pretty Severn-side village. **Geology** N - Permian; NW and rest of S - Coal Measures intersected at Shatterford by NE-SW aligned Basalt and Dolerite fault. **Highest point** 594 feet near the summit of the ridge S of Shatterford. **Lowest point** 91 feet by the Severn below Hawkbatch. Upper Arley was **76th most-populated Staffordshire parish in 1801** with 693; **81st in 1811** with 691; **86th in 1821** with 715; **86th in 1831** with 735; **93rd in 1841** with 667; **92nd in 1851** with 678; **79th in 1861** with 886; **86th in 1871** with 793; **91st in 1881** with 731; **91st in 1891** with 647; **90th in 1901** with 670.

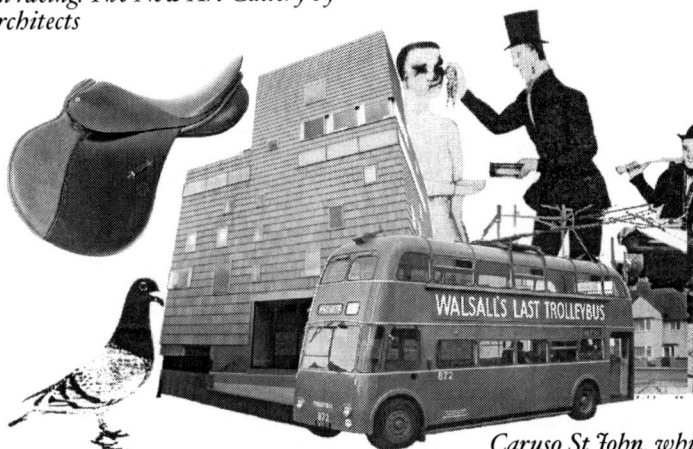

A saddle and a pigeon representing Walsall's prowess at making saddles and pigeon racing. The New Art Gallery by the architects

Caruso St John, which the Queen opened at Walsall in May 2000. Walsall pugilist George Holden

Walsall
Did you know that...

Walsall's top folklore The legend of the Hand of Glory or Arm of Glory. In 1870 what looked like an embalmed child's arm was found at White Hart Inn, a substantial Jacobean brick house at Caldmore Green. It cannot be decided if the arm is that of a dwarf child chimney sweep or a hanged villain pickled and dried. Or what the object was used for. Perhaps it was a candle holder, or used in witchcraft, or as a medical specimen for students of anatomy. It has also been linked to the ghosts seen in the house which has been haunted by a young girl and an elderly maid who both committed suicide here at different times, and the print of a small hand which was found in the locked attic. **Bloxwich's top folklore** Perhaps the ghost of a young girl who stayed at Wallington House, Wallington Heath, when it was a coaching inn called the King's Arms's in the 1720s, and was murdered in her room, perhaps, by an ostler, who made off with her roll of French silk. **What Walsall is famous for** Its leather trade. **Saddest place in the country** Walsall; in a 2007 poll of 6,000 people only 46% said they were happy (BBC Midlands Today March 8 2007). The **name Walsall first appears** in possibly in the C11, certainly in 1163. **'Middle of the Midlands'** Title of a series of booklets about Walsall by Billy Meikle (1858-1943), appearing c1938. **First meeting of the Bloxwich Rifle Volunteers** Took place on Nov 1 1859. This was preceded in Spring 1859 by the formation of the Walsall Rifle Volunteers (SA Jan 14 1860 p5 col 4). **Britain's most important terrorist trial of the late Victorian period** The trial of members of the Walsall branch of the Social Democratic Federation, alias the

Walsall Anarchists accused of bomb-making, Stafford Assizes, spring 1892. **Walsall's first 'Savings bank'** Opened May 1824 (HOWW) (TEBC2). **2nd town in the country to adopt the Free Libraries Act** Walsall in 1857, and a library building was opened in Goodall Street in 1859 (SA Aug 14 1897 p4 col 5) (VCH vol 17 p251). **Walsall's first cinema** Opened in 1908. **First junior full-time art department in any English art school** Was created at the Walsall Municipal School of Art, Goodall Street, 1912; out of this emerged the Walsall Secondary Art School, which itself closed in 1954 (VCH vol 17 p263). **One of the earliest Woolworth branches in the country** Opened in Park Street, Walsall, 1914 (The Iron Elwells. CJL Elwell. 1992 (2nd ed) p36 note). **14th largest co-operative society in Great Britain 1961** Walsall Society, formerly Walsall and District New Co-operative Society, founded 1886; The Midcounties Co-operative, which incorporates Walsall Society, was 4th largest co-operative in the UK in 2007 (Documenting the Workshop of the World Newsletter. Jan 2007). **2nd biggest public autumn illuminations display in UK** Walsall Illuminations, after Blackpool (So you think you Know? Walsall. Francis Frith Collection. 2005. p20), and has also been claimed the **largest light show in the country**, only cancelled on two days in its history (BBC Midlands Today Oct 16 2007). **First Walsall Illuminations** 1951 (Black Country Breaks. Black Country Tourism. 2005?). **First College of Education to have all its courses approved by the Council for National Academic Awards** West Midlands College of Education, Gorway, Walsall, 1974 (VCH vol 17 p266). **National home (2002) of the British Export Accessory & Design Association** Old Sandwell House, Sandwell St, Walsall. National home (2002) of the Association of Directors of Public Health Walsall Health Authority, Lichfield St, Walsall.

Municipal life...

Most complete Roll of Mayors of any borough in Staffordshire Walsall, dating back to 1377 (Staffordshire County Handbook c1958). **First named mayor of Walsall** Nicholas Flaxhall in 1452. **First recorder of Walsall** John Byrch - Bishop Hough of Lichfield was his grandson. **First professional police force in the Black Country formed** Walsall on July 6 1832 (TEBC2). **First Black Country town to have a police force under the Municipal Corporation Act 1834** Walsall in 1835, with no other Black Country town able to have a force until 1839 (TEBC2). **Walsall's first Medical Officer of Health** Dr James McLachlan, 1870s (Walsall (NW) 1902. Old OS Maps. Godfrey. 1992). **'Probably few towns other than Walsall have been served through anxious years of war by a Mayoress so youthful'** Miss Mildred Slater (b c1897) daughter of Mayor Slater, who took on her mother's role as mayoress, after she died from wounds received on No. 16 tram hit by an enemy bomb on Jan 31 1916. In her role Mildred was very active in the borough in child welfare, servicemen's parcels to the Front, the POW committee, Girls Club, Girl Guides, and YWCA (SA June 8 1918 p3). **First place in West Midlands to hold a demonstration to show the public what might happen in war time** The Borough Surveyor's staff in 1938 who covered gas contamination, and fire bombing (So you think you Know? Walsall. Francis Frith Collection. 2005. pp3,4,17).

Buildings & utilities...

'like Ceausescu's Romania with fast-food outlets'/ 'It is possible that there are uglier towns in the world than Walsall, but if so I do not know them...' Theodore Dalrymple, critic, in New Criterion, 2001. **Staffordshire's best hostelry 1834** The George Hotel, on Digbeth and Bridge Street, according to White's directory (1834) which says 'its internal arrangements and its external appearance rank second to none in the county.' **'The most beautiful building in Walsall?'** Walsall Science and Art Institute, Bradford Place, built 1887-8, which became Walsall Technical College, in the opinion of Mark Dabbs (Oct 16 2003 p13p). **Harden's oldest building** Perhaps Cromwell Cottage, existed in c1800 when a shop (BY p26) (SNBP p31). **Pevsner's most acclaimed Staffordshire building of the 1960s** Former West Midland Teachers' Training College, Broadway and Gorway Road, 1961-4, by Richard Sheppard, Robson & Partners (BOE pp43,200). **Walsall's first telephone exchange** Was opened as an independent exchange in the evening of Sept 30 1881 over the shop of a photographer, F Brown, at 3 The Bridge (A History of the Birmingham Telephone area. RE Tupling. 1978 p10). **Country's second town to have overhead wire electrification** Walsall, 1893, country's first town to have electrical wire running down on one side of the road Walsall, 1893 (TEBC) (TEBC2 p136). **Walsall's first council house** No. 98 Blakenhall Lane, 1920 (BCM Winter 2001 p44). **Last surviving Black Country Co-operative Society** Walsall Co-operative Society, which was by 2003 West Midlands Co-operative Society (BCM Spring 2003 p22). **England's only tenant-controlled housing association** Beechdale Community Housing Association, formed by Beechdale housing estate tenants, March 1995 (The Guardian. Society Section. Sept 23 1998 pp6-7). **UK 'Memorial of the Month'** Walsall cenotaph in Bradford Place for April? 2005, awarded by the War Memorials Trust website (TB April 28 2005 p11p). **Walsall's most popular piece of public art** The Walsall hippo, as described by the website Walsall/Wonderland (The Daily Telegraph Sept 29 2005 p8p). **Largest solo mural painting in the world** 'Hole in the Wall' depicting Walsall scenes painted by local graffiti artist CHU, covering 2,800 sq feet at Upper Rushall St, Walsall, using 700 cans of spray paint and taking 320 hours in Sept 2007 (BBC Midlands Today Sept 11 2007).

Challenges...

World shorthand record Arnold Bradley who achieved 309 wpm without error using the Sloan-Duployan system, with 1,545 words in five minutes in a test at Walsall on Nov 9 1920 (GBR 1998 p24). **British squatting on a barrel on top of a pole record** Set by Victor Reeves, 23, of Walsall, who squatted on a barrel 28 inches in diameter on a 40-foot pole for 31 days seven hours, ending on Aug 19 1952 (GBR 1962 p220). **World record for brick carrying** Set by Reg Morris of Walsall when he carried a 9 lb brick in a nominated ungloved hand in an uncradled downward pincher grip over 61.75m on July 16 1985 (GBR 1991 p176). **World record for fastest sausage meat eating** Set by Reg Morris when he ate 2.72 kg (6 lb) in three minutes 10 seconds at Walsall in 1986 (GBR 1999 p60). **World record for fastest kipper eating** Reg Morris when he ate 27 kippers in 16 minutes 52.66 seconds at Walsall in 1988 (GBR 1999 p60). **Woman's record for brick-carrying** Set by Wendy Morris of Walsall when she carried a 9 lb 12 oz brick over a distance of 22.5m on April 28 1986 (GBR 1991 p176).

Churches...

The ancient parish church in Walsall is St Matthew, the **only such county dedication** (of ancient parish churches); **61st= oldest ancient parish county church** dating from the C13 or roughly 1250. **Earliest silver flagon in the Archdeaconry of Stafford** At St Matthew's, dated 1698 (BAST vol 73 1955 p1). **'Finest set of medieval misercords in the Black Country'** 'The choir stalls contain the finest medieval wood carving in the old county of Staffordshire!'; there are 18 misercords in total (four were remade in 1880), and the originals are of C15. Tradition has it that the choir stalls come from Halesowen Abbey, but Jeavons cannot find any written authority to prove this (SHOS vol 2 p878) (W p641) (JMW pp48,49-50) (WOPP pl4) (CHMS p74) (TB Aug 8 2002 p10ps). **Also note** A carving on a capital of one of the tower pillars of a Jack in the Green (TB May 27 2004 p32p). A mutilated effigy to the memory of Sir Roger Hillary, died c1399. It was in the garden at Haunch Place 1821-75, when removed to Rushall Hall, and returned to the church in 1888 and placed in the crypt, before being moved to its present position (SHOS vol 2 p78 pl p 13 at back) (GNHS p173) (LGS p248) (JME part 1 p25) (CHMS p74) (BCM Jan 1977 p48). There was also a brass to his memory, as well (SHOS vol 2 p78) (BMMB p182) (Dugdale MS F:1 or N. ii fol. 1546). **In the churchyard** In the old part, under a Norman arch, apparently lay a mortuary and collection of bones. A tale used to be told of a bragging swash buckler who made a bet that he would go at midnight, knock a nail into a coffin, and bring away a scull. His companions waited for his return an hour, and, finding he did not come, went to look for him. They found him in a state of abject fear: He had driven the nail through his coat tail into the coffin, which on his attempt to return held him back (The Autobiography of Thomas Newton. Elwell & Cockin. 2008 p114). **St Matthew's longest serving vicar** William de Bermyncham, who served 37 years, 1376-1413. **Other churches** St Paul (1892-3), St Paul's St (VCH vol 17 p236). A memorial to Sgt Major William Purvis (see above); St George (1873-5), Persehouse St (VCH vol 17 p239); R.C. St Mary (1827), Glebe St. On **BEECHDALE ESTATE** is St Chad (1958), Edison Rd. At **BIRCHILLS** is St Andrew (1884-7), Birchills St. **Most saints portrayed in glass in Staffordshire** Perhaps St Andrew's, Birchills, with 70 images of saints in its stained glass (VB p60). Top Lock Church, Birchills. St Peter (1839-41), Stafford St. R.C. St Patrick (1965-6), corner of Green Lane and Blue Lane East (VCH vol 17 p241). At **BLAKENALL HEATH** is Christ Church (1865-

72). At **BLOXWICH** is All Saints (early C15, 1791-4), High Street. **In the churchyard** Grave of Samuel Wilks (d1764) successful campaigner who fought against the plan to combine Foreign and Borough rates, compelling the Foreign to pay a greater proportion of the rates (SHOS vol 2 p81). R.C. St Peter (1869), High St. At **CALDMORE** is St Michael and All Angels (1870-1), Bath Rd. At **THE CHUCKERY** is St Luke (1879, 1934, 1989), Selbourne St. At **COAL POOL** was St Mary (1892, closed 1965, dem 1970). At **DAISY BANK** is St Martin (1960), Sutton Rd. At **MOSSLEY** is St Thomas (1959), Cresswell Crescent (VCH vol 17 p235). At **LEAMORE** is St Aidan (1964), Hawbush Rd; St John (1883, rebuilt 1931, dem 1970). At **LITTLE BLOXWICH** is St Paul (1876, closed in 1960s). On **LOWER FARM ESTATE** is The Holy Ascension (1968), Sanstone Rd. At **PALFREY** is St Mary and All Saints (1901-2), Sun St. At **PLECK** is St John the Evangelist (1857-8, rebuilt 1976), Pleck Rd. At **RYECROFT** is St Stephen (1890, closed by 1946). At **SHELFIELD** is St Mark (1895 at School St, closed 1964, rebuilt in Green Lane). At **WALSALL WOOD** is St John (1837), High St, built 'in a plain Gothic style' (VCH vol 17 p282), called **'The little Tabernacle in the Desert'** described in 1849 as "... is neat: but for the same money the bricks might have been worked together into more Gothic' (SA Nov 3 1849 p8 col 7).

Collections..

One of the most exiting new galleries to open in UK 1985-2005 The New Art Gallery, Walsall (Black Country Breaks. Black Country Tourism. 2005?). **Man who caused the word 'grabatologist' to be created, UK champion grabatologist** Tom Holmes of Walsall whose tie, started in 1928, amounted to 10,624 in 1998 (GBR 1996 p218. 1998 p70). **Largest private toy collection in Britain** About 10,000 toy bus and car toys collected by Geoff Price of Walsall (BBC 1 Midlands Today. Feb 27 2003).

People...

Walsall's most famous old worthy (male) John Robinson McClean (1813-73), born Belfast, an originator and first engineer of the South Staffordshire Waterworks Company, who did much to raise the industrial prowess of Walsall, according to a contemporary in the town, Thomas Newton (who thought he rated higher than Sister Dora). McClean was a great speculator on projects in Staffordshire including railways, coalmining and waterworks, specifically benefiting Walsall (The Autobiography of Thomas Newton. Elwell & Cockin. 2008. pp106-108). **Walsall's most famous old worthy (female)** See Sister Dora heading below. **26th and 28th Chief Justice of the Common Pleas** Sir Roger Hillary (d c1399), in 1341-42 and 1354-56 respectively (Wikipedia 2007); he has had memorials in St Matthew's, Walsall. **First guardian appointed by the Assay Act of 1773** Joseph Adams, a manufacturer of silver shoe-buckles, snuffers, sugar tongs, etc, who lived in a half-timbered house at the junction of Adams' Row and Hall Lane. He, and other manufacturers of silver articles, formerly sent their goods to London to be assayed.

Complaint was made to the government that goods were lost (perhaps stolen on the road). Adams application to assay and stamp his own and his fellow-manufacturers' goods was not granted, but it led to the establishment of an Assay office in Birmingham with Adams, the first guardian appointed by the Assay Act of 1773 (Street Names of Walsall. 1992. p5). **Falkland Island's first Colonial Surgeon** Dr Henry Joseph Hamblin (c1810-1864), 1843-64; surgeon in Walsall by 1835. Walsall's heroine Sister Dora (see below). **Walsall's villain** Rev Richard Gleadow, dreaded and tyrannical early C19 master of Queen Mary's School, who flogged boys with a knotted cat o' nine tails (WOb Dec 31 1887, 8 Sept 1888 - Annals of Walsall). **Walsall's last survivor who fought at Waterloo** David Stanton (d1873) (SA Nov 8 1873 p7 col 6). **Walsall's Charge of the Light Brigade hero** Sgt Major William Purvis (d1899), who served in the 17th Lancers and Walsall Troop of Q.O.P. Yeomanry, and took part in this action in the Crimean War, buried at Ryecroft Cemetery (TB Dec 1979 p9p) (BCM Oct 1992 pp54-58ps); his memorial in St Matthew's was unveiled on June 16 1900 (SA June 23 1900 p5 col 3) (KES p220). **Walsall's WWI hero** Ordinary Seaman John Henry Carless awarded a postumous V.C. in 1917. He was born Nov 11 1896 at Renwick Terrace, spending his childhood in the Caldmore area. He displayed great heroism continuing as Gun Rammer for No. 2 gun on HMS Caledon against intense enemy fire in The Heligoland Bight action of 1917, despite being fatally wounded. A bronze bust of him was unveiled as a memorial outside Walsall public library in Feb 1920 (TB June 1995 p11p. Sept 29 2005 p21p. Feb 8 2007 p15p). **Walsall's Iraq War hero** Gunner David Lawrence of Walsall who died in Basra in Sept 2004 whilst serving with the 1st Regt Royal Horse Artillery (E&S March 20 2008 p24). **Walsall's bravest** Jack Stanley (1899-1966), Gunner, of Junction Street, Palfrey, worked for the Walsall Goods Dept of Midland Railway before WWI. In the War he won the Military Medal for 'marked steadiness and gallantry' for action on March 12 1917 in Pigeon Wood on the Hindenburg Line with the 46th (North Midland) Division Ammn, and later also won the Croix de Guerre (TB Jan 22 2004 p27p. Feb 5 2004 p25). **Thrice recipient of the Military Medal** Pte James Gavin (1880-1947), 2nd South Staffs Regt, of Walsall but originally from County Mayo; one of only 180 individuals thrice so awarded in WWI. The first M.M came in March 14 1917 for action in Loupart Wood.; second during the Battle of Cambrai in late Nov 1917; third in 1918 for carrying his C.O. to safety when under heavy fire. After the war Gavin was a boiler man at Walsall Workhouse (TB Nov 22 2007 pp20-21p). **Bloxwich's villain** Joseph Dace of Bloxwich, executed along with Samuel Hames for burglary, committed on March 13 1818 at Walsall, and stealing four gowns and other articles of clothing belonging to John Broomhall (TB Jan 1981 p5). **Bloxwich's 'Jack the Ripper'** George Hawkes of Ladywood Road, Birmingham, who drunk and disorderly with his shirt removed and kicking about the road, went about shouting in Bloxwich High Street he was 'Jack the Ripper' on Oct 15 1888. He claimed he had been affected by sunstroke when in the army in Africa, and was discharged, pending surety of his good behaviour for a month (SA Oct 20 1888 p2 col 7). **Bloxwich's unluckiest** William Cunningham was killed by lightning in Aug 1870. Two others were injured at Yieldfield Hall where they were mowing the lawn. The violent thunder storms over Bloxwich also caused damage to properties (SA Aug 6 1870 p7 col 7). **1st= murderer hung at Stafford Gaol not sent for dissection** Mary Smith of Bloxwich who killed her illegitimate daughter, Mary Ann; she was executed 19 March 1834. She was buried in the precincts of Stafford Gaol. Hitherto murderers were sent for dissection at the County Infirmary. **Staffordshire's longest newspaper nom de plume** 'Autobiographies Verbosperimpateaubiquitos' under which Thomas Newton (1810-89) wrote for the Walsall Observer (1887-9). In his column he noted he once told a stranger who confused Warsaw with Walsall he was not a Pole from Poland, but 'only a stick from

WALSALL PEOPLE - Nick Gillingham, Garath Marshall, Sister Dora, John Henry Carless, Thomas Newton, Noddy Holder, Mark Dabbs, Jerome K Jerome

Staff-shire' (WOb Jan 14 1888 p8). **'one of the Black Country's biggest attractions'** Christine Bailey, born Bescot by 1910, she grew to be nearly 28 stones, a weight only rivalled by a few other women in Britain. She appeared as a spectacle in Pat Collins' fair, and some Hollywood 'freak' films c1932 (TB Sept 4 2003 p5p). **'The Female Jack Sheppard'** Mrs Elizabeth Allcroft (alias Gwilliams, Williams) (b1833), thief and burglar, who exuded the demean of middle-class respectability. In 1859 she earnt this nickname, like Sheppard she escaped from gaol - Walsall Borough Gaol, having already been imprisoned at Stafford Gaol no less than six times. At the Borough Gaol she pretended to suffer from some dreadful illness so was removed to the Union Workhouse hospital where she proceeded to escape out of a window with tied up bedding (TB Dec 16 2004 p13). **'Probably the most scandalous case ever before the bench'** Mr Evans barrister for Henry Simms in the Walsall Observer before Walsall Petty Sessions, Aug 22 1888. Simms at his home in Rowley St had been assaulted by his wife's lover William Neville (of Lower Forster St), found upstairs in the bedrooms, supposibly - as Neville claimed - trying to eradicate bed bugs, but Simms' wife was in a state of undress; Neville got fined and two months imprisonment (WOb Aug 25 1888 p5). **Strange but true!** George Holden, a butcher at Walsall in the C17, suffered badly from periodical asthma. A postmortem after his death revealed no phlegm on his lungs nor any natural cause for the asthma, but many stones in his gall bladder which may have upset the nerves to his lungs or to some part of his breathing apparatus (NHS pp301-302). **'one of the first Englishmen to fly', First pioneer of Walsall aviation** Ernest Maund who built his own aircraft at his factory at Wisemore (near present Leather Museum). It was flown as early as 1904 from a field near Stokesay, Craven Arms, Shrops (Walsall Chronicle Oct 27 2005 p16). **'Walsall's most famous policeman'** PC Dudley Edwards, over 6 feet tall, and probably weighed some 20 stones; his feet and hand were almost twice normal size, earning him the nicknames 'hand, feet and maulers', 'Dudley Maulers' and 'hands across the sea' (TB Aug 30 2001 p14). **One of the first to demonstrate a suspected hybrid had undergone chromosome doubling in the course of evolution** Charles Leonard Huskins (1897-1953), geneticist in the field of cytogenetics, born Walsall, who emigrated to Canada with his family in 1906 (Wikipedia, 2008). **First Bloxwich Carnival Queen** Miss Edna Holden crowned 1926, and again 1927 (and is the only queen to have reigned in successive years). **President of Rotary in Britain and Ireland 1933** J.A. Crabtree (1886-1935), born Rochdale, but had the renowned electrical Lincoln Works in Walsall (BCM Winter 2003 pp61-64). **'one of the towns with the fattest population in the country'** Walsall, according to health statistics (The Daily Telegraph Sept 29 2005 p8). **Greatest concentration of people in Britain with the surname Cooper** Walsall in 1999 (Daily Mail July 17 1999 p35). **Manor Hospital's 1st Millennium baby** Bethany Jade Horgan at 12.11am Jan 1 2000 (E&S Jan 3 2000 p13). **Freedom of the City of London recipient** Colin Harrison born Church St, Bloxwich 1937, Chairman of Open Learning Foundation, in 2000 (TB Sept 7 2000 p21p). **The man who walked from Walsall to India** Tara Bariana, Walsall resident from the age of 13, who walked from his home in Walsall to Amritsar, 1996 (BBC Radio 4 Excess Baggage Sept 16 2006). **Midlander of the Year 1992** Phil Drabble (d2007), naturalist and wildlife author, and original presenter of the long-running TV show 'One Man and His Dog', born Bloxwich 1914; retired to Goat Lodge, Abbot's Bromley (The Daily Telegraph July 31 2007 p15p). **Youngest person in the country to be electronically tagged** A 12-year old girl from the Beechdale Estate in May 2002. She could not be named for legal reasons. The device was fitted to her leg after breaching conditions of bail imposed after being charged with assault and theft (E&S Dec 31 2002 p39). **Slimmer of the Year 2003** Simon Walters (b1973), of Penderel St, Bloxwich, in a competition run by Rosemary Conley Diet & Fitness magazine, starting with a weight of 22 stone 12lbs, and losing 10st 7lb (E&S Jan 3 2003 pps). **The man who has run in a marathon on all six inhabited continents, St George's Hero 2007** Mark Dabbs a nurse from Walsall who takes part in running events round the world for numerous charities and has donated gifts to schools, churches, hospitals and Walsall itself. He completed his marathons feat in 2001. In 2007 he was picked as one of the five heroes for the St George's Heroes, an award instigated by the English Beef and Lamb Executive for English heros (BCM Spring 2003 pp79-82p) (TB Feb 19 2004 p27p) (BBC 1 Midlands Today 21 March 2007) (SN March 22 2007 p19. April 19 2007 p12pc). **UK's No. 1 Computer Games Player** Gareth 'Garpy' Marshall, 21, professional computer games player of Walsall in 2007 (BBC Midlands Today 30 April 2007). **Walsall's kindest** Henry Boys (1832-94), brick manufacturer born in Wolverhampton Street, who had erected the Henry Boys Almshouses on Wednesbury Road, Walsall, 1886, at a cost of £10,000, and in his will he left about £3,500 to provide annual gifts of Witney blankets for poor widows over the age of 50, boots for unemployable men over 50, and shoes for children. To quote the epitaph on his grave in Queen Street Cemetery, he was "In his prosperity he forgot not the poor or suffering, but generously gave his wealth for their comfort and benefit.' (TB Aug 24 2006 p6il). **Walsall's poorest** There were poorhouses in the C17 and earlier C18, apparently in the Ditch. From 1717 there was a workhouse in Hill Street, Walsall. There was another workhouse at Elmore Green, Bloxwich (for the Foreign), by 1752. Former buckle maker and insurance agent James Gee (1746-1827), who wrote his life story from 1797, was governor for Bloxwich briefly in 1798 but resigned after only three days because he did not like the place. In 1801 he was appointed governor for Walsall (VCH vol 17 p212) (TB Oct 26 2006 p18). Walsall Union workhouse, opened 1838 in Pleck Road (known derisively as **'The Spike'**), later became known as Beacon Lodge, and St John's Hospital from 1950, becoming a part of the present Manor Hospital (TB Dec 23 2003 p19p. Nov 22 2007 p21). **The 'Humming Idiot'** John Rowley, a workhouse inmate c1888, who tried to feign idiocy by humming in order to be sent back to Burntwood Lunatic Aslyum, from whence he had been formerly discharged for being perfectly sane. He was said to be copying 'a humming idiot' he had seen there - but doing it with too much method - to be believed. He was charged with neglecting to do workhouse prescribed tasks (SA Feb 25 1888 p7 col 2). **'the poorest part of the poorest parish in Walsall'** How Walsall North district of St Peter's parish (formed 1842) was described in 1879 (Walsall (NW) 1902. Old OS Maps. Godfrey. 1992). **Walsall's earliest recorded will** Belongs to Agnes Myllis, and is dated Oct 9 1523. **Staffordshire's 3rd will proved in a civil District Probate Registry** Belongs to Charles Mason of Walsall, Gentleman, proved on Jan 20 1858. Before Jan 12 1858 wills were proved in an ecclesiastical court. **First person in the parish register (St Matthew's)** Elizabeth Norrys baptised March 25 1570. **(Walsall R.C.)** Suzanna Sylvester daughter of Thomas and Mary Sylvester, baptised Oct 27 1762. **(Bloxwich)** Hannah Tranter daughter of Edward and Ann, baptised Dec 25 1721. **Choicest quote** Jerome K Jerome, Walsall native and novelist, whose greatest work is Three Men in a Boat 1889 in My Life and Times 1926, wrote 'Later, the leading Nonconformists in the town got together, and the Congregational church in Bradford Street, which is still one of the features of the town, was built for him, my father giving his services as architect. It stands on the top of the hill, and in those days looked out over fields to Cannock Chase.'

People in politics...

MP who wished that the world's dust might be swept by Walsall brushes Charles S Forster, MP for Walsall 1832-41, in a speech nominating a parliamentary candidate in 1841 (HOWW p417). **First socialist to hold elected public office in Britain** Reputedly, Hayden Sanders, elected to Walsall BC, 1888 (On the Trail of the Walsall Anarchists. Barrie Roberts. 1992). **Country's first female to chair a junior chamber of commerce** Miss Mollie Orgill at Walsall, 1939 (Old Walsall and district in years gone by. Walsall Observer. March 1999. p19p). **'The Mayor of Bloxwich'** Sidney Aldridge (fl1920s-68) styled himself as this. He was proprietor of Hunts Cycles in Bloxwich and a keen mandolin player (TB Nov 9 2000 pp1,10). **'Staffordshire Joe the Human Cocktail'** Joe W Harper (d1935) who stood as a Christian Socialist for the Walsall seat in the General Election 1935. He ran his own laughable campaign, including styling himself as the above. After the election he committed suicide (TB March 1 2001 p10ps). **Mysterious billposters** appeared all over the Black Country in 2005, for instance on Lichfield Rd, Walsall, simply proclaiming 'ARTHUR BALFOUR WAS THE 33rd PRIME MINISTER OF GREAT BRITAIN'. Various theories have been forwarded as to who is behind them - descendants of the Balfours, or Wolverhampton Wanderers (because of the colour of the poster), or Freemasons, or they are just a cryptic conspiracy (TB March 17 2005 p27p).

People in the Arts...

'Walsall's most distinguished literary son' Jerome K Jerome (1859-1927), famed for his novel 'Three Men in a Boat' (1889) (TB Feb 1995 p21). **Man who drew the Peter and Jane pictures for the Ladybird Books Key Words Reading Scheme** John Henry

'Harry' Wingfield (1910-2002). After retirement he continued to live in the semi-detached house in Walsall where he had spent his working life as an artist (Wikipedia 2008). **One of Morecombe and Wise's best known catchphrases and longest-running gags** The phrase "Not now, Arthur" told to Arthur John Stone Tolcher (d1987), born Bloxwich April 9 1922, as he would appear on their show about to play his harmonica, the duo would call out to him "Not now, Arthur" (TB Aug 30 2007 p7p). **3rd person to get a star on the Birmingham Hall of Fame** Noddy Holder of Walsall, lead singer with the Wolverhampton rock group, Slade (BBC 1 Midlands Today Dec 5 2007). **TV's Pop Idol runner-up 2003** Mark Rhodes of Walsall, aged 21 (BBC website). **'a voice from the Black Country as authentic as baltis and Bank's bitter'** Time Out magazine on Paul McDonald, born Walsall 1961, whose novels about the industrial Midlands include 'Kiss me softly, Amy Turtle' 2004.

Sister Dora...

Walsall's most famous old worthy (female) Dorothy Wyndlow Pattison (1832-78). Born Hauxwell, Yorkshire. Nurse extraordinary in Walsall where she was noted for her work at Walsall Cottage Hospital, Bridge Street, 1865-78. She took charge of the isolation hospital in Hospital Street, 1875; attended the wounded of the Pelsall Colliery disaster, 1872, and those of the blast furnace explosion at Jones & Son in Green Lane, 1875. She died on Dec 24 1878. She was compassionate and highly admired becoming affectionately known as Sister Dora. Queen Street cemetery where she was buried became the Sister Dora Garden; the Cottage Hospital became Sister Dora Hospital. **First statue erected in England to an uncrowned lady** Sister Dora statue, Bridge St, 1886 (TB Jan 3 2002 p23. Feb 3 2005 p22). **Walsall's Florence Nightingale** (and Florence Nightingale's brother attended the unveiling of her statute) (BBC website, 2006).

Sport...

BOXING Walsall's pugilists George Holden (TB Jan 1994 p30il), and Thomas Farrell (TFBC p163). **Midland 'Young Boxer of the Year' 2006** Martin Gethin, lightweight boxer born Walsall 1983, awarded by the Midland Area Council. **World Middleweight Bodybuilding champion 2006** John Harris, born Walsall, resides Leics (BBC Midlands Today Nov 23 2006). **CYCLING Walsall's earliest cycling contest** Perhaps that in the Arboretum grounds between E Shelton of Wolverhampton and R Thomas of Portsmouth (who won) in a 10-mile match for £25 on April 15 1876 (SA April 22 1876 p7 col 7). **Most cycled in six days by 1876** Perhaps when a cyclist rode 600 miles in six days at the Arboretum in Sept 1876 (WOb Oct 25 1968) (TEBC2). **HORSE RACING Man with extraordinary memory for horseracing statistics** Joe Newman of Barleyfield, Walsall, c1830 (WOb Jan 28 1888 - Annals of Walsall). **'The Bloxwich Pony'** A famous racehorse of c1766 belonging to James Green of Bloxwich, who beat the noted horse 'Silvertail' hollow in one ten mile heat for 50 guineas, after giving him one mile start (SOB p219). **'Walsall's favourite jockey'** George Whitehouse, born less than a mile from Walsall racecourse, and went on to ride more winners there than any other jockey; his first win was in 1834; 16 more wins followed (TB April 7 2005 p31p). **FOOTBALL Footballer who allegedly played in heavy rain holding an umbrella** Charlie Athersmith of Bloxwich, who signed for Aston Villa in 1891-2, achieved 12 English caps (TB June 24 2004 p30). **FA Cup winner 1893** Harry Allen, born Walsall 1866, when playing for Wolves against Everton; indeed he scored the winning goal. He made over 150 appearances for Wolves 1886-94. He won five England caps and retired to become a Wolverhampton licensee (TB Aug 23 2007 p30. Feb 7 2008 p30 cartoon). **FA Cup winner 1894/5, FA Cup and League Cup winner 1895/6** WC Athersmith winger for England and Aston Villa, who became licensee of the Red Lion Inn, Green Lane, Bloxwich (SNBP p30). **First Schoolboy International match (Football)** Was played at Hillary Street ground, Walsall, between England and Wales on April 13 1907 (TB April 21 2005 p35) (BCM Spring 2006 pp18-20). **Walsall FC's most famous result** Their 1933 FA Cup win against Arsenal 2-0. **Walsall's FC's last match at Fellows Park** Against Rotherham in May 1990. **Walsall FC's first league match at Bescot Stadium** Against Torquay on Aug 25 1990. **Walsall FC's biggest ever signing** Paul Merson (Arsenal, Aston Villa, England) in 2003 (E&S Aug 28 2003. Past & Present p4). **Oldest player ever for Walsall FC** Des Bremner 37 years 240 days against Bristol City on May 5 1990. **Youngest ever player for Walsall FC** David McDermott 16 years 200 days, against Sheffield Wednesday in 2004 (E&S Aug 28 2004); the previous holder was Geoff Morris 16 years 218 days against Scunthorpe United on Sept 14 1965 (TB Aug 23 2007 p30). **OTHER World record for three forward spring jumps (barefoot)** Joseph Darby (1861-1937) at Bloxwich on July 11 1891, when he cleared 40 feet 11 inches (TB Aug 5 2004 p13). **Air speed world record for fastest lap, Schneider Trophy Race winner 1927** Air Vice Marshall Norman Sidney Webster (1902-1982) in a Supermarine S5, at 284.1 mph. He was born at No. 41 Borneo Street (BCM Oct 1984 pp60-62) (Walsall Chronicle Oct 27 2005 p16). **World record for 200m 1960, Olympic (100m) bronze medalist 1960, (4x100m relay) bronze medalist 1960, European Championship (4x100m relay) silver 1958, (100m) bronze medalist 1958** Peter Frank Radford, athlete, born Walsall 1939. His world record time was 20.5 seconds (Wikipedia 2008). **Snooker European champion under-19 2001, English Open champion 2005, English Amateur championship 2006** Mark Joyce (b1983), lives in Walsall (Wikipedia 2007). **PIGEON RACING Highest number of pigeon fanciers in Britain** Walsall ('Woman's Hour' BBC Radio 4 Oct 12 1993). **Best racing pigeon world career record by 1992** The pigeon 'Champion Breakaway' owned by R Green of Walsall Wood, having won 59 first prizes between 1972 and May 1979 (GBR 1992 p285). **SWIMMING Waterpolo national champions 1922** Walsall (TB May 24 2007 p35). **3rd in world for 220 yards, 'Walsall's Champion Swimmer'** Edward Gilbert (1883-1932), swimmer, waterpolo captain and publican of Walsall. He held the title of 220 yards Staffordshire County champion for many years from 1902 (WOb Jan 2 1932) (TB May 10 2007 p10p. May 31 2007 p35). **'one of Britain's finest breast-stroke swimmers', Olympic (200m) silver 1988, bronze 1992, World Championship (LC) (200m) bronze 1991, World Championship (SC) (200m) gold 1993, (4x100m) bronze 1993, Commonwealth Games bronze 1983, bronze (100m and 200m) 1990, European championships (LC) (200m) gold 1989, 1991, 1993, (100m) silver 1993, bronze 1989, (4x100m) 1993** Nick Gillingham, born Walsall 1967, breast-stroke swimmer (TB July 21 2005 p30). **Cross Channel record swimmer** Bill Pickering (b1921), manager of Bloxwich swimming baths 1951-, who completed the 21-mile crossing in 14 hours 6 minutes on 26-27 Aug 1955, but he only held the record for two months (TB Jan 9 2003 p13p).

Transport...

Walsall's most famous coaching inn George Hotel, junction of Digbeth and Bridge St, Walsall, built 1781 (MR p357). **Walsall's last coach driver** Stephen Howes, who may have been working local coaches at Walsall to c1850 (The Autobiography of Thomas Newton etc. Elwell & Cockin. 2008. p142). **First electric trams in the Black Country** Began on Jan 1 1893 running on Wednesbury to Darlaston and Walsall to Bloxwich lines (TEBC2). **One of Walsall borough's most noteworthy features in connection with transport** Central Bus Station and Transport Offices, built 1950s, which - complete with shops, washrooms, a cafe and special services to outlying collieries - was ahead of its time (Staffordshire Handbook c1966 p39) (TB Oct 5 2000 p13ps). **Only female driving examiner for the driving test in the Black Country** Mrs Kate Wilson in the late 1930s, and after WW2 to 1960s. In WW2 she was the Petrol Controller for Walsall and District at Collins' transport garage, Walsall Wood (TB Dec 8 2005 p31p). **First woman ambulance driver in West Midlands Ambulance Service** Mrs Shelia Hawkins of Fallowfield Rd, Orchard Hills, Walsall, former nurse at St Margaret's Hospital, Great Barr on Feb 11 1974 (E&S Feb 13 1974 photo). **Worst roads of any local authority in England and Wales** Walsall (BBC website, Jan 16 2002).

Work...

'Saddlery Town' 'The Town of A Hundred Trades' Walsall as it had so many different industries, a chief one being saddlery. The slogan 'The Home of Craftsmen and the Town of One Hundred Trades' appears in an advertisement of 1929 placed by Walsall Borough Council (Walsall guide 1949, Walsall & District Incorporated Chamber of Commerce) (MIW p91p). **First leather dresser in Walsall** Vaughan Barber c1800 (WOb Dec 31 1887 p7). **First improved Australian saddle-tree** Made out of raw hide by one Leveret of Thomas Newton's Saddlery, it was sent as a pattern by him from Melbourne (WOb Jan 14 1888 p8). **Walsall perfecters** Walsall operatives perfected, if not invented, the method of tinning, annealing, castings, and nickel plating (WOb Jan 14 1888 p8). **Provider of all British Army saddles in First World War** Reputedly all saddles used in the War had been produced in Walsall (Staffordshire: Shire County Guide. Peter Heaton. 1986). **Last Walsall furnaces to operate** Hatherton Furnaces, Fryer's Rd and Leamore Lane, SW of Bloxwich, were blown out in 1948 (SNBP p27p). **Largest works of their kind in the country** The works of Messrs Job Wheway & Son Ltd of Green Lane, and from 1894 their subsidiary company at West Bromwich, a cart hame manufacturer 'S Marsh & Son', later 'S Marsh & Son Patent Hame Works' (Walsall Archives, 2007). **First to produce electrically welded chains in UK** Messrs Job Wheway & Son Ltd, Green Lane by 1902 (Walsall Archives, 2007). **Longest-established workers' co-operative in Britain 1985** Walsall Locks & Cart Gear, which went into receivership in 1985 (MIW p109p). **Walsall's biggest factory, 'the largest and best-equipped factory of its kind in the British Empire'** The Lincoln Works, set up by John Ashworth Crabtree (1886-1935), in 1919 makers of electrical components (switches) in Rushall Street, and from 1923 in Lincoln Road (WOb 1935) (BCM Winter 2003 pp61-64). **First to make tubes in 'Staybrite'** Talbot Stead Tube Co Ltd in operation in Green Lane by 1913; they supplied boilers and tubes for many famous ships; Staybrite is a special stainless steel alloy (SNBP p55). **World's first stainless-steel toast rack, World's first stainless-steel teapot** Made 1928 and 1930 respectively, by J & J Wiggin, Old Hall Works, Bloxwich; the latter by William Wiggin. The firm, who could claim in 1978 they had made the world's first stainless steel tableware, closed in 1978 (MIW pp64p,74). **Britain's largest tent manufacturer 1980s** Probably JJ Hawley of Lichfield Road, Walsall (MIW p120). **Longest needle in the world** One six feet one inch long made by George Davies of Thomas Somerfield, Bloxwich, made for stitching on mattress buttons lengthways (GBR 1992 p218). **'World's largest producers of stamps and security documents', World's first self-adhesive postage stamp** Designed, developed and printed by Walsall Security Printers, Wednesbury Road, for the government of Sierra Leone, 1964 (MIW p123p). **Fancy that!** In 1896 a Government expert was forecasting the Walsall horse equipment trade had nothing to fear from the introduction of the motor car for another 50 years (SA Dec 5 1896 p4 col 7).

The area...

Walsall is the **county's 24th largest parish**, consisting of 8,314 acres; **76th closest parish to the county town**, 12.05m SSE; **extremist length** 6.1m, making it **17th longest parish in the county**; **extremist width** 5.1m, making it **26th= widest parish in the county**. **Chief settlement** Walsall, a large market and corporate town. There was also a detached part of Walsall, 13.4m SSE of the county town; its extremist length is 2.7m; its extremist width is 2m. **Chief settlement** Walsall Wood, a straggling residential area on the Walsall-Lichfield road. Famed for Organs (built and repaired at Walsall Wood). **Geology** BRIDGE ward - Silurian (Wenlock) Limestone (all); FOREIGN ward - Middle Coal Measures (all); ST GEORGE's ward - Middle Coal Measures (most), Silurian (Wenlock) Limestone (E fringe); WALSALL Wood - Upper Coal Measures (all). **Highest**

points Walsall - 550 feet at Great Bloxwich. Walsall Wood - 551 feet on E boundary on Lichfield Road. **Lowest points** Walsall - 367 feet by the Tame at Bescot. Walsall Wood - 410 feet on S boundary by Ford Brook. Walsall was **4th most-populated Staffordshire parish in 1801** with 8,314; **4th in 1811** with 10,399; **5th in 1821** with 11,189; **6th in 1831** with 15,066; **6th in 1841** with 20,852; **6th in 1851** with 26,822; **4th in 1861** with 39,690; **3rd in 1871** with 48,524; **3rd in 1881** with 58,453; **3rd in 1891** with 71,397; **3rd in 1901** with 87,464.

Wednesbury
Did you know that...

Wednesbury's top folklore That a Wednesbury prize fighter, George Clifton (1704-1789), turned from mob-leader haranguing John Wesley to aiding him, becoming a true Methodist. On Oct 20 1743 Wesley was being returned to the town by a mob who had tried to present him to magistrates in Walsall when another mob intercepted and succeeded in capturing him. Clifton, now so impressed by Wesley and converted that day to Methodism, led others in rescuing him. A few days later Clifton presented himself to a member of the Society, became a Methodist, and received the alias 'Honest Munchin'. The incident so impressed several local inhabitants, including John Rosley, vicar of Darlaston, he promised to join any measures to punish the rioters. **What Wednesbury is famous for** Iron working and Methodism. The **name Wednesbury first appears** in Domesday Book, 1086. **One of the oldest markets in the Black Country** Wednesbury, established by Queen Anne by Charter 1709 (WDOP p19); excepting those at Wolverhampton and Walsall. **Place where finches were first cross with canaries** Moxley, c1778, and so they became known as Moxley Mules (BCM Oct 1978 p52). **'Capital of the Black Country'** In c1834 Wednesbury was considered so, according to TH Gough in Black Country Stories, 1934, 5th volume, p66. **Wednesbury's earliest newspaper** The Wednesbury Observer published by T. Proverbs, High St, which first appeared on Sept 19 1857 (WP p90). **First meeting of the Wednesbury Rifle Volunteers** Took place on Jan 3 1860 (SA Jan 14 1860 p5 col 4). **One of the world's largest collections of 1930s Ruskin pottery, the largest public collection of Ruskin pottery** There are 300 pieces of Ruskin pottery in Wednesbury Museum and Art Gallery (Black Country Breaks. Black Country Tourism. 2005?) (BBC Midlands Today Sept 26 2006). **Last LMS Parade for Horses and Motor Vehicles (Wolverhampton & District)** Was held at The Goods Yard at Wednesbury, July 1947, as the era of cart horses was nearing an end (TB June 1 2000 p1). **Only wing at a children's hospice for adolescents in Europe** Acorns Children's Hospice in Walstead Road, 1999 (BBC 1 Midlands Today June 21 1999) (info Jessia Foster). **'one of the tallest and best proportioned (chimneys) in the country'** The great chimney stack at Elwell's iron works at Wednesbury Forge, built after 1817, and demolished in 1880s due to subsidence (The Iron

Elwells. CJL Elwell. 1992. p72). **The most famous of English provincial ballads** 'The Wedgebury Cocking' a famous C19 broadside ballad, relating a barbaric cockfighting match at Wednesbury (The

The mob in Wednesbury harangues Methodist leader John Wesley; St Bartholomew's church is in the background

Faber Book of Ballads' edited by Matthew Hodgart). **Oldest pub in the Black Country** It is generally thought The Leathern Bottle is (Q&ABC no. 200). **Largest celebrity entertainer autograph collections in Staffordshire** Belongs to Wednesbury librarian Paul Voyce, who has over 2000 signed photographs collected from c1980 (BBC Midlands Today Jan 3 2007).

People...

Wednesbury's most famous old worthy William Paget (1505/6-1563). Very prominent statesman in the reigns of Henry VIII and Edward VI, created Baron Paget of Beaudesert, 1549. He was born in London, the son of William Paget, a serjeant-at-mace of the city of London, long believed to be a native of Wednesbury. **Man who tunnelled himself out of a collasped mine shaft at a rate of 9 yards an hour** The collier, Dashfield, of the C17, who fell down a disused mine shaft in Wednesbury and astonished the local people he was able to tunnel himself out, by transferring the soil above him to beneath him, for about nine yards in an hour. His neighbours were so suspicious of his extraordinary tunnelling powers they named him 'Witch' Dashfield (NHS p306). **Staffordshire town John Wesley visited first and most** Wednesbury, which 'The best loved man in England' is said to have visited at least 33 times, 1743-90, including six at which he did not appear to preach. His first visit to Staffordshire and to Wednesbury was on Jan 5 1743 as guest of Francis Ward, the under manager of John Wood's Colliery at Wednesbury, when he preached in the Town Hall, while his brother Charles spoke in High Bullen (HOWY p211) (SOB p141) (VCH vol 17 pp64,65) (BCM Winter 2001 ppp29-34). **'Apostle of the Black Country'** Rev Richard Twigg, rector of St James, Wednesbury, who is said to have caused at least 30 young men to enter the Ministry (The Iron Elwells. CJL Elwell. 1992. p103). **Wednesbury's villains** William Beards, aged 35, who murdered Ann Griffiths, a maid of Mr Crowther, at Wednesbury on March 16 1844. He declared at the gallows on Aug 17 1844 he was 'as innocent as a child'. However, he had confessed to cutting her throat when she came to him to seek work, and she had shunned his advances (Calendar of Prisoners). Enoch Knowles of Wednesbury, who wrote the abusive letters sent to the Edalji family of Great Wyrley, signed by the fictitious 'Wyrley Gang' from 1903. Knowles was not arrested and convicted until 1934 (TB Oct 18 2006 p7). Bridget Macfarlane of Wednesbury who came before Stafford borough bench in Oct 1898. The Mayor of Stafford, one of the magistrates, believed she had the longest record of any prisoner who had come before him public misconduct and assaulting police officers (SA Oct 15 1898 p7 col 4). **Wednesbury's Charge of the Light Brigade hero** John Ashley Kilvert (1833-1920), born High Ercall, Shrops. He survived Balaclava in the 2nd line of the Brigade on Oct 25 1854, one of 25 of the 110-strong regiment to do so, and one of 2 of 14 of his tent. In 1861 he married Elisabeth Aston Hayes of Wednesbury, opened a pawnbrokers business in Union St, and served as Mayor of Wednesbury 1905-07; buried Wood Green Cemetery (Wednesbury Local History Society). **One of Wednesbury's best known public figures** Chad

Jackson (1896-1986), born in Union Street, Wednesbury, retail chemist, co-founder of Wedenesbury Rugby Football Club 1921; created Wednesbury Sports Union 1936; Mayor of Wednesbury 1942-44, and 1945; founder of Wednesbury Society of Arts 1947; founder of the Staffordshire Magic Circle; borough alderman and opposer of dissolution of the borough in 1966; leading light in Wednesbury Orchestral Society (TB Oct 26 2006 p26p). **'one of the best known of Wednesbury's worthies', Wednesbury's favourite son** FW Hackwood (d1926), the Black Country's most prodigious local history author, and to whose initiative Wednesbury really owes its charter of incorporation and its Borough Bench. The first claim is from SA Nov 26 1898 p7 col 7, the second is from TB Sept 13 2001 p4. **Wednesbury's poet** TF Bissell in FW Hackwood's opinion. In 1871 he published his 'Original Poems'. Hackwood's gem of the collection is a 'Serenade'. Later work includes 'A Reverie in Wednesbury Old Churchyard', 'Time and Eternity, a poem in black verse' and 'Ravenscourt, a novelette' (WP p83). **Man who introduced the cholera to Wednesbury** 'Jemmy the Tinker' who lived in Beggar's Row, and the infection was said to have been caught at Tipton Wake, where he had spent a week of debauchery (WP p126). **Man who discovered the first hormone** Sir William Maddock Bayliss (1860-1924), born in Butcroft, with EH Starling, discovered Secretin, 1902 (TB April 24 2003 p11). **Wife of the co-founder of Lloyd's Bank** Sarah, daughter of Richard Parkes, a Wednesbury ironmaster, who married Sampson Lloyd II (1699-1779) (WDOP p8). Taylor and Lloyd's Bank (later Lloyd's Bank) was set up in 1765. **Strange but true!** Wednesbury solicitor Saunders Smith was found dead in his office. No one knew how he had died, so a verdict of accidental death was returned. The case would have ended there but was reopened, July 13 1893, after the deputy coroner was tipped off. A post mortem revealed nothing, but then the determined deputy coroner ordered an unusual examination of the stomach which revealled strychnine. It was found Smith had greatly speculated on the Stock Exchange and lost all his own, and some others, money (SA Aug 26 1893 p5 col 3). **Tallest (and heaviest) children of their ages, in the world 1907** Ruby Westwood, 13, and Wilfrid Westwood, 11, of New Zealand who visited relatives in Wednesbury in summer 1907; Ruby weighed 17 stone and 4lbs, whilst Wilfrid, weighed 20 stone 6lbs (TB Annual 1999 pp41,42ps). **Strange but true!** Jack Ebsworth, a sailor turned barrister of Wednesbury, settled in Sydney, Australia. Returning with a novel he was seeking to have published in England, he went down on the SS Waratah in July 1909 on route from Adelaide via Cape Town. The Waratah was lost without trace in a violent storm after leaving Durban. Strange to say a business man from Sydney, one Jack Sawyer, who he befriended on board suspected the ship was top heavy and disembarked at Durban without returning to the ship (BCM Oct 1973 pp50-52). **The 'Tramway King'** Joseph Smith, later Ebbsmith (1849-98), first clerk to the Wednesbury Local Board of Health, leaving the town in 1888 to be the managing director of the Electric Construction Corporation in London, where he became devoted to seeing the spread of the electric tramway throughout the country. Resided at Oakswell Hall. Author of 'The Tramways of Great Britain; their past, present and future' (1897) (Evening Mail April 2? 1972 photo). **Wednesbury men who went down on the Titanic** The first class passengers Richard Fraser White, ticket number 111, and Percival Wayland White, ticket number 110, of 65 Bridge Street, Wednesbury; both drowned, only Richard's body was identified (Who Sailed on Titanic? The Definite Passenger Lists. Debbie Beavis. 2002). **'one of Wednesbury's most famous sons'** Richard Wattis (1912-1975), actor and comedian, born Hollies Drive, Wednesbury, but moved to Birmingham when he was four. He has appeared in classic films such as 'Inn of the Sixth Happiness,' 'The Longest Day' and St Trinians and Carry On films, and several Norman Wisdom films (TB June 3 2004 p16p. May 25 2006 p18ps). **'oldest labour leader of prominence in the country' 1912** William Aucott (b1830), JP, of Wednesbury, born Hickley, Leics, who had been involved with labour relations for 60 years by 1912 (Hackwood - Newspaper cuttings vol 2. Sandwell Archives. Familiar Faces No. 13 photo). **'Empire Jack'** Nickname for Sir John Norton Griffiths, Conservative MP for Wednesbury 1910-18, presumably in recognition of his high imperial aims (Evening Mail May

WEDNESBURY PEOPLE - FW Hackwood, Norman Deeley, Meg Hutchinson, Richard Wattis, Janice Nichols

19 1970 photos of campaign posters) (Black Country Stories. 1934. Vol 2. TH Gough pp80-81). **Solicitor General 1974-79** Peter Archer, born Wednesbury, serving March 7 1974 to May 4, 1979. **Ladder safety device inventor** Sid Lester born Foley St, Wednesbury, 1909, moving to Cape Hill, Smethwick in early life. He patented an A-frame clip for the bottom rung of ladders devised at his workshop in Beakes Road, Smethwick, 1947 (TB Feb 27 2003 p11p). **Woman who composed the 'The Women's Institute Song'** Emillie Hammond, who was born in Wednesbury (VFC p59). **The Black Country Catherine Cookson** Meg (nee Astbury) Hutchinson, former teacher at Lyng, and novelist. She was brought up in Dangerfield Lane, Wednesbury, and has since moved to Shrops. Her first novel was 'Abel's Daughter', subsequent ones are:- 'For the Love of The Child' 'Pit Bank Wench' 'Peppercorn Woman' 'Pauper's Child', and 'A Penny Dip' (semi-autobiographical) (TB 11 March 2004 p7p. Aug 3 2006 p7p). **Man who wrote Jack and the Beanstalk** Was from Wednesbury (West Bromwich Local History Fair 2008). **Woman who said "Oi'll give it foive" on TV's Thank Your Lucky Stars** Janice Nichols, born Wednesbury, achieving national fame on the show 1962-5, recorded at Aston Studios (Wednesbury Local History Society) (E&S July 9 2003 pp1,8ps). **Tiptonian of the Year 1998** William Haynes, born Wednesbury 1939, silversmith, who made the statue of 'The Tipton Slasher' 1993 (BCM Spring 2002 pp45-46). **6th biggest lottery win by 2001, biggest lottery winner to go public by 2001** Tom Naylor, 46, a lorry driver of Wednesbury, winning £15.5 million in the National Lottery Extra drew (The Times Nov 17 2001 p6pc) (The Daily Telegraph Nov 17 2001 p19pc). **'the Wednesbury Blobber'** Fred Barnfield, artist and provocateur, who created barcode paintings, and parodies of Blue Plaques for ordinary people (TB Jan 24 2008 p16p). **Wednesbury's saddest** Selina Price, aged 12, of Elwell Street, Wednesbury, who was tragically decapitated in front of her friends on June 12 1888 as they were walking home from school on a footpath in the Walsall road near Oakeswell-end with hands held together. Selina was nearest the kerb, slipped, overbalanced, and fell straight into the way of the hind wheels of a loaded railway wagon, which cut her right across the neck, severing her head (SA June 16 1888 p5 col 3). **Wednesbury's kindest** The Parkes family - Thomas of Willingsworth Hall, and his son Richard and his wife Dorothy: Thomas is supposed to have given almshouses, 1602; the latter gave money for four sermons to be preached in church on four festival days forever, which at length got transmuted to a bread dole on Good Friday. **Wednesbury's poorest** Four cottages for paupers in Meeting Street were purchased on behalf of the vestry in 1715. In 1766 a workhouse there was enlarged. It was vacated in 1857/8 (HOWY pp105,164,258) when the poor were removed to West Bromwich Union workhouse. **Wednesbury's earliest recorded will** Belongs to Ralph Poole, and is dated May 4 1537. **First person in the parish register** Avis Jeynyns buried July 12 1561. **Choicest quote** Georgiana Elwell, a member of the iron forging family of Wednesbury Forge, in her diary 30th November, captures Victorian life of some

the Black Country well-to-do "I went to the funeral of Widow Fielding at St James's church with Mrs Twigg and stayed to tea at the Parsonage afterwards. Mr Twigg brought me from Wednesbury for the Night School." (from A Lady of Wednesbury Forge: The Diary of Georgiana Elwell 1868-1869. Edited by CJL Elwell).

Municipal Life...

Only borough in Black Country still served by county magistrates 1890 Wednesbury, whose Town Council were then considering a borough bench of magistrates, like had the boroughs of Dudley, Walsall, West Bromwich and Wolverhampton (SA Jan 11 1890 p4 col 6). **Youngest mayor of Wednesbury** CWD Joynson JP, CC (1862-1943), born Kings Hill, architect, mayor 1898-1900 (TB June 15 2006 p6p. July 20 2006 p3). **First council houses to have built-in bathrooms in the country** Wednesbury, with their houses built 1919 in Meryhurst Road, Wood Green (Peter Nichols, Wednesbury Local History Society). **1000th house on Fallings Heath Estate** Erected in Beebee Road, opened on Oct 29 1931 and inspected by the Prince of Wales (Wednesbury Local History Society). **Wednesbury's 2,000th municipal house** Was erected in Price Road, Crankall Lane (West) Estate (TB Feb 20 2003 p15p).

Education...

One of the first towns in the country to take advantage of the Elementary Education Act 1870 Wednesbury, with election (without contest) of its first School Board on March 15 1871; the first meeting held on Thursday 30 March 1871, Richard Williams being chairman (WP p45) (WAM p117). **First City & Guilds certificates in the non-destructive testing of metal awarded in UK** To Alan Glover and Peter Bryan, both of Great Barr, at West Bromwich College of Commerce and Technology at Wednesbury in 1970 (Evening Mail Nov 2 1970). **One of the first batch of 48 schools to successfully bid for training school status** Mesty Croft Primary School, receiving £100,000 per year for three years, May 2000 (BBC website). **Earliest Staffordshire state school radio station** Perhaps Radio Woden, broadcast from Wodensborough High School during school 45-minute lunchbreaks from Nov 4 1970, with one listening room in the school, with relays possible in the future (E&S Oct 26 1970. Nov 3 1970). **First school in the country to wake up its pupils with text messages** Wodensborough Community Technology College, Wednesbury, 2007, as many pupils complained there was no one at home in the mornings to wake them (Daily Telegraph May 16 2007 p12). **'one of England's most successful - and business-focused - head teachers'** Kevin Satchwell of Wednesbury, head teacher of Thomas Telford School, Salop, 2001 when knighted (BBC website, June 15 2001).

Sport...

Wednesbury's pugilists Dreadnought, a prize-fighter (BCM July 1972 p45), and George Clifton (see above). **The first of the Black Country towns to host an Amateur Athletic Meeting** Perhaps Wednesbury, organised by Wednesbury Town TC at Crankhall Lane

Grounds, Sept 1875 (WP pp66-67). **When the Champion Middle-Weight of America came to Wednesbury** George Rooke who appeared in a benefit fight at the Theatre Royal, 1876 (WP p66). **Fancy that!** In Dec 1896 a cripple's 100 yards race was held at Harding's Recreation Grounds, between Buffin, a wooden-legged man of Windmill End, Rowley, and Winchurch of Dudley, a cripple on crutches. The stakes were £10 a-side. Buffon, backed by the champion jumper Darby, won easily by 20 yards. A large number people watched (SA Dec 12 1896 p6 col 7). **Scored nine goals in 18 full internationals for England** Billy Walker (1897-1964), England football striker, born Wednesbury. He scored an amazing 80 goals in Walsall Boys League in the season 1910-11; played for Aston Villa 1919-31, claimed 11 hat-tricks (9 in the League, 2 in the FA Cup); played for England 1925-33 (TB Dec 4 2003 p31p. June 9 2005 p30 see cartoon). **The Morland England's Glory Cup (Golf) winner 1937, Churchman (cigarette) Cup (Golf) winner 1937** Henry Russell of Wednesbury (TB March 23 2006 p6p). **A Cricket Test Record World Cup team score** of 348 for 9 was achieved by Bermuda v. Malaysia in the ICC Trophy Matches at Wednesbury on June 16 1982 (GBR 1983 p261). **Walsall FC Player of the Year 1977** Brian Caswell, born Wednesbury 1956, played for Walsall FC 1971-95, during which time he scored 19 goals in 458 first-team matches; later he played for Doncaster, Leeds United, and Wolves (TB Jan 17 2008 p31). **'The Wednesbury Whippet'** Norman Deeley (b1933) of Wednesbury, English Schoolboy International footballer 1948, Wolves 1948-62. In 2007 Harry Harrison conducted an interview with him for his Harry Harrison's 'Off The Cuff' Black Country Stuff in The Bugle. But before the piece appeared the pair had died, two weeks apart; Harry passed away on Aug 21 2007, Norman on Sept 7 2007 (TB Sept 13 2007 p20. Dec 7 2006 p23).

Work...

'Tube Town' Wednesbury (HOS 1998 p100). **'Wednesbury Dirt'** a local reference to coal (BCSG vol 4 pp68-69). **One of the first constructed Newcomen engines** Was developed and tested at Broadwaters near Moxley by Thomas Newcomen (1663-1729) and Thomas Savery (c1650-1715), for extracting water out of collieries; but the water here was too powerful for the machinery (SHOS vol 2 p120) (THS p154). **Only windmill built for metal bashing purposes in the country** One of c1730 at Wednesbury Forge, excavated c2005 (Peter Nichols, Wednesbury Local History Society). **First velocipede (bicycle) maker** Cornelius Whitehouse of Wednesbury Forge, c1818 (WOb Jan 14 1888 p8). **Earliest gas-piping** A piece was at the Museum & Art Gallery, Holyhead Road (KES p224). **World's first axle** Was made at the Patent Shaft Works, Wednesbury (Q&ABC no. 152), of the Patent Shaft & Axletree Company, founded 1838. The axle's originator was Rev James Hardy who invented the faggoted axle of forged iron - patented 1835 (see below). **First Staffordshire firm to adopt the hot blast furnace** The Lloyds of the Old Park Works, 1849 (WW p71) (HOWY p242). **One of the earliest examples in industrial history of 'vertical integration'** At the Old Park

Works, Darlaston Road, King's Hill. This was the participation by one firm in several industrial processes and the making of a varied range of related products (WMLB p105). **Largest merchant bar ever rolled by 1855** Probably that rolled on April 5 1855 for the Paris Exhibition at Messrs John Bagnall & Sons, Imperial Iron Works. It was 25 feet 3 inches long, 7.25 in diameter, weighing 1 ton, 10 cwt, 2 qrs, 12 lbs. In 1851 Bagnalls produced a 20-feet 1-inch long, 7-inch diameter, 1 ton 2 cwt 3 qrs 12 lbs bar roll for the Crystal Palace in Hyde Park, which won a prize (SA April 7 1855 p5 col 4). **Largest establishment in Wednesbury and one of the largest in the area 1862** The Old Park Works (Lloyd Foster), Darlaston Road, King's Hill, with a total number employed there and the Monway Axle and Tyre Works together with those in the company's collieries, was over 3,000 in 1866; in 1851 it had been 1,200 (HOWY p242). **First Bessemer Steel Plant in the Midlands** Installed at the Old Park Works in 1864 (TEBC2). **One of the last and largest contracts carried out by Lloyds Fosters** Was that for supplying the parts for Blackfriars Bridge (HOWY p243). **Queen Victoria's invalid carriage maker** The axle was made by Wm Richards & Sons of Wednesbury, possibly identifiable in Richards & Co. of Eagle Axletree Works, Hobbins Street (formerly Queen St) (TB July 27 2006 p17). **Oldest tube manufacturer in the South Staffordshire district 1901** Edward Smith (1822-1901), of Brunswick House, Bridge St, Wednesbury, having been in business upwards of 60 years. In 1850 he erected the Brunswick Tube Works, Potters Lane (SA Dec 21 1901 p5 col 5). **One of the biggest engineering companies in the Black Country 1971** Patent Shaft Steelworks, Brunswick, Monway and Old Park; it closed in 1980 (WMLB p102) (WDOP p8). **UK's only major producer of stainless nuts and bolts, late 1978** FH Tomkins of Wednesbury (E&S Sept 29 1978). **Biggest steel foundry in Europe** FH Lloyd, covering 38 acres (Carl Chinn BBC Midlands Today March 29 2006). **'Mother likes it, so do I'** Motto for Hickinbottom & Sons Ltd, Wednesbury, bakers 1893-1977 (BCM Autumn 2003 pp19,23). **'One of the biggest independent vending companies in the Midlands' 1978** Vendaid, Stafford Street, Wednesbury (E&S Feb 21 1978).

Some patentees...

Patentees for 'making malleable iron from pig, or sow metal' No. 759,25 John Wood with Charles Wood of Low Mill near Whitehaven, Feb 1761, also 'making all kinds of fused or cast iron, as also scull or cinder iron malleable with raw or pit coal', No. 794,29, July 1763 (WAM p129). **Patentee of an iron axle for carts** A local Baptist minister Rev James Hardy, 1835, after which the Patent Shaft Steel Works, Wednesbury, got its name (BCM Summer 2002 pp14,46). The idea is said to have come him after noticing the divisions of an orange with it is cut transversely. It was not until a few years later when it passed into new hands that the business prospered, but the invention was an exceedingly important one having world-wide impact and was applied to the fullest extent in the manufacture of axles for railway rolling stock (Wednesbury Local History Society). **Patentee for**

'separating cadmium from its ores' No. 12,970 John Stephen Woolrich and others of Wednesbury, Feb 21 1850 (WAM p130). **Inventor of the mandrel for rolling wrought-iron tubes, the service pipe**, and **patentee of the butt-welded tube** Cornelius Whitehouse (1795-1883) of Oldbury, employee at Wednesbury Forge (WOb Jan 14 1888 p8) (WDOP p8). **Patentee of the wrought iron round elbow No. 2959** Samuel Bentley and William Elcock of Elcock & Lowe, Holyhead Rd, Wednesbury, Nov 27 1857; the device helped in the manipulation/bending of tubing (TB Aug 16 2001 p5p). **Patentee of the first rotary steam engine, inventor of the metallic pump** Henry Davies, third of six sons of William Davies of Wednesbury. The rotary steam engine was patent no. 7,688, June 14 1838 (WAM p131) (WW p30) (VCH vol 2 p168; called James Davies and was of the Meeting Street engine works).

Churches...

Wednesbury's ancient parish church is St Bartholomew, **one of 6 such county dedications** (of ancient parish churches); **61st= oldest AP county church** dating from the C13 or roughly 1250. **'One of the most beautiful Perpendicular churches in the Midlands'** St Bartholomew's (Staffordshire County Handbook c1958), about which Rev James White (c1813-1900), curate 1870-79, wrote in his 'The Seasons and Miscellaneous Poems' (1873) a 20-verse poem entitled 'The Old Parish Church, Wednesbury'. The first verse goes:-

> 'UPON the hill, and pointing high,
> With spiral form to yonder sky,
> There stands, to greet and please the eye, -
> the Old Parish Church.

(TB Jan 18 2007 p20. Feb 8 2007 p20). **Earliest flagon in the Archdeaconry of Stafford** At St Bartholomew, dated 1673, of pewter (BAST vol 73 1955 p1). **Oldest wooden pulpit in Staffordshire** At St Bartholomew, dated 1611 (SHOS vol 2 p87) (BAST vol 68 p53). **Unique lectern** That at St Bartholomew's is believed to be; it is a gilded fighting cock made of plaster on an oak pedestal (KES p223). **One of the best sets of C19 church plate in Staffordshire** At St Bartholomew, dated 1829; along with that of Wombourne (BAST vol 73 1955 p1). **Also in the church** The memorial of John Ashley Kilvert (d1920), JP, sergeant major in 11th Hussars who took part in the charge of the Light Brigade at Balaclava (TB Oct 1979 p11). **OTHER CHURCHES** St James (1847-8), St James's St, united with St John in 1980. **The vicarage Hackwood thought 'a model of ugliness'** The Vicarage House, erected c1867, opposite St James', but it was not the fault of the architect, says Hackwood, but that of the Ecclesiastical Commissioners (who didn't provide enough or any funds?) (WP p126). St John (1845-6, redundant by 1980 when united with St James), Lower High Street. **2nd earliest ecclesiastical districts created in the UK under Sir Robert Peel's Act, 6th & 7th Victoria, Cap 37** St John EP and Moxley EP, which were said to have been created 'by the zeal and energy of the respected vicar' (SA Nov 17 1849 p6 col 5). **Staffordshire's second Wesleyan 'preaching house'** Wednesbury, opened 1760 (HODW p132). R.C. St Mary (1873-4),

Church Hill. At **DELVES** is St Gabriel (1939), Walstead Rd; St Luke and the Good Shepherd (records from 1857). At **KING'S HILL** is St Andrew (1893), Darlaston Road. At **MESTY CROFT** is St Luke (1894, rebuilt? 1973), corner of Elwell and Oldbury Streets. At **MOXLEY** is All Saints (1850-1), Holyhead Rd. At **WOOD GREEN** is St Paul (1874), 70 Wood Green Rd. **'unique in the annals of campanology'** In 1926 the bells of St Paul's had a band of ringers made up entirely from one firm, Messrs Edward Elwell Ltd of Wednesbury Forge (The Ringing World. Feb 12 1926) (IE pp99-100). On the **YEW TREE ESTATE** is The Annunciation of Our Lady (1956-8), corner of Redwood Rd and Thorncroft Way.

The area...

Wednesbury is the **county's 110th largest parish**, consisting of 2,287 acres; **49th= farthest parish away from the county town**, 16.6m SSE; **extremist length** 2.1m; **extremist width** 4.3m. **Chief settlement** Wednesbury, a Black Country industrial town. **Geology** ALL - Middle Coal Measures. **Highest point** Church Hill at 520 feet, of which it has been claimed **'There is no spot in Staffordshire from which so extensive and striking a panorama of the mine and metal district can be viewed, as from Wednesbury hill'** (SA Nov 17 1849 p6 col 5). **Lowest point** 370 feet by the Tame at Wednesbury Forge. Wednesbury was **17th most-populated Staffordshire parish in 1801** with 4,160; **15th in 1811** with 5,372; **14th in 1821** with 6,471; **11th in 1831** with 8,437; **11th in 1841** with 11,625; **10th in 1851** with 14,281; **10th in 1861** with 21,968; **10th in 1871** with 25,030; **13th in 1881** with 24,566; **14th in 1891** with 25,347; **14th in 1901** with 26,554.

Wednesfield See Wolverhampton...

West Bromwich
Did you know that...

West Bromwich's top folklore A servant girl who had become trapped in a secret room of Hill House, at the north end of Dagger Lane, had died there of either starvation or suffocation, and her ghost returns to haunt the house. **What West Bromwich is famous for** Iron working and forming. **Only 'holme' in the Black Country** Bustleholme Lane, north of Wigmore (NSFCT 1916 p81). The **name Bromwich first appears** in Domesday Book, 1086; West Bromwich in 1293 (OWB p33). **Staffordshire's 11th earliest commutation of tithes when they were dealt with under a parliamentary enclosure act** The great and small tithes of West Bromwich, by allotments of land, 1801. **'The Chicago of Modern England'** West Bromwich as described by FW Hackwood (WBY p6). **World's first washing powder** Hudson's Dry Soap Powder, invented by Robert Spear Hudson (d1884), son of John Hudson, minister of the Congregational chapel at Mayer's Green, 1801-43. Robert founded his business

A Jensen car, West Bromwich Albion match programme for Albion vs. Arsenal March 2nd 1957, The Public community arts centre designed by Will Alsop due to open summer 2008, Hud-

son Dry Soap package, an illustration from the 'Illustrated Police Budget' June 1894 depicting the murder of Mrs Hall, housekeeper, by her employer Mr Hassall with a kitchen knife at Herbert Street, West Bromwich; this represents the high number of interesting murder cases in the parish

in 1837, probably in the High Street where he was trading as a chemist by 1845, but the date of his invention is unknown (VCH vol 17 p42) (West Bromwich Local History Fair 2008). His most renowned slogan was "A little of Hudson's goes a long way." **County Archivist, Thea Randall's least favourite lost country house in Staffordshire** Sandwell Hall, as Thea states in her lecture 'Staffordshire's Vanished Country Houses'. **'Throstles'** A designation to many West Bromwich institutions (not only West Bromwich Albion FC); said to have arisen when a passenger in a coach travelling over West Bromwich Heath is supposed to have been confused by a donkey braying. The explanation of the noise was 'it is only a West Bromwich throstle singing' (BCM Autumn 2003 pp19,23). **'Jacques's bulldogs'** were the pupils with a place at 4th Earl of Dartmouth's school for deserving children, called

'Jacques' School' in New Street, later in Hill Top (WBY p17). **First meeting of the West Bromwich Rifle Volunteers** Took place on Dec 9 1859 (SA Jan 14 1860 p5 col 4). **West Bromwich Spitfire** Mk1z X4918, ordered June 9 1940, with monies raised at West Bromwich in the Spitfire Fund. Its first flight was on Jan 3 1941 from Eastleigh airfield, Hants. It crashed near Kemsey, Worcs, Feb 26 1943 and was written off May 31 1943 (West Bromwich Local History Society). **One of the first council-run dog schools in the country** West Bromwich Central School of Dog Training, set up by councillors in Sept 1957, In 1978 it was being run as an evening class once a week at Red House Park, Great Barr (Sandwell Evening Mail Feb 17 1978). **First R.A.S.C. anywhere to be awarded Freedom of Entry and permitted to wear their town's badge** 904 Company, R.A.S.C. (Motor Ambulance) (T.A.) and the R.E.M.E. workshop corp based at Carters Green Drill Hall, who were granted Freedom of Entry in West Bromwich in April 1963, and given permission by the MOD in 1964 to wear a badge on their tunic with the arms of West Bromwich borough (Evening Mail Nov 24 1964). **One of the first local authorities to set up a new careers services advisory committee** Sandwell; the first meeting of the new committee took place on Nov 13 1974 (E&S Oct 22 1974). **First broadcast of BBC Radio 4's 'Any Questions?' from West Bromwich** On Nov 3 1978 from West Bromwich Community Centre (Sandwell Evening Mail Oct 14 1978). **National Boys Brigade band champions 1978** 12th West Bromwich Company at Bingley Hall, Stafford, beating reigning champions Halifax, and were crowned by the Earl of Elgin, president of the Boys' Brigade (E&S May 2 1978).

Feats of achievement...

Longest duration of frost ever in the Black Country West Bromwich where there was a continuous frost from 3-24 Feb 1947, with the exception of a few hours on the 10th (TB Jan 25 2001 p16). **Oldest living dog in UK by 1998** Taffy, a Welsh Collie, owned by Evelyn Brown of Forge Farm. He was whelped on April 2 1952 and died on Feb 9 1980, aged 27 and 313 days (GBR 1995 p31. 1998 p240). **Highest Staffordshire lottery syndicate win** Perhaps £1.9 million for ten staff of Nicholl Grange residential home on Jan 11 2003 (BBC Midlands Today Jan 17 2003). **Largest spinach plant ever 1976** Perhaps that grown by Aubrey 'Happy' Henry, aged 49, of Hanbury Rd, West Bromwich, which was still growing at 5 feet 8 inches tall (E&S Oct 26 1976 photo).

Churches & temples...

West Bromwich's ancient parish church is All Saints, **one of 19 such county dedications** (of ancient parish churches); **88th= oldest ancient parish county church** dating from the C14 or roughly 1350, but is mainly of 1871-2; the last full day of worship in the old church was Sunday, June 25 1871. **In the church** Under arcading between chancel and Lady Chapel are C17 effigies of Ann (d1599), wife of Sir William Whorwood, and their fourth son Field (d1658). Field lost a hand which possibly held a book; the two figures were discovered in a coal hole during the rebuilding of 1872. It is generally believed they are the sole survivors of seven alabaster tombs of prominent local families. Some of the lost effigies include memorials to the Stanleys, Sheldons, Pages, Turtons and Addenbrooks (VCH vol 17 p54) (All Saints' - A Short History and Guide. GW Hannah. 1975. pp19,21p). The parish chest, perhaps of Norman origin, was lost in the C19 and found in 1932. The Lady Chapel Screen, erected 1893, is a memorial to Job and Mary Haines. It has intricate carved bosses which represent primroses, snowdrops and the correa speciosa, which Mr Haines is reputed to have introduced into England (HOWB p36). **In the churchyard** There is a longish epitaph on the tombstone of Mary Jesson, wife of Richard Jesson, daughter of Thomas Willets of Caversham, Oxon, d1779 aged 25, and left three children Richard, Thomas and Elizabeth (SHOS vol 2 p133). The grave of James Eaton (d1857) (see below). **West Bromwich's longest-serving vicar** Muirhead Mitchell Connor, who served 49 years, 1881-1930. In **HIGH STREET AREA** is Christ Church (1821-9), **Staffordshire's only Commissioners' Church funded out of the first grant** (BOE p34); Holy Trinity (1840-1), Trinity St, serves the SE part of the town. St John the Evangelist (1876-8, Sams Lane, redundant 1960, rebuilt as Good Shepherd with St John Evangelist in Lyttleton St, 1968). R.C. St Michael and the Holy Angels (1875-7), corner of High and St Michael Streets. At **CARTERS GREEN** is St Andrew (1867), Old Meeting St. At **CHARLEMONT** is St Mary Magdalene (1964), Beacon View Rd; the first confirmations took place on Feb 18 1979 (Sandwell Evening Mail Jan 15 1979). At **DARTMOUTH PARK** is St Philip (1898-9), Beeches Rd. **Vicar of 'one of the largest "parishes" in the country** Rev Edgar Daniels, a former vicar of St Philips, when he took on in 1967 the additional task of Vicar of the Midlands area of the Company of Compassion, covering nine counties - Worcs, Warws, Northants, Derbys, Notts, Leics, Ches, Staffs and Shrops - ministering to a few separated or divorced women by correspondence (E&S April 1967). At **FIVE WAYS Staffordshire's only early Congregational church with preserved records from beginning of the C18** Ebenezer Congregational church (1839, before when it was known as Old Meeting), Old Meeting St (Congregational Churches of Staffordshire. AG Matthews) (WBY p13). It closed in 1971 and became the Shree Krishna temple (HOS 1998 p70). **Staffordshire's first Hindu temple** Shree Krishna temple, 1974 (HOS 1998 p70). At **FRIAR PARK** is St Francis of Assisi (1940), Freeman and Keir Roads. At **GOLDS HILL** is St Paul (1881-2), Bagnall St. **Note the W window** to Mariann Purser's memory, whose image is shown at the foot of Christ; it was given by her husband Charles Purser in the 1920s (TB March 23 2006 p20p). At **GREETS GREEN** is St Peter (1857-8), Whitehall Rd. At **HILL TOP** is St James (1844). At **LAMBERT'S END** is St Michael and All Angels (1881, closed 1953, dem earlier 1970s), Bull Lane. At **LYNG** is The Good Shepherd (1902), Spon Lane, united with St John in 1966. At **STONE CROSS** is The Ascension (1938, abandoned 1958), Walsall Rd.

Crime & Society...

'First women's anti-slavery society in Britain' The Ladies' Society for the Relief of Negro Slaves, founded at the home of Lucy Townsend of West Bromwich in 1825. She was the daughter and wife of vicars of the town. She was joint secretary with Mary Lloyd, wife of Samuel Lloyd, ironmaster of Wednesbury (E&S Feb 21 2008 Black Country People p20). **England's first club for the purpose of encouraging emigration to the British Dependencies and Colonies** The Emigration Club founded by Rev Frank Duerdin Perrott when curate of St Peter's, Newtown, Great Bridge. His curacy there ran 1883-85 (STELE OSm March 10 1951. March 17 1951). **'A disgrace to civilisation'** Housing conditions in the West Bromwich County Court district according to Judge Tebbs addressing the Birmingham Architects Association in 1930 (WBY p38). **'one of the highest rates of juvenile delinquency in the country'** West Bromwich at sometime before 1958 (WBY p4). **'one of the highest rate poundages in the country'** West Bromwich at sometime before 1958 (WBY p4). **'one of the highest rates for maternal mortality in the country'** West Bromwich at sometime before 1958 (WBY p4). **'one of the most highly publised Black Country murder cases'** of the C20, first time the BBC broadcast a description of a murderer on the radio** The stabbing to death of Charles William Fox, 24, at his home in Moor St on Aug 27 1933, by Stanley Eric Hobday of Sams Lane, hung in 1933 (TB Aug 2 2001 p5). The broadcast brought a response from the Cheshire police, as Hobday's vehicle had been abandoned at High Legh near Lymm, Cheshire, and he was seen by a landworker at Townsend Farm near Carlisle. He was arrested at Radcliffe, Cumberland. **West Bromwich's most intriguing unsolved murder case** The murder of Dorothy Mills of Bernard Street, aged 32. Her body was found by a shed at Wesley Tennis Club in Bratt Street, where she had been to play tennis on Jan 21 1961. The motive for the killing was at first thought to be robbery; her handbag was found in a nearby street minus four pounds. But a postmortem revealed that Dorothy, a reserved, single person with no known boyfriend, was 13 weeks pregnant. **'Probably the most absurd case we have had in the United States with regard to airport security'** US lawyer John Elbert to BBC WM on his client Sarah Johnson of Crankhall Lane, Friar Park, 22, a hairdresser on her way to work on a cruise liner leaving from Puerto Rico. She was arrested as a suspect terrorist for unwittingly running through a restricted area at Philadelphia Airport, charged with trespass and fined, April 2002 (E&S Aug 12 2003 p11) (BBC website).

People...

West Bromwich's most famous old worthy Walter Parsons (c1580-1620s). Royal porter and giant, of at least 7 feet 4 inches tall. Born Hall End. Generous and gentle, after employment as a blacksmith, he served James I and Charles I as porter, occasionally using his immense size to the playful detriment of others, lifting a man onto a hook high in a street who had challenged him to fight and taking two of the tallest yeomen of the guard under his arms and carrying them about the Guard's Chamber. Portraits, reputedly of him, hung there, and at the Popeshead Tavern in Popeshead Alley, London; a piece of wainscot at Bentley Hall may have been embossed with his handprint. **'one of the ablest men of his time', inventor of an alloy of copper and zinc with a small admixture of iron, 'the greatest man the parish of West Bromwich has ever known'** James Keir, FRS, (1735-1820), chemist and member of the Lunar Society. Resided by 1791 at Finchpath Hall, West Bromwich, formerly of The Grove, Smethwick. In sole charge of the Soho Works of Boulton and Watt from 1778. The alloy discovery was made and patented in 1779. The last claim is by Rev Samuel Lees, a West Bromwich historian (STELE SARA Dec 10 1954). **Signal midshipman who relayed Nelson's famous 'England Expects' battle-cry to the fleet at Trafalgar** James Eaton (1785-1857) on HMS Temeraire that fateful day Oct 21 1805; by 1837 he was residing in West Bromwich, by 1839 at Hill House (alias Dagger Hall), Dagger Lane, where he died (VCH vol 17 p4) (TB Oct 1997 p25). **Man who was three handshakes from King Charles II** Frederick Willett (d1939, aged nearly 101), vicar of West Bromwich 1865-82, who claimed as a small boy he shook hands with a very old man, who had as a boy shaken hands with another elderly man who had seen Charles II walking in Whitehall (WBY pp7-8). **Man who was the first to offer King Louis Philippe a meal at Newhaven on his arrival in exile in England** The grandfather of Frederick Willett, vicar of West Bromwich 1865-82, in 1848 (WBY p8). **Woman who wrote down all the sermons she heard and rose regularly at 4am** Mary Henry, daughter of the famous Presbyterian divine Matthew Henry, author of 'Commentary'; she married William Brett of West Bromwich (WBY p13). **Strange but true!** In the earlier C19 Robert Plunger of West Bromwich had amorous desires for his fiancee Anne, and her sister Isabel. At the wedding Anne fainted in the aisle and was taken off unwell; Isabel, there and then wed her sister's bridegroom instead (WOb June 30 1888 in the Annals of Walsall). **Pleasant Sunday Afternoon founder** John Blackham (1834-1923), a Congregationalist deacon at Ebenezer chapel at Five Ways (see above) in 1875; his testimonial from the first members is dated Sept 5 1875 (West Bromwich & Oldbury Chronicle Aug 27 1897 p1p) (VCH vol 3 pp133-134. vol 17 pp67-8). **First woman to publish a Staffordshire parish history** Mary Willett who wrote A History of West Bromwich, 1882. **'the real historian of modern West Bromwich'** W Ellery Jephcott in the opinion of RD Woodall in his book West Bromwich Yesterdays (1958); Jephcott's articles on the town appear in Midland Chronicle newspaper 1945, 1946 (WBY p3) and Smethwick Telephone 1950s. **'one of the best known authorities on mining in the Midlands...'** Description of John Field (1831-1913) of Hill Top in his obituary in the West Bromwich Newspaper, Aug 29 1913. It continues, 'his advice being sought in many important mining undertakings. For many years he was mining agent for Lady Scott and for 25 years he was a director (and for a portion of this period, chairman) of the Sandwell Park Colliery Co'. Buried in the family grave in St Bartholomew's, Wednesbury (TB Jan 3 2008 p20). **The West Bromwich men who went down on the Titantic** The Davies brothers, iron-

WEST BROMWICH PEOPLE - Madeleine Carroll, Walter Parsons, Jeff Astle, Phil Lynott, W Ellery Jephcott, David Christie Murray, John Blackham, Robert Plant, James Keir

workers moving jobs to Michigan - Joseph, 17, of Maxstoke Cottage, John, 21, whose bodies were never found, and Alfred HJ, 24, all travelling 3rd class on ticket numbers 409, 408, and 411 (Who Sailed on Titanic? The Definite Passenger Lists. Debbie Beavis. 2002). In addition, Jack Wesley Woodward, a cellist from Hill Top, in the ship's orchestra also drowned (TB March 1997 p20). **One of the oldest practising solicitors in the country 1920s** Edward Caddick of West Bromwich, who started practising in 1856 (WBY p40); his brothers, fellow lawyers, and sister were:- Robert, Alfred and Helen Caddick (see below) (TB June 1 2006 p6). **First president of the Soroptimist International association** Mrs Mary Siddons (d1976), West Bromwich magistrate, made Freeman of West Bromwich in 1970; the Soroptimists were founded in 1943 (E&S Jan 16 1976. Jan 21 1976). **First woman elected to West Bromwich Education Committee, the 'White Woman in Central Africa', Only female Keeper of Art in a British School of Art 1900, one of the first governors of Birmingham University 1901** Helen Caddick (1842/3-1927), daughter and sister of West Bromwich lawyers (see above and below); travelled to the Middle East (1889), Egypt (1890), Japan (1891), South Africa, India, Japan, USA (1892), Java, Australia (1895), China (1914). She kept dairies and her 'A White Woman in Central Africa' appeared in 1900. Resided in Herefordshire until 1883, and at Edgbaston from 1886 (TB June 1 2006 p6p). The School of Art was that at West Bromwich, then part of West Bromwich Institute, Lodge Road; one of her roles there was to give lectures upon the works of art under her care (Edgbastonia: A Monthly Illustrated Magazine. March 1900 p46). **'The Grand Old Man' of West Bromwich Congregationalism** Simeon Williams, aged 83 in 1930, a pattern maker for a Swan Village firm, and was a leading figure on the Hospital Sunday Fund Committee (WBY p39). **Wood-wittling champion of the world** Samuel Wilkes (1860-1933), carver in wood, originally of Great Bridge, later of Dudley Port. He achieved the title by carving a 472 link chain in wood. He could take a Glory match and leaving the brimstone at the head carve the shaft into 22 tiny moveable links (BCM Summer 2007 pp57-61). **First West Bromwich victim of WW2** Stoker AE Hall of 1 Bilhay Lane, who went down on the 'Courageous' (West Bromwich Local History Society). **Western Australia's Artist of the Year 1974** Mrs Diana Johnstone, 30, formerly of West Bromwich (E&S April 2 1974 photo). **Staffordshirian who has taken the driving test the most times** Perhaps Sue McIlwraith (b1957) of Hill Top, who passed in 2003 on the 20th occasion after 300 lessons (E&S Aug 1 2003 p8p). **First woman (and officer) outside the Royal Army Medical Corps responsible for career planning of Army medics; first woman in British Army sent on a NATO course** Col Audrey Smith of Great Bridge, 1987 (57 Black Country People. Stan Hill. 2002 pp92,93). **West Bromwich's hero** Capt Robert Edwin Phillips of Holyhead House, Hill Top, who won a V.C. on Jan 25 1917. Born Queen Street, Hill Top, 1895. Then as a lieutenant he went to the assistance of his commanding officer who was lying in the open, mortally wounded while leading a counter-attack. Phillips went out with a comrade, and under the most intense fire they succeeded in bringing him back behind the lines (TB Feb 8 2007 p15) (E&S March 20 2008 p15p). **West Bromwich's heroine, youngest recipient ever of the George Medal by 1970** Miss Charity Anne Bick of Maud Road, West Bromwich, who performed astounding feats during the air raid over the town on Nov 19 1940 aged 14. Indeed, she was so young her father forbade her to give her real age at the time, and she was reported as being 16 in the press. On the night she was the sole messenger link between a wardens' post in

Sams Lane and the control centre at the town hall about a mile away, once being blown off her bicycle by flying shrapnel, and urgently borrowed another. She also helped her father, the senior warden, to put out an incendiary bomb in the roof of a nearby pawnshop. Then charred timbers gave way and Charity fell into a bedroom. Two other George Medals were won in West Bromwich during that air raid, awarded to Dr Walton (the Medical Officer of Health) and to the Matron of the District Hospital for their valour in evacuating the patients from the Hospital, whilst the roof was ablaze (E&S Aug 15 1966 photo) (trans of the West Bromwich LHS 1970). **West Bromwich's 'Quiet Hero'** Sergeant William Shuker of Osborne Road, a West Bromwich Corporation Transport Dept employee, who gained a Military Medal for bravery fighting in the Far East in WW2 at Bishenpur and Oinam in May 1944, and again at Ningthoukhong in July 1944 (TB July 28 2005 p17p). **West Bromwich's bravest, 'Blind Dave', 3rd man to run 7 marathons on 7 continents in 7 days** Dave Heeley (b1958), blind athlete with West Bromwich Harriers, who runs marathons to raise money for charities (TB Sept 4 2004 p25. Jan 11 2007 p25p). He ran 7 marathons on 7 continents in 7 days April 7-13 2008, becoming the 3rd person to do this, and the first blind man to do this. He was accompanied throughout by his guide Malcolm Carr (BBC Midlands Today Oct 1 2007) (The Sunday Telegraph April 13 2008 p33p). **West Bromwich's poorest** A parish workhouse in St Clement's Lane opened in a former nail warehouse in 1735. Not far to the north, West Bromwich Union workhouse, Hallam Street, opened in 1857. Later it became Hallam Day Hospital; West Bromwich was the last Black Country Poor Law Union to form, forming in Dec 1837 (VCH vol 17 p45 - says it formed 1836) (TB Jan 6 2005 pp19-20p). **First person in the parish register** Jane daughter of Walter Stevens baptised Jan 4 1609. **Last West Bromwich town crier** James Richards (1850-1927) (info Sandwell archives A 436). **West Bromwich's earliest recorded will** Belongs to Thomas Sumbecke, and is dated May 27 1530. **Staffordshire's last wills administered by the bishop's consistory court** Belong to James Colley of West Bromwich, and others from Pensnett, Stoke-upon-Trent, and Wolverhampton, all proved on Dec 31 1860. This was after the Probate Court Act (1857) became law from Jan 12 1858, replacing ecclesiastical courts with civil District Probate Registries. **Choicest quote** Betty Boothroyd, MP for West Bromwich West 1974-2001, in her Betty Boothroyd: The Autobiography, 2001, says 'Queen Victoria is said to have ordered the curtains of her railway carriage to be closed when she passed through the town on her way north because of the smoke pouring from its factory chimneys. Pollution remained a problem when I first went there, but the spirit of its people was unbroken and we created a partnership that endured for twenty-seven years.'

People in Politics...

'The Man who made West Bromwich' Reuben Farley JP (1826-99), born Great Bridge, Mayor of West Bromwich for several periods, and first Freeman of West Bromwich Borough, created Dec 20 1895 (TB Jan 31 2002 p25). **First to have Freedom of Entry in West**

Bromwich South Staffordshire Regt, July 23 1949. **First MP for West Bromwich** John Horton Blades, Liberal 1885-6 (WBY p44). **First Town Clerk of West Bromwich borough 1882** Alfred Caddick, lawyer of West Bromwich; his brothers and sister were:- Robert, Edward and Helen Caddick (see above) (TB June 1 2006 p6). **First Labour member of West Bromwich borough council** Joe Holland, sometime before WW1 (WBY p39). **First woman mayor and alderman** Mrs Grace Cottrell, daughter of FT Jefferson (d1920), first elected councillor in 1918 for the Tantany ward, served as mayor 1926-28; the former mayor was her husband (West Bromwich & Oldbury Midland Chronicle etc Nov 12 1926 pp4-5p) (WBY p40). **Last mayor of West Bromwich** Sidney ET Martin of Greet's Green, who served 1973-74 (Evening Mail Jan 9 1973).

People in the Arts...

The 'English Paganini,' only English violinist to match foreign artistes William Henley born Hill Top, Jan 28 1874, considered the 'English Paganini' by some by 1897. His first concert tour was in 1886 through Gloucestershire and the Forest of Dean, when he was announced as the 'Boy Paganini' (West Bromwich & Oldbury Chronicle April 16 1897 p1p) (WBOP p154p). **'England's Gem', first of the Victorian 'male impersonators'** Bessie Bonehill, international superstar of the Victorian Music Hall; born into poverty she 'trod the boards' of her native West Bromwich; took London by storm; conquered New York; toured the American West with sheriffs riding shotgun on her luggage; fled South Africa on the outbreak of the Boer War. Only her death which prevented her from touring Australia. In impersonation she was a forerunner of Millie Hylton, Vesta Tilley and Ella Shields. Her ability to instantly 'buttonhole' and captivate audiences earned her the title of 'England's Gem' (England's Gem. Richard Bonehill. 1st edition sold out by 2008). **'A drunken blackguard'** David Christie Murray, novelist, born High Street, West Bromwich, 1847, according to QC Dr Edward Kenealy in 1868; Murray replied in print and discovered that he could write (WBY p44), going on to produce 50 books relating to the industry and life of the area. His best known novel is Capful o' Nails (1896). Murray Road, off Kelvin Way, was named after him in 1972 (Evening Mail July 13 1972). **One of the first to play Jack Judge's 'Tipperary'** Jimmy Timmins, who worked at the Kingfisher Works in Great Bridge and played the piano at the 'Hen and Chickens' New Street, West Bromwich, as confirmed in a letter to RD Woodall from Jack Yorke, 1954 (WBY p36). It is said that 'It's a long way to Tipperary' was the song that Jack Yorke of West Bromwich came up with after being challenged to write, produce and perform a song on the same day on New Year's Day 1912. Yorke was sometime manager of the Eight Locks Inn, Greets Green (West Bromwich Yesterdays. RD Woodall) (SOWB p22). Others have attributed Jack Judge of Oldbury with writing the song. **Musician who 'helped perhaps more than any other artist to create the "god of rock and roll" or "rock god" archetype'** Robert Plant, born West Bromwich on Aug 20 1948, with his mane of long blond hair and powerful, bare-chested appearance, when lead vocalist of the rock group Led Zeppelin, according to Wikipedia. Grew up in Halesowen and co-founded Led Zeppelin in 1968. In 1975, he was reported to have exclaimed the phrase "I am a Golden god!" from the balcony of the Continental Hyatt House in Los Angeles, California (reference to which was later made in Cameron Crowe's film, Almost Famous). Adrian Chiles on BBC 1's 'The ONE Show' on Feb 25 2008 called him the "second best thing to come out of West Bromwich". **Musician who composed the 'Top Of The Pops' theme tune** Phil Lynott (1950-86) born in Hallam Hospital (later Sandwell General Hospital) of a black Brazilian father and an Irish mother. His father returning to Brazil he adopted his mother's surname. Brought up in Manchester, then Dublin where c1970 he formed the rock group Thin Lizzy. In a solo career from c1980, his song "Yellow Pearl" (1982), was a Top 20 hit and became the theme tune to Top Of The Pops (Wikipedia 2008).

Madeline Carroll...
'West Bromwich's Star of the Silver Screen', "the most beautiful woman in the world", Legion of Honour medalist 1946, Medal of Freedom (U.S.A.), one of the first ambassadors for UNICEF (in 1946) Madeleine Carroll born at 32 (later renumbered 44) Herbert Street on Feb 26 1906, died Oct 2 1987; the allusion to her beauty was made by James Montgomery Flagg, film director, in 1937. A memorial to her was unveiled in a new square in West Bromwich on Feb 21 2007 (TB June 24 2004 p19p. March 1 2007 p4p) (BCM Summer 2007 pp44-45); **probably the biggest female star of 1930s Hollywood** (TB Oct 26 2006 p17p). **Her most famous film** 'Thirty Nine Steps' 1935; **her first screen work** 'Guns of Loos' 1929; **her first appearance on cigarette cards** No. 50 of Cinema Stars, the 3rd series of Wills Cigarettes, 1930s, where she appears with Frank Lawton in 'Young Woodley', also No. 14 of the same series relating to 'Escape' and showing her, Marie Ney, and Sir Gerald Du Maurier (TB March 22 2001 p19p. March 22 2007 p19p. April 5 2007 p4 il on a Player's Cigarette card).

Transport...
West Bromwich's first car registration number EA 1 in 1889 (E&S Oct 28 1970). **West Bromwich's last gas-lamp lighter** Henry Knight (b1889), responsible for a 100 manually-operated gas lights in Bromford and Spon Lanes, and Birmingham Rd 1924-30; he was still living in 1976 (E&S March 30 1976 photo). **Last trams to run in West Bromwich** On Saturday April 1 1939; on April 2 they were replaced by buses. Tram lines were erected in 1881 and converted to electricity in 1902 (Midland Chronicle & Free Press March 31 1939 p7). **Sandwell borough's first Pelican crossing** Officially installed between Brickhouse Lane and Fisher Street, Great Bridge, on Feb 27 1975 by Percy, a pelican, and his keeper from Dudley Zoo (E&S Feb 24 1975. Feb 27 1975). **West Bromwich's last rear-entry buses** The last two buses (double-deckers) were withdrawn on May 26 1978, having done more than 400,000 miles (E&S May 26 1978).

Pubs & food...
West Bromwich's oldest building which had a license in 1971

Manor House, Hall Green Road, built 1290-1310 (West Bromwich Mail Sept 8 1971 p2). **West Bromwich's longest known-licensed pub** Swan Inn, Swan Village, built 1550, but the original building was demolished in 1860, although some of the old stone was incorporated into the new building (West Bromwich Mail Sept 8 1971 p2). **West Bromwich's oldest pub in the same building 1971** The Dartmouth, Dartmouth Square, which was known as the Bull's Head in the C18 (West Bromwich Mail Sept 8 1971 p2). **'one of the original Real Ale houses'** Holden's Black Country Ales Brewery, Swan Village (MR2 p103). **Most pubs visited** The Black Country Ale Tairsters of West Bromwich (Peter Hill, Joseph Hill, Rob Jones) drunk in 4200 different pubs in Britain 1984-92 (GBR 1993 p93). **'Britain's Champion Pub Crawler'** Peter Hill of West Bromwich, author of 'A Black Country Pub Crawl' and founder member of the Black Country Ale Tairsters, 'BATS' who started pub crawling in 1984 and visited their 12,000th pub (The White Swan, Digbeth, Birmingham) on Jan 7 2005; that is every pub in every Midland county and some pubs in every UK county (BCM Winter 2003 pp25,39. Spring 2005 p23). **One of the AA's 1001 Great Family Pubs** The Vine Inn, Roebuck St 'The Vine boast the Midlands' only indoor barbeque' (book of the above title, 2005). **53rd McDonald's restaurant to open in England, 1st in the Midlands** West Bromwich Town Centre, which opened on March 2 1981 (Sandwell Evening Mail Feb 2 1981).

West Bromwich Albion...

The day the club was formed Sept 20 1879, a decision by George Salter Spring Workers. **Original name** West Bromwich Strollers, becoming West Bromwich Albion in 1880. **'The Baggies'** Informal name for the fan, on account of in c1883 the supporters were ironworkers in moleskin trousers fastened with belts not braces, and periodically the ironworkers would give a 'Sailor's hitch' to their unmentionables when they began to sag over their boots. Aston Villa supporters were said to heckle the WBA fans at their old ground at Perry Barr "Here come the Baggies from Bromwich" (Midland Chronicle & Free Press April 30 1943 p2 col col 4). Another accounts says, originally the team were miners and they often played in their 'baggy' working trousers (Q&ABC no. 22). **The first game** Took place on Dec 13 1879 against Black Lake Victoria, with Albion winning 1--0 (Albion! A Complete Record etc. Tony Matthews with Colin Mackenzie. 1987 p9). **First club to head the Football League** WBA going to the top of the table on the opening day of the competition, 8 Sept 1888, after winning 2-0 at Stoke, with an all-English-born team (and they were the first to do this). **English Cup winners 1887-8, 1891-2, 1930-1** WBA; in 1930-1 they were the first (and by 1987 only), side to win the FA Cup and promotion from the Second Division in the same season (TB Feb 10 2000 p33) (BCP p23). **First team to win the the Football League championship by playing 42 matches in a season, to score more than 100 goals in Division One in a season, first team to register 60 points** WBA in 1920 having 28 wins, and scoring 104 goals (TB July 27 2006 p35). **Highest score by one side in a Football League (Division 1) match by 1974** 12 goals when WBA beat Darwen 12-0 at West Bromwich on March 4 1892 (GBR 1974 p269). **WBA's greatest player to 1958, 'finest right-winger in the game between 1887 and 1895'** William 'Billy' Isaiah Bassett (1867-1937), born West Bromwich, playing for WBA 1887-95, retiring from football in 1899. The first claim was made by RD Woodall (WBY p55), the second by Tony Matthews (TB Oct 11 2007 p31). **'Prince of Goalkeepers', Albion's first international** Bob Roberts (1859-1929), 'a giant of a man' who played three times for England, born West Bromwich (TB Nov 16 2006 p34 il. Nov 23 2006 p30 il). **'one of the greatest names in the annuals of West Bromwich Albion Football Club', Albion's most capped England player** Jesse 'Peerless' Pennington, left back, born West Bromwich 1883, died Kidderminster 1970; played for WBA between 1903-22 (TB Feb 19 2004 p31p), making 496 appearances for the club (BCM Spring 2003 p68). **WBA's oldest player ever** George Baddeley (1874-1952), when 40 years old starred in his 157th and final game for the club against Sheffield Wednesday in April 1914 (TB Oct 4 2007 p31). **WBA's youngest player ever** Charlie 'Tug' Wilson, 16 years 73 days when he played against Oldham Athletic on Oct 1 1921 (TB Aug 23 2007 p30). **WBA's most famous player, 'King of the Hawthorns', 'King of Wembley'** Jeff Astle (1942-2002), born Eastwood, Notts, former England striker, playing 5 times for his country, and was the first player to score a goal in both the FA Cup Final (1968 v Everton) and in the League Cup Final (1970 v Manchester City), at Wembley. The last appellation appears in the title of a Bugle article by Tony Matthews (BBC website) (King of the Hawthorns: The Jeff Astle Story. Willmore & Homer. 2002) (TB May 10 2006 p35p). **Last home match of Johnny Giles, the 'little Irish wizard'** Saturday before May 16 1977 against Stoke, who from joining WBA in 1975 took them from the depths of the 2nd Division to the top half of the 1st (Sandwell Evening Mail May 16 1977). **First European professional club side to play in China** WBA in May 1978. **First British professional football team to win a match in the Soviet Union** WBA when they played Dynamo Tbilisi on June 7 1957 winning 3-0. **First player to reach 100 goals** Fred Morris (1893-1962) of Tipton (see). **First club to be relegated from the First Divisions of the Football League and the Central League in the same season** WBA in 1985-6. **Fastest goals scored in a football match by 1995** Those by William 'Ginger' Richardson of WBA when he scored four goals in five minutes from 'kick-off' against West Ham United at Upton Park on Nov 7 1931 (GBR 1995 p253). **Worst dressed football supporters in the country 2000** WBA (BBC 1 Midlands Today. April 25 2000). **WBA worst day** May 11 1991 when they were relegated to the 3rd Division (BBC Midlands Today March 7 2008). **Only Staffordshire F.C. with its own railway station** WBA; the station was named 'The Hawthorns' (Q&ABC no. 4). **First person to give his name to a tram on the Midland Metro system** The late Jeff Astle in 2003 (BBC website). **The 'Bard of the Baggies'** Andrew Detheridge (b1969), poet, and lecturer at Sandwell College (E&S Jan 16 2003 p8p).

Leisure & Sport...

Rare formal garden of limited dimensions Has been found at the Oak House; it possibly dates from the C17 (WMARCH 1994 p111). **Last maypole dancing in West Bromwich** In a field near to Stone Cross Inn, 1915 (BCM April 1969 p54). **West Bromwich's pugilist** Tass ('Hazard') Parker, beaten in an 133-round fight with the Tipton Slasher in 1844 (BCM July 1972 p45) (TB Nov 1980 p31) (TFBC p159). **Five members of one family who have all played professional football** The Bowen family of Walsall and West Bromwich: George (born Walsall 1875), Wolves player 1899-1901, 1901-04; Tommy (born West Bromwich 1900), Wolves player 1924-28; Tommy jnr (born West Bromwich 1924) WBA player in WW2; David (born Walsall 1903), Walsall player 1925-26; Stewart (born West Bromwich 1972, a relation to Tommy jnr) WBA player in 1990s (TB Nov 8 2007 p31). **One of the historical golf courses of the British Isles 1910** Sandwell Park Golf Club, founded May 11 1895 (Historic Golf Courses of the British Isles. Bernard Darwin. 1910. p141). **Finest sports centre in the Midlands** Ellesmere Athletic Club Sports Centre by Dartmouth Park, with access at end of Thynne Street, 1920-46 (BCM Autumn 2003 pp53-57). **Wembley FA Cup final's first referee** David Asson, born West Bromwich, who refereed the Bolton Wanderers and West Ham United game, April 1923. He was a former amateur with WBA (1898-99) (TB March 2 2006 p33). **Olympic gold medalist 2000, bronze medalist 1996 (and GB's only medal), Commonwealth Games gold medalist 1994, 1998** Denise Lewis, born West Bromwich 1972, heptathlete; twice runner-up in BBC's Sport's Personality of the Year (BBC website, 2006) (TB Sept 22 2005 p34. June 22 2006 p30p). **Midland Light Welterweight champion, English Light Welterweight champion, WBF International Light Welterweight champion, British Welterweight champion Jan 28-June 1 2006** Lee Woodley (b1976), alias Young Mutley, born West Bromwich (TB July 5 2007 p34p). **When West Bromwich hosted the Fly-weight boxing championship of Great Britain** On Sunday Oct 13 1929, fought between Bert Kirby of Birmingham and Jack Brown of Manchester; the latter won (West Bromwich Free Press Oct 18 1929 p6). **European Junior Cycle-Speedway champion 2006** Jack Hibberd of Sandwell Caterline. A.C.C. Lions (TB July 27 2006 p33). **World Junior Pairs Cycle-Speedway champion 2007** Tom Hibberd of Sandwell Caterline. A.C.C. Lions, brother of Jack. His partner was Tom Colling (Southampton) (TB July 26 2007 p33).

Work & utilities...

'The City of A Hundred Trades' Subtitle of RD Woodall's book 'West Bromwich Yesterdays: A short historical study of "The City of A Hundred Trades"' (1958). **'Famed throughout the world'** West Bromwich for the manufacture of springs (Staffordshire County Handbook c1958). **'No. 1 spring works in the world'** West Bromwich Springs of Lyng Estate, makers of the heaviest and largest suspension springs in the world (TB June 15 2000 p21). **Inventor of corrugated iron** John Spencer, ironmaster of Phoenix Ironworks, Spon Lane, in 1844, by accident during the rolling of iron rail (Birmingham Post Dec 11 1965). **Inventor of a patent slide valve** Isaiah

Vernon in 1862 whilst at the Meadow Steam-engine Works (VCH vol 2 p168). **National home (2002) of the Confederation of British Metalforming** 47 Birmingham Rd, West Bromwich. **Largest gas works in the country and 'consequently in the world'** Claimed of The Birmingham & Staffordshire Gas Light Company works at Swan Village, built 1825, by a guide book dated 1838 (W p682) (WAM p111) (VCH vol 17 p8) (Portrait of the Black Country. Harold Parsons. 1986 p105) (WBOPP pl 77). **Britain's biggest producer of cast iron hollowware** At one time it was Izons and Co. Ltd, of West Bromwich (TB June 22 2006 p18). **First woman elected chairman of a British Steel stockholders' association** Mrs Connie Taylor, chairman and joint managing director of Hall Brothers, West Bromwich in 1973 (Birmingham Post April 14 1973). **Largest rice mill in Europe** Built by East End Foods PLC, founded 1972, of East End House, Kendrick Way, by 2006 (BBC 1 Midlands Today. Nov 6 2006). **Central British-Business & Commerce Award winner 2003** Sukhjinder Khera, Managing Director of East End Foods Ltd.

Jensen cars...

One of the first cars to have a fibreglass body, one of the first cars to have disc brakes on all 4 wheels Jensen 541 model of the 1950s. The firm was founded by Alan and Richard Jensen in 1935, who started building cars under their own name in 1931 when they bought out a local garage in West Bromwich. **One of the ugliest cars in the world** Jensen C-V8, made by Jensen in 1962-4. **World's safest automobile, 1st passenger car in the world to offer all-wheel-drive and anti-lock brakes** Jensen Interceptor FF made in 1966. **'ranks among the world's best cars'** Road & Track magazine Oct 1973 on the Jensen Interceptor. The new owners from 1971 went bankrupt in 1976; into liquidation in 1992. The marque, regarded as one of the classic sports car makers, ranking alongside names like Aston Martin, was bought by a British conglomerate in 1998. **Last Jensen car produced** A 7.2 litre coupe with unique design alterations finished summer 1976, and expected to sell for over £12,000 (Sandwell Evening Mail July 30 1976 photo). **First new Jensen of the new Jensen company** Jensen S-V8 of 1999 built on Merseyside with an imported US Ford V8 engine (Website - Jensen Interceptor, Mopar-powered English touring car by TJ Higgins) (BBC Online News).

The area...

West Bromwich is the **county's 44th largest parish**, consisting of 5,851 acres; **42nd= farthest parish away from the county town**, 17.7m SSE; **extremist length** 4m; **extremist width** 3.7m. **Chief settlement** Lyndon, before 1801, then the town of West Bromwich that grew on Bromwich Heath. **Geology** SWAN Village, Greets Green - Upper Coal Measures; WEST BROMWICH parish church, Charlemont, Hill Top - Middle Coal Measures; WEST BROMWICH Heath, Guns Village, Lambert's End - Permian. **Highest point** 571 feet in Sandwell Park, alternatively, at the junction of Beeches Road and Thynne Street at 567.83 feet (Q&ABC no. 140). **Lowest point** 344 feet by the Tame at Forge Mill. West Bromwich was **8th most-populated Staffordshire parish in 1801** with 5,687; **8th in 1811** with 7,485; **8th in 1821** with 9,505; **4th in 1831** with 15,327; **3rd in 1841** with 26,121; **3rd in 1851** with 34,591; **3rd in 1861** with 41,795; **4th in 1871** with 47,918; **4th in 1881** with 56,295; **4th in 1891** with 59,474; **4th in 1901** with 65,114.

Willenhall See Wolverhampton...

The Wolves FC badge, lock and keys representing Wolverhampton as a centre of the lock

manufacturing industry, statue of St Wulfrun by Sir Charles Wheeler by St Peter's church, Molineux House and grounds (with St Peter's in the distance), a model of the Sunbeam car which broke the world speed record, a 1920s traffic light

Wolverhampton, Bentley, Bilston, Pelsall, Wednesfield, Willenhall
The best folklore...

Wolverhampton's top folklore The cult of Lady Wulfrun, Wolverhampton's foundress. Her exact identity, burial place and beneficence has always been a mystery so creating Wolverhampton's oldest and growing legend. All that is known is she received estates at Wolverhampton in 985, and in turn granted estates to a 'monastery' there in 994. From her 'monastery' probably derived the name of the town. By 1880 there was this rhyme:

> A thriving town, for arts Vulcanian famed
> And from its foundress, good Wulfruna, named.

(S&W p366). In 1974 a statue of her was erected in front of St Peter's church. **Bentley's top folklore** A spectral cavalier allegedly haunts the site of Bentley Hall, on which now stands a public library. **Bilston's top folklore** After the death of John Wilkinson, Bradley ironmaster (see below Iron working), he became something of a folk-hero and on July 14 1815 several thousand people assembled on Monmore Green 'expecting his ghost to make an appearance, riding his grey horse'. **Hatherton's top folklore** That Sir Hugh de Hatherstone's ghost use to haunt Hatherton Hall. A C19 lord of the manor made his skull into a goblet lined with silver. Whilst a dinner party was taking place, and the goblet containing wine was passed round, the headless figure of Sir Hugh in armour appeared and snatched the goblet away. The next day, a silver ball was found in the grounds and it was presumed Sir Hugh had only need for his head back and not the silver lining. **Hilton's top folklore** Shares the same folklore with Essington, see Bushbury. **Pelsall's top folklore** By old tradition Lady Wulfrun made her way to Pelsall after escaping from the sacking of Tamworth in 943. At Pelsall she rested her horses and was treated kindly by the local inhabitants. **Wednesbury's top folklore** By another old tradition, a Saxon noble wanted to build a church at Church Hole, an unlocated place between Bilston and Wednesfield, but as it was being erected by day, fairies, who lived there, carried the stones away by night. **Willenhall's top folklore** That a glowing red handprint on a wall in a corner of Love Alley, near Bilston Street, Willenhall, beside the Railway Tavern, is the spectral blood-stained hand of policeman Enoch Augustus Hooper, for this is the spot where he was stabbed to death on Dec 8 1865, in pursuit of some involved in disturbances at the Royal George Inn, Walsall Street.

Did you know that...

The **name Wolverhampton first appears** in 985 as Hampton, 1070-85 for Wolverhampton. **What Wolverhampton is famous for** Wool, locks and keys, Catholic recusancy, immigration, railways and engineering. **How Black Country people pronounce Wolverhampton and Bradley** 'Wolvo' and 'Braydley' (Where I Live: The Black Country BBC website). **First record of the Bay-leaved Willow (Salix Pentandra) for Britain** Made by Thomas Johnson at Wolverhampton in 1639 (NSFCT 1946 p82). **Most important of the ancient fairs of Staffordshire** Wolverhampton Wool Fair, held on days surrounding July 10, according to Hackwood (SCSF p100). **One of the world's most sought-after autographs, world's most-valuable autograph 1927, 1979** That of Button Gwinnett (d1777), Wolverhampton tradesman, and a signatory of the United States' Declaration of Independence; by 1937 there were only 36 Gwinnett autographs known to exist; 27 of these were already owned by collectors. One appears on his record of marriage in St Peter's PR; an autograph sold in 1927 (making $51,000) and 1979 (making $100,000 (KES p235) (SLM March 1952 p21p) (WF p45) (VB p56) (BCM summer 1995 p48) (GBR 1965 p137. 1981 pp95-96). **Largest and most populous town in Staffordshire in 1827** Wolverhampton (Smart's Trade Directory). **First use of 'Wolves' in association with Wolverhampton** Perhaps the caption to a cartoon in Figaro in London, a satirical magazine, which appeared on June 6 1835 inscribed 'The Wolves let loose at Wolverhampton' about soldiers sent in to quell local rioting (TB Oct 10 2002 p1p). **Staffordshire Yeomanry's last public order duty** Patrolling Wolverhampton streets in anticipation of riots against anti-Catholic activist Murphy, come to give a speech in the town, on Feb 22 1867 (The Uniforms of the British Yeomanry Force. 15: Staffordshire Yeomanry. RJ Smith & CR Coogan. 1993 p13). **Strange but true!** Two performing circus elephants broke down the doors of the coach-house in which they were lodged after their keeper left, shortly after arriving at Molyneux Grounds on Jan 15 1888. They broke into a storeroom where some casks of ale were, and rolled the barrel about until it smashed and the contents flooded the floor. In the yard they pulled down the entrance gates and escaped into North Street, wandered about the neighbourhood, causing £30 worth of damage, until the keeper was called to secure them (SA Jan 21 1888 p5 col 5). **'the Peter Pan of Staffordshire villages'** Bentley, according to W Byford-Jones (Quaestor in E&S) in 1930s, for never having grown up since at least 1830s, void of any modernity, and containing nothing higher than 16 feet, and the trees, though neat and pretty, being mostly not very tall (QBSS pp195-198). **First telephone in Wolverhampton** Is believed to have linked Graiseley Old Hall in Claremont Road with Ironmongers' rope factory in Salop Street (StE). **Staffordshire's 1st recorded heavier-than-air-flight** When showman Samuel Franklin Cody demonstrated one of his 'kites' in West Park, 1902 (SAWW2 p9). **'one of the oldest private flying clubs in the country'** The Midland Aero Club, established on 3 Sept 1909, which held its first displays at Dunstall Park (Documenting the Workshop of the World. May 2007). **Wolverhampton's first aviation meeting** Dunstall Park June 27 to July 2 1910 (TB Dec 1993 p17). **Oldest operative computer in Britain/ the world by 1978** The WITCH (Wolverhampton Instrument for Teaching Computing at Harwell), built 1949-50 at the Atomic Energy Research Establishment at Harwell. In 1956/7 it went to Wolverhampton and Staffordshire College of Technology (Staffs County Handbook. c1958 p157) (GBR 1973 p95. 1977 p156p. 1978 p153) (University of Wolverhampton Web Page. 1998). **Largest surviving dog litter** Set by 'Trudi' an Irish Setter owned by Alan Jenkins of Wolverhampton, when she gave birth to 17 puppies in Feb 1977 (GBR 1978 p32). **National home (2002) of the British Society of Comedy Writers (1981)** Parry Rd, Ashmore Park, Wednesfield.

Fifth most haunted place in England 1998 Wolverhampton (Wolverhampton Chronicle Sept 11 1998 p5). **Only planned German air raid in WW2 on a Staffordshire place** Wolverhampton in 1940; but it never happened (info Dr Philip Morgan, 2006). **Most playing card jokers in the world** Have been collected by Derek Haddon (b1938) of Willenhall (GBR) (TB June 1996 p4p).

Culture...

Wolverhampton's **first subscription library** 1813, the former County Court Building, Queen St (BBC website). **'one of the finest (theatres) designed by the theatre architect Charles Phipps'** The Grand Theatre, Lichfield Street, Wolverhampton, opened Dec 10 1894. The first performance was Gilbert & Sullivan's opera 'Utopia Limited' (Wolverhampton City Trail, Wolverhampton City Council, 2006). **Only British town to participate in the Brussels International Exhibition 1935** Wolverhampton (WF p26). **First public performance of Benjamin Britten's 'Let's make an opera'** Wulfrun Hall June-July 1949 (info Richard Wisker) (Civic Hall Quarterly). **European Small Museum of the Year 1978** Bantock House Museum, Merridale. **Best museum of Fine Art, Museum of the Year Awards 1998** Wolverahmpton Art Galley. **Biggest Pop Art collection in a UK public art gallery** Wolverhampton Art Gallery (take a brain sip website, 2006). **Largest circulation of any provincial daily evening newspaper in UK/ 'one of the most widely read provincial newspapers in Britain'** Express and Star (BBC, and take a brain sip websites, 2006).

Education...

One of the oldest active schools in UK Wolverhampton Grammar School, 1512 (take a brain sip website, 2006). **Worst Further Education college in the country** Bilston Community College in 1999 (BBC website Aug 5 1999). **One of the first Beacon Schools in the county** New Invention Primary School (see Berkswich) (BBC Midlands Today July 7 1998).

Buildings and hospitality...

'The best street of Wolverhampton' Queen Street in architectural terms according to Pevsner, 1974 (BOE p319). **Wolverhampton's oldest building c2000** Perhaps Graisley Old Hall, Penn Road, parts of which pre-date 1485, and not No. 19 Victoria Street, a former inn, which bears the date on a gable 'A.1300.D'. Graisley was built probably for Nicholas Rydley, a wealthy wool exporter (Wolverhampton (SW) 1901. Old OS Maps. Godfrey. 2004). **'most famous of all the town's inns'** The Swan Hotel in High Street, according to CJL Elwell (BCM Spring 2001 p17). **Wolverhampton's largest public meeting room in C19** The Agricultural Hall, Snow Hill, which could seat 2,000 (Wolverhampton (SW) 1901. Old OS Maps. Godfrey. 2004). First telephone exchange in Staffordshire Probably that at Garrick Street, Wolverhampton, opened by the Midland Telephone Company in 1880; it moved to Powlett Street in 1890 (A History of the Birmingham Telephone area. RE Tupling. 1978 p93). **First annual meeting of the Midland Counties Confederation of**

Church Guilds Wolverhampton on Aug 4 1873. The meeting commenced with Holy Communion at Christ Church, then promenading in Molineux Grounds and the meeting there in a tent. The confederation consisted of 17 guilds, numbering 400 members (SA Aug 9 1873 p7 col 6). **Willenhall's first council houses** Were 32 houses which ran from Mill Lane to Spring Lane, completed Dec 12 1921 (BCM Winter 2001 p41). **Most haunted house in Willenhall** Wellington Villa, which stood on the corner of Walsall and Bilston Roads (GPCE p60). **'Wolverhampton's favourite park'** West Park, opened 1881 (TB June 1 2006 p18). **'one of the most complete surviving inter-war cinemas in England'** Odeon cinema, Skinner Street, Wolverhampton, designed by Harry Weedon; it became a bingo hall in 1983 (Wolverhampton City Trail, Wolverhampton City Council, 2006). **One of the best B&Bs in Britain** The Old Chelsea Hotel, 58-60 Tettenhall Rd, Wolverhampton (The Good Bed and Breakfast Guide: Over 1000 of the best B&Bs in Britain. 1990. p317). **One of the last or last inn in Wolverhampton area to brew it own ale on premises** Angel Inn, High St, Wednesfield, until it passed from Jim Howe to Wolverhampton and Dudley Breweries in 1958 (TB Aug 1 2002 p5). **National home (2002) of the Brewing, Food & Beverage Industry Suppliers Association (1907)** 85 Tettenhall Rd. **Couple who won their home in a TV gameshow** Adrian Wright and Louise Harrison of Willenhall, who won a 3-bedroom semi in John Riley Drive, Willenhall in the Channel 5 show 'Hot Property' in July 2003 (E&S July 5 2003 p1pc).

Mander Centre...

'one of Britain's first purpose-built shopping centres' The Mander Centre, bounded by Queen's Sq, Victoria, Bell and Dudley Streets, 1968 (Daily Telegraph Aug 25 2006 p31). **Largest Woolworth's store in Europe** Mander Centre, c1965 (MR2 p366) (Nostalgic Wolverhampton. True North Books Ltd. 1999. p18). .

Municipal life...

First Black Country town to have Improvement Commissioners Wolverhampton in 1778 (BCM Autum 2003 pp19,23). **One of England's finest Victorian municipal parks** West Park, opened 1881 (The History of West Park. Wolverhampton Council). **Staffordshire's largest borough prior to 1910** Wolverhampton (LGS p256). **10,000th post-war council house** Completed July 1965 (Staffordshire Handbook c1966 p41). **Among the most industrious and efficient local authorities in the country** Wolverhampton's rate of 9s. 10d in the £ for 1965/66 compared with the average for all county boroughs of 11s. 2d. (Staffordshire Handbook c1966 p41).

People...

47th Archbishop of Canterbury, 25th Lord Chancellor and Lord Keeper of England Hubert Walter, whose tenure ran from 1193 to 13 July 1205, dying in office; he was Lord Chancellor between 1199-1205 (Wikipedia 2007). He is supposed to have been born in Wolverhampton (SMC p166). **One of the most romantic figures**

of his time Francis, Lord Lovell, lord of Stowheath from 1485. He appears in Shakespeare's Richard III. **243rd Lord Mayor of London** Sir Stephen Jenyns, founder of Wolverhampton Grammar School, who served in 1508-9. **316th Lord Mayor of London** Sir Richard Pipe of Bilston who served in 1578-9. **118th Governor of the Bank of England** Mervyn A King (b1948), economist, becoming Governor on June 30, 2003 (and reappointed 2008), son of a railway clerk. He attended Wolverhampton Grammar School; founder member of the Monetary Policy Committee in 1997 (Wikipedia, 2007) (The Sunday Telegraph. Business. Dec 16 2007 p7p). **First to issue rum to the Royal Navy** Admiral 'Grog' Vernon, kinsman of the Vernons of Hilton Park (VB p126). **'King of Little London'** William Morgan (c1715-99), of Little London so described in church records; apparently he is referred to as this as he was the eldest son of a Welsh clan here (TB Jan 13 2005 p27). **Strange but true!** The four daughters of Rev George Browne MacDonald of Waterloo Road 1862-3 went on to have either famous husbands or children: Georgiana (1840-1920) married the painter Sir Edward Burne-Jones: Louisa (1845-1925) married Alfred Baldwin MP and was the mother of Stanley Baldwin: Agnes (1843-1906) married the painter Sir Edward John Poynter, President of the Royal Academy: Alice (1837-1910) married John Lockwood Kipling and was the mother of Rudyard Kipling (BCM Summer 2006 p39). **9th oldest Staffordshire man ever** William Hyven of Lapley Hayes, near Wednesfield who died c1810 aged 115 at Little Bloxwich; he married a third wife at the age of 105 saying it was 'better to marry than burn' (W p57). **Queen Victoria's first public appearance after Prince Albert's death** Wolverhampton, where she unveiled the statute of Prince Albert in Queen's Sq, 1866 (BBC website). **Discoverer of 'respiratory pigments' in cells** Charles Alexander MacMunn, M.D. (1852-1911), physician and spectroscopist, born Easkey, Sligo, Ireland. Practised at 14 Waterloo Road, Wolverhampton 1872-99, returning to Wolverhampton in 1902. The discovery, first published 1880, lay fallow until 1925, when it was noted indeed myohaematin and histohaematin were in fact the cytochromes, which are an integral part of the respiratory chain within mitochondria, the location of internal cellular respiration. MacMunn was also first pathologist to the South Staffordshire General Hospital. Buried Jeffcock Road Cemetery (DNB) (TB May 27 2004 p18. June 17 2004 p4p). **Wolverhampton's best known eccentric (male), 'Fred alias Trampee alias Shakespeare'** Josef Stawinoga (1920-2007), Polish hermit who lived on the same spot on the central reservation of the St John's section of the inner ring road between PC World and a bathroom showroom for 40 years. He came to Britain of WW2, settled in Wolverhampton, 'dropped out of society' for unknown reasons in the 1960s. By the 1970s he had moved into a makeshift tent under a weeping willow on the ring road, shunned all worldly possessions, rejected all council attempts to rehouse him, never bathed, and only spoke Polish. Hindus and Sikhs came to revere him as a saint showering him with gifts, Wolverhampton Polytechnic staff awarded him an honorary degree, and finally there was a Facebook

WOLVERHAMPTON PEOPLE - Emma Lloyd Sproson, Jonathan Wild, Richard Attwood, Tessa Sanderson, Maggie Teyte, Button Gwinnett, Peter Broadbent, John Wilkinson, Charles Pelham Villiers

fansite. After his death on Oct 28 at his tent it was rumoured he had been in the German SS in WW2, and became a recluse in repentance (Daily Mail Oct 5 2007 p15p) (Daily Telegraph Nov 17 2007 p33p). **Wolverhampton's best known eccentric (female), 'Singing Margaret'** Miss Margaret Gibson, who walked the streets of Wolverhampton singing at the top of her voice, and earning a few shillings from passers-by, 1920s; one of her favourite pastimes was to attend the bible class at Pountney Street Chapel. It was rumoured she

Josef Stawinoga, Henry Newbolt, Rev William Moreton, Violet Gordon
Charlesworth, Lisa Potts, Catherine Eddowes, Derek Dougan, Admiral
'Grog' Vernon, Enoch Powell

was related to some wealthy family, who had 'turned her out' for a
youthful misdemeanour (MMBCC pp74-75p) (TB Jan 10 2008 p25p).
'Jackie Wack' The Bilston barber who suffered severely from religious mania and would ask new customers about the state of their
soul (MMBCC p77). **'champion rat-catcher of the world',**
'Hairy' Kelly William Kelly of Blakenhall, rat catcher, fl1910-30,
noted for catching rats with his teeth. In an Express & Star article in
1930 he proclaimed himself 'champion rat-catcher of the world'

(TFBC pp153, 154il). **Highest recorded aggregate score in marksmanship in the Staffordshire Rifle Association to 1898** Corp Fisher of Wolverhampton with a score of 191 achieved in 1898; the association was formed in 1861 (SA June 25 1898 p4 col 5). **England's oldest vet 1900** Richard Pritchard (1800-1900), died aged 99 on May 30 1900; his Cleveland Street practise was one of the largest in the Midlands (SA June 2 1900 p5 col 4). **'smallest and smartest policeman in New Zealand'** Thomas Hickman (1847-1930), born France but brought up in Bilston. He emigrated to New Zealand in the 1860s, becoming a policeman there in 1886, retiring in 1911 and employed to do intelligence work among the Maori. Being only between 5 feet 2 inches and 5 feet 4 inches tall Margaret Carr in her 'Policing in the Mountain Shadow' acclaimed him thus (Dictionary of New Zealand Biography) (TB Aug 3 2006 p28p). **'the ogre of Wolverhampton'** Sir Charles Mander (1921-2006) called by a group opposing his building housing estates on his land in the 'green belt' at Perton in 1960s (Daily Telegraph Aug 25 2006 p31p). **Bilston's historian**, or **'The unknown Staffordshire historian'** George Thomas Lawley (1845-1935), born Bilston, overshadowed by FW Hackwood, who drew on Lawley's earlier work. Commercial traveller for Butler's Priestfield Brewery, Wolverhampton. Author of 'Price and Beebee's History of Bilston' (1868) (which gives the first biography of ironmaster John Wilkinson), and 'Bilston in the 17th Century' (1920); contributor to Wolverhampton Chronicle, The Midland Counties Express, The Bilston Mercury (BCM Spring 2002 pp33-37p). **Greatest British concentration of Turners** Wolverhampton (Daily Mail July 17 1999 p35). **Wolverhampton man killed in the Airship R101 disaster** W Moule, an engineer, aged 30. This airship, the world's largest, was en-route to Egypt and India, when it crashed in a ball of flames at Allonne, near Beauvais, Northern France, on Oct 5 1930 (TB Aug 17 2006 p17). **Most and oldest living siblings in Staffordshire** All 12 Holmes bothers and sisters ages were alive in 2000 when their ages computed to 932. They were born in Bray St, later moving to Gough St, Willenhall - Ida (91), Phylis (90), Leslie (860, Reg (81), Glenis (79), Ralph (77), Iris (75), Marjorie (74), Hazel (73), Cynthia (70), Pearl (69), Ray (67) (TB March 2 2000 p6p). **UK's oldest mother by 1980** Mrs Winifred Wilson (nee Stanley), born Wolverhampton (1881/2-1974), who gave birth to her tenth child, a daughter, Shirley, in 1936 aged 54 or 55 and 3 days (GBR 1980 p16). **Wolverhampton's longest serving landlord in 2004** Geoff Bangham, having kept six pubs in and around Wolverhampton, and elected in 2004 Citizen of the Year by Wolverhampton Lions Club (TB April 29 2004 p1p). **Youngest member of MENSA 2004** Chloe Bennion of Wednesfield, aged 6, with an IQ of 138; MENSA don't usually test children under age of 10 (BBC Midlands Today Feb 23 2004). **Miss UK runner-up 1988** Angela Newland, 22, the then reigning Miss Wolverhampton (Daily Telegraph Aug 25 1988). **Last Bilston Carnival Queen** Leanne Demming 1997-8 (TB May 16 2002 p23). **Last Willenhall town crier** Charles Lawrence (1869-1956); his bell went to the Walsall Museum and Art Gallery (TB

March 1988 p15p). **Young Florist of the Year 2003** Adele Copson (b1980) of Bilston, student at Robaston College, Penkridge (E&S Feb 24 2003 p5p). **Wolverhampton's 1st Millennium baby** A girl to Anna Rhodes, 19, of Bradley, Bilston, at New Cross Hospital at 12.37am Jan 1 2000 (E&S Jan 3 2000 p13). **Bentley's kindest** Alfred Ernest Owen (1869-1929), partner in the firm of Rubery, Owen and Co, Darlaston, sole owner from 1910. He funded the building of Emmanuel church, Bentley, dedicated to his memory in 1932 (TB June 10 2004 p23). **Willenhall's kindest** Dr Joseph Tonks (1835-91), born Spring Bank. His kindness, courtesy and good humour earned him the soubriquet in Willenhall of 'The Poor Man's Doctor'. He died young and curiously. On Aug 29 1888 he was persuaded against his better will (saying to the crowds "You can say what you like, but it is safer on land than in this car!") to ascend in a balloon at Willenhall Horticultural Society's show. The balloon hit a chimney and Tonks descended on a rope to the ground with a gash to his thigh. It shortly got contaminated by water from the body of a recovered drowned child and he died of the infection in 1891; in the meantime however he added to his workload becoming Medical Officer for the Guardians of the Poor and Public Vaccinator for Willenhall and Short Heath. On May 10 1892 a drinking fountain and four-faced clock was unveiled to his memory in Willenhall Market Place (TB Sept 15 2005 p17p). **Bilston's saddest** Ann Phillips, of Salop Street, Bradley, aged 67, suffering from partial deafness and defective eyesight believed the Dudley to Bilston train she was on had arrived at Bilston opened the carriage door and leapt from the train, while it was still in motion. She died in the Wolverhampton Hospital from injuries (SA Dec 8 1888 p5 col 4). **Wolverhampton's kindest** Sir Stephen Jenyns found of the free Grammar School, 1512/3, alderman of London. **Wolverhampton's poorest** To 1837 the poor could have been accommodated at a poorhouse at Horseley Fields, which went on to be used as Chubb's Lock Manufactory (TB April 19 2001 p21il). Wolverhampton Poor Law Union came into being on Dec 11 1836, and its workhouse was built in 1838 on Bilston Road. It was so overcrowded in 1885 some inmates were sent to Westbury-upon-Severn's workhouse. In 1897 a female inmate, aged 38, and a male inmate, aged 30, eloped, quit, leaving the woman's children behind in the workhouse. A new workhouse was built at New Cross in 1903 (SA June 26 1897 p5 col 1) (TB Jan 6 2005 pp19-20p). **First persons in the parish register (St Peter's)** Richard Poultney and Jane Leveson married June 15 1538. **(R.C. SS Peter & Paul)** John Barney, son of John and Frances baptised April 26 1788. **(Bilston)** Jane, daughter of Daniel Whitehouse and Margaret his wife, Dec 14 1684. **(Pelsall)** Andrew son of of Michael and Ann Cox born Aug 17 1746. **(Wednesfield)** Mary daughter of John and Mary Webb baptised May 19 1751. **(Willenhall)** Elinor daughter of Will. Eaton al. Fletchers buried, baptised? 1642. **Earliest recorded wills (Wolverhampton)** Belongs to Richard Lydeat, and is dated 1612: **(Bentley)** John Hen, Aug 28 1629: **(Bilston)** Thomas Lanson, 1631: **(Featherstone)** Ralph Traunter, 1626: **(Hilton)** Thomas Meeke, 1634: **(Wednesfield)** Michael Podmore, 1630: **(Willenhall)**

Nicholas Harrison, April 6 1624. **Staffordshire's last wills administered by the bishop's consistory court** Belong to John Lewis of Wolverhampton, and others from Pensnett, Stoke-upon-Trent, and West Bromwich, all proved on Dec 31 1860. This was after the Probate Court Act (1857) became law from Jan 12 1858, replacing ecclesiastical courts with civil District Probate Registries. **Choicest quotes (for Wolverhampton)** The populous town of Wolverhampton has long been a place for lectures. In 1830 William Cobbett came for that purpose as he records in Rural Rides: Midland Tour, "I set off from Lutterworth early on the 29th of April, stopped to breakfast at Birmingham, got to Wolverhampton by two o'clock (a distance altogether of about 50 miles), and lectured at six in the evening. I repeated, or rather continued, the lecturing on the 30th and on the 3rd of May. On the 6th of May went to Dudley, and lectured there:" **(for Hatherton)** Cannock writer, Diana Hallchurch, captures Hatherton in the first two lines of one of her poems

> Hatherton whispers of dangling woodsmoke
> tangling into acid black trees.

(VB p80). **(for Wednesfield)** The author of the Towns of South Staffordshire in The Staffordshire Advertiser writes 1849 'Wednesfield Heath is becoming rapidly depopulated of its rabbits, and covered with houses' (SA Dec 15 1849 p7 col 1). **(for Willenhall)** he writes 'May Willenhall retain a trade as secure as if it was under her own lock and key, and with all the locks she makes, may she never lose the key to her own moral and mercantile prosperity!' (SA Dec 1 1849 p7 col 1).

People in the Arts...

'father of art photography' Oscar Gustave Rejlander (1813-75) who set up as a portraitist in Wolverhampton c1846 (WA no. 1 vol 1) (WJO March 1908 pp69-72). **Sir Henry Newbolt's best-known work** 'Admirals All' (1897) which contains the poem 'Drake's Drum.' Newbolt was born in St Mary's Vicarage, Bath St, Bilston, 1862. **Alfred Noyes' best-known poem** 'The Highwayman'; Noyes was born at Chapel Ash, 1880. **James W Tate's biggest hit** Was the song 'A Bachelor Gay' which he composed for 'The Maid of the Mountains' (1916), which went on to be one of the most popular songs in British concert revue. Tate was born in Wolverhampton in 1875; he was half-brother of Dame Maggie Teyte. He caught pneumonia on a tour and died in Stoke-on-Trent on Feb 5 1922 (TB April 5 2007 p15p). **She inspired Elgar's 'Dorabella' variation** Dora Penny (b1874), daughter of Rev Alfred Penny, rector of St Peter's (1891-), and friend of composer Edward Elgar. 'Number X, Dorabella' is part of the Enigma Variations, first performed 1899 (TB June 2 2005 pp16-17p. June 30 2005 p17). **'The Portobello Poet'** Thomas Bratt (1852-1929), his 1000 poems or so on news stories and football clubs of his day, received no publication beyond Willenhall's Cartwright's Monthly Review c1895-1905 (info Maureen Hunt author of a book of his poems on football clubs) (TB Jan 22 2004 p13. Sept 2 2004 pp16-17p). **'one of Britain's greatest illuminators'** Daisy Alcock (1903-96), Calligrapher of New Cross Farm, Wednesfield; her greatest work is the 'Battle of Britain Roll of Honour' at Westminster Abbey July 1947 (TB March 20 2003 pp10-11. March 27 2003 pp10-11. April 3 2003 pp4-5. April 10 2003 p17). **She sang in the first British performance of the medieval Spanish opera 'Play of Elche'** Miss Angela Whittingham, born Wolverhampton, soprano soloist, a member of the Handel Opera Society (1970) (Staffs Illustrated. May 1970. Staffs Scene). **Bilston's greatest rock and roll group** Danny Cannon and the Ramrods, active in the late 1950s (The Black Country: The Changing Face of the Area & Its People. New Williams. 2002. p97p). **UK's first female breakdancer** Hanifa Hudson (b1969) of Wolverhampton, alias Bubbles, who toured with Wolverhampton's B-Boy Crew in the 1980s, and was the first girl worldwide to compete on the same level as boys (BBC website). **Most prolific graffiti artist in a Staffordshire town** Aaron Bird alias 'Temper', 35, who over 24 years graffitied 180 buildings in Wolverhampton (BBC Midlands Today Feb 16 2007).

Maggie Teyte...

One of the greatest British operatic sopranos Dame Maggie Teyte (d1976), born in Exchange Street, Wolverhampton on April 17 1888. **Her real name** Margaret Tate. **Her first public appearance** Paris, March 1906, as Cherubino in the Marriage of Figaro, and Zerlina in Don Giovanni (TB April 12 2007 p23ps). **Her first professional debut** Opera House, Monte Carlo, Feb 1 1907, as Tyrcis in Offenbach's Myriame et Daphne (TB April 12 2007 p23). **Her first New York appearance** 1948. **"She is the only singer today who can sing"** Sir Francesco Paolo Tosti, singing master to the royal household and friend of Edward VII (TB April 12 2007 p23). **Only singer Debussy accompanied on the piano with an orchestra in public** (The Staffordshire Society AGM order of service 2007). **First Maggie Teyte Prize winner** Jane Cockell 1996. A Musicians Benevolent Fund prize of £2,000 to women singers under the age of 30 (TB April 12 2007 p23).

People in Politics...

Oldest 'father' of the House of Commons by 1995 Rt Hon Charles Pelham Villiers (Wolverhampton South) (b1802) when he died on Jan 16 1898 aged 96 years 13 days; but of whom it was claimed he never once visited the town! (GBR 1995 p186) (TB July 1 2004 p11p). **The woman who voted in the 1908 General Election (before women had the vote!)** Lois Dawson who claimed she was the Louis Dawson on the electoral register for Wolverhampton East and successfully voted (TB March 20 2003 p7). **'last of the Midland radicals'** Sir Geoffrey le Mesurier Mander, Liberal MP for Wolverhampton 1929-45, distinguished for his stance against Appeasement and a supporter of the League of Nations (BBC website, 2006). **Oldest member of the House of Commons by 1983** Robert Edwards MP (Labour) for Wolverhampton South East (b1905) (GBR 1983 p212). **First woman councillor in Wolverhampton** Emma Lloyd

Sproson (d1936), 'Red Emma' who won the Dunstall Ward in 1921 (TB March 20 2003 p7. March 27 2003 p7). **Youngest member of the House of Commons 1974-79, first woman to breastfeed at Westminster, first Lord Speaker of the House of Lords** Baroness Hayman (Helene Valerie Hayman (née Middleweek)), born Wolverhampton 1949, attended Wolverhampton Girls' High School, Labour politician. Lord Speaker, which Hayman has held since 2006, was instituted under the Constitutional Reform Act 2005, and was formerly a role of the Lord Chancellor (Wikipedia, 2007). **First Labour alderman elected on Staffordshire County Council** Richard Clift in 1934 on the death of Alderman Thompson. Clift had represented Willenhall East 1922-34 (SA May 19 1934 p10).

Heroes, villains & victims...

Wolverhampton's most famous old worthy, Ireland's villain William Wood (1671-1730), hardware manufacturer. Born Shrewsbury; married Margaret Molineaux in 1690, daughter of Willenhall iron founder, Richard Molineaux (Wikipedia 2008). The family lived at the Deanery Hall 1692-1713 (Wolverhampton Civic Society). He was the first man ever seriously to attempt the substitution of coal for wood in the smelting of iron; he reputedly mined iron and copper in 39 counties (KES p238), given a contract as a mintmaster to strike an issue of Irish coinage, and the famous 'Rosa Americana' coins of British America. For Ireland he was authorised to produce 360 tons of halfpence and farthings (derisorily termed **Wood's halfpence**) at 30 pence to the pound 1722-36, but in reality the coins were too heavy to be profitable and were withdrawn. Wood received some government compensation before he died (Wikipedia 2008). All Ireland needed was small change to the value of £15,000, but Wood put out £100,000 worth. A fury of indignation was excited there in 1723; denunciation by the Irish Parliament; protests the coins would involve Ireland in a loss of £150 on every hundred pounds of copper coined. Jonathan Swift in letters written in the character of a Dublin draper predicted the ruin of his country; and Wood's effigy was burned in the streets of Dublin (KES pp238-239). **Wolverhampton's villain, 'one of the most notorious criminals in British history' 'The Prince of Robbers'** Jonathan Wild (c1682-1725). Born Walsall Street, Wolverhampton, the son of a wig maker. Buckle-making preceded a life as thief ringmaster in London. Eventually he was arrested for receiving some stolen lace. He was hung at Tyburn on 24th May, and buried in St Pancras churchyard beside his third wife, Elizabeth; his skeletal remains became an exhibit and he was immortalised in the saying 'Staffordshire had produced the three greatest rouges ever known in England - Jack Sheppard, Jonathan Wild and Tom Parker (of Leek)' (MR2 p367). Another villain of the time was William Duce, Wolverhampton-born highwayman, executed on Tyburn Tree in 1723 (TB Aug 17 2006 p22il). **Wolverhampton's villainess** Alice Grey, the famous fraudster, who about 1855 was committed for trial at Wolverhampton. Outside the court a crowd of 4,000 is said to have gathered and no fewer than 24 magistrates attended. She was accused of perjury, that she had had her purse stolen by boy purse-snatchers in various towns in the country in order to secure alms from officials in the towns. She was tried at by the Grand Jury at the assize court, Stafford in 1855. An anonymous ballad, after the style of Macaulay's lays was printed in Wolverhampton in 1856; its theme was a satire on the mass hysteria of her trial. The print is very rare (only two copies being known) (OP pp5-8). **Jack the Ripper's 4th victim, his only victim killed within the City of London, 'Kidney Kate', 'The Mitre Square Victim'** Catherine Eddowes, daughter of a tin plater of Wolverhampton (b1842), alias 'Kate Conway' 'Kate Kelly' and 'Mary Ann Kelly' when perhaps working as prostitute, murdered Sept 30 1888. She was called 'Kidney Kate' because the Ripper had removed her left kidney (The Penny Illustrated Paper Oct 13 1888) (TB Jan 1995 pp1,16-17. May 30 2002 p20. July 3 2003 p11) (Wikipedia). **'The George Street Tragedy'** The case of Edward Lawrence, wine and spirit merchant of George St, Wolverhampton, who shot his lover Ruth Hadley dead with a revolver on Dec 29 1908, but claimed he acted in self defence. Despite the case looking black for Lawrence, a notorious drunkard and prolific philanderer, he was wealthy enough to employ the brilliant advocate Edward Marshall Hall, K.C. and a verdict of not guilty was returned at his trial in March 1909 (TB Sept 16 2004 p5). **'Vanishing Violet'** Miss Violet Gordon Charlesworth (b1884) a 'woman of means' who lived at 34 Sweetman St, Whitmore Reans, (originally from Stafford) who mysterious vanished in her car in Jan 1909. The case became known as the 'Welsh Cliffs Mystery'. She was reported to have been involved in a tragic car accident in Wales, and said to have been hurled to her death over the cliffs near Penmaenmawr, but no body was found. Later, there were sightings of her boarding a ship at Holyhead, or sightings of her in Sussex and Ireland. She left debts of £13,000, and the case remains a mystery (TB March 4 2004 p7. Sept 2 2004 p11p). **1st= hung using the 'New Drop' on the Lodge of the New Gaol at Stafford** Ebenezer Colston, 21, a soldier, for the wilful murder of Henry Yates at Wolverhampton, executed 17 Aug 1793. **Last woman condemned to transportation at Stafford Quarter Sessions** Emma Vaughan, 27, committed 17 May 1853, appeared at the June Sessions 1853, for stealing the silver watch of Thomas William Porter from him at Wolverhampton, after a previous conviction of felony; seven years transportation. **Wolverhampton's heroine, George Medalist** Lisa (nee Potts) Webb (b1975), nursery teacher at St Luke's Primary School, Blakenhall, who protected her class in 1996 from a machete wielded by Horrett Campbell, severe paranoid schizophrenia, who had intruded into the school. She suffered severe scarring, depression and post-traumatic stress disorder and was awarded £68,000 compensation more than four years after the attack; she was awarded the medal for bravery in 1997, and has also received 11 other awards; subsequently she worked as a counsellor and in 2001 started a charity, Believe To Achieve, based in schools in Wolverton (Behind the Smile. Lisa Potts. 1998) (BCM Summer 2006 p69p) (Wikipedia, 2007). **Bentley's hero** Col John Lane who allowed Charles II to hide from parliament forces in his house Bentley Hall between Sept 9-10 1651 after the battle of Worcester, whilst his daughter Jane Lane must be **Bentley's heroine**. She dared and succeeded taking Charles (disguised as a servant) with her as his foil out of the district on her proposed visit to her cousin at Bristol. **Bilston's villainess** Joan Coxe, who allegedly bewitched the Boy of Bilston. She was tried in Aug 1620 at the Bishop's consistory court for witchcraft by the chancellor of the diocese, and afterwards at the assizes at Stafford where she was acquitted (NHS p281) (HOL p287) (SHOS vol 2 p171). **Pelsall's hero** Second Lieut Sidney Thomas Fox, Royal Garrison Artillery, killed in action in France 1917 interred in the Military Cemetery at Zillebeke (from his memorial in Pelsall church). **Pelsall's heroine** Dorothy Wyndlow Pattison, 'Sister Dora' Walsall nurse-extraordinary, who came to the aid of the bereaved in the Pelsall Hall Colliery disaster, Nov 1872; 22 men died. **Wednesfield's heroine** Tessa Sanderson (b1956), former Wards Bridge Comprehensive School pupil, the only British athlete to compete at five Olympic games from her tenth place in 1976 to fourth in 1992. She was the Olympic javelin champion in 1984 and awarded the MBE in 1985. **Last man condemned to transportation at Stafford Quarter Sessions** Charles Weaver, 55, committed 5 July 1853 for stealing one hammer and one saw off Samuel Ikin at Wednesfield, after a previous conviction of felony; seven years transporation. **Willenhall's villain** Rev William Moreton (b1759), who became curate in Willenhall in 1789 and vicar in 1795, seems to have had the worst reputation of any Staffordshire clergyman that ever lived. He would deliver his sermons inebriated and then go off to cock fights. His nickname was 'Old Mowton' and he is remembered in this rhyme

> A tumbledown church
> A tottering steeple
> A drunken parson
> And a wicked people

In 1791 he was even fined 'for sporting with a gun and two setting dogs upon the manor of H Vernon of Hilton Park.' Moreton was declared bankrupt in 1812 and died in July 1834 and was buried in St Giles' churchyard, Willenhall. At his funeral his curate, Rev George Fisher, contrived not to mention him in the sermon. His pedigree was unknown, and some have thought he was a 'nephew' of George III. **First person 'privately' hung at Stafford Gaol** Christopher Edwards of Church Street, Willenhall, on Aug 13 1872 for the murder of his wife Rosannah (TB April 13 2006 p25). **First Wolverhampton tramp given an ASBO** David John Savage, 33, of no fixed abode, on March 24 2003, banned from entering Wolverhampton city centre and begging anywhere in the country (E&S March 25 2003 p12).

War heroes...

Wolverhampton's heroes RN Petty Officer Alfred Sephton (1911-41), attended Dudley Road Council School, Wolverhampton. On May 18 1941 he was in a director tower of his ship, The Coventry, on patrol in the Mediterranean trying to aid Aba, an hospital ship, when it came under heavy enemy fire. He carried on at his instruments despite a bullet passing through his body, thus maintained the efficiency of the director, helping to save both ships. He lost his life and was awarded with a posthumous V.C. Dec 2 1941 (TB Feb 21 2008 p16p). William Mitchell (b1894) of St John's Square, Wolverhampton, Royal Marine who received an illuminated certificate from the Borough of Wolverhampton to commemorate his gallantry in the raid on Zeebrugge on 22-23 April 1918; he narrowly missed receiving the V.C. (TB May 20 2004 pp12-14p). **Bilston's heroes** L-Corp George Onions, 1st Batt Devon Regt, born Bilston 1883, awarded the V.C. for action on Aug 22 1918, south of Achiet-le-Petit. On an errand he unwittingly came upon and repulsed an enemy counter-attack. Only aided by another man, the pair took 200 prisoners and marched them back to their company commander (SA Dec 21 1918 p3 col 3). Harold Edwards of Wolverhampton Street, Bilston, 1st Batt South Staffs, a Messrs Sankey & Sons employee, was awarded the Croix de Guerre and D.C.M in WW1 (ELSONSS p90p). **Wednesfield's hero** Sgt W Birchall of 64 Neachell's Lane, whose D.C.M. and M.M. were announced on Jan 4 1917, aged 27. He was a former Patent Axle Box works employee, having been employed there from a boy as a chipper and filer. He was the first Wednesfield man to obtain the duel honour (ELSONSS p178). **Willenhall's hero** Ike Howell (1896-1978), born Walsall Rd, Willenhall, won the Medaille Militaire in France in WW1, presented Jan 6 1918; also considered one of the most respected and memorable of policemen of Wolverhampton (MMBCC pp35-37). **2nd Staffordshire casualty due to WW2 black-out regulations** John Edward Felton, 46, a casement maker of 32 Penn Road, knocked down on Sept 9 1939 by a trolley bus near Graiseley Hill. A verdict of accidental death was recorded; the coroner warned there ought to be some modification to the lighting restrictions. The first such casualty was at Longton (SA Sept 16 1939 p8 col 9). **'one of the first to join the SAS'** George Edwards, born Derry St, Wolverhampton, 1912, who joined Special Air Service in 1942; unit disbanded 1946. Died Wednesfield 1984 (TB Feb 17 2005 p21p). **First officer to land by parachute in France on D-Day** Lieutenant J.S. Jeavons (b1918) of Bilston, of the 13th Battalion Parachute Regt part of the British 6th Airborne Division who arrived in the middle of the night to pave the way for the invading armies (TB May 13 2004 p15). **'The man who saved Wolverhampton'** Reginald Victor Jones (d1997), Chief of Air Scientific Intelligence with MI6, who worked out from German codes that the enemy were going to raid Wolverhampton on the night of Nov 14 and 15 1940. He subsequently ordered the town be heavily ringed with Anti-Aircraft guns. The Germans received intelligence of this and called off the raid. But Jones was criticised at the time by his superiors for leaving the defences of nearby towns significantly depleted. The BBC's 1977 series 'The Secret War' was based primarily around his work (TB Jan 24 2008 p17p).

Record breakers...

Keeping a see-saw in constant motion Martin Ashton and Graham Stokes for 100 hours at Willenhall from June 1-5 1971 (GBR 1971 p308). **Most flame torches extinguished in a mouth** 20,035 by

Reg Morris on March 17 1987 in one hour 48 minutes 14 seconds at Cinders Night Club, Willenhall (GBR 1988 p20). **The longest odds win** On Feb 11 1984 Edward Hodson of Wolverhampton landed a 3,956,748 to 1 horse racing bet for a 55p stake. But the bookmaker had a £3000 payout limit (GBR 1993 p253). **Longest Rugby 'try' ever executed** That over 166.5 miles from Wolverhampton Polytechnic to Cardiff Arms Park, Wales, by 15 players from Wolverhampton Polytechnic RFC in 23 hours 29 minutes on March 9-10 1973 (GBR 1974 p277). **Blowing clarinet for longest time** Phil Palmer (b1953/4) of Ashmore Park, owner of Music Land in Wolverhampton, blow into a clarinet for 1 minute 16 seconds on Nov 27 2006; the previous world record had stood at 49 seconds (E&S Nov 28 2006 p5). **Fastest 100-mile run on a treadmill** Glyn Marston, 40, of Sneyd, Willenhall, in 19 hours at Bluewater shopping centre, Kent on July 2 2003, breaking the former world record by about 13 minutes (E&S July 5 2003 p39).

Society...

2nd oldest district Freemason lodge in Staffordshire The 'Ancient' or 'Athol' Lodge of Wolverhampton founded 1764 (SA Dec 29 1917 p7 col 7). **Earliest parish register entry in Staffordshire of a black person** George John Scipio Africanus baptised 31 March 1766 in the register of St Peter's, Wolverhampton, a slave to the Molineux family of Wolverhampton. He lived to 1834 aged 71. There is an earlier reference to a black person: A Molineux family diary recalls in 1762 'Pluto came to Wolverhampton - his age between 9 and 10 years old' (TB July 24 2003 p7. July 31 2003 p7). **Staffordshire's largest concentration of Catholics 1767** Wolverhampton with 491, according to a return of Roman Catholics in England and Wales (HOS 1998 p64). **Youngest recorded death from alcoholic poisoning** Four year old, Joseph Sweet, in Wolverhampton in 1827 reported in the Stafford Assizes case R. v. Martin (GBR 1979 p21). **First and last deaths of the 1849 Cholera outbreak in Willenhall** Occurred on 17th August and 4th October (TB April 29 2004 p6p). **First meeting of the Wolverhampton Rifle Volunteers** Took place on June 3 1859. The first meeting of the Bilston Rifle Volunteers was on Nov 29 1859 (SA Jan 14 1860 p5 col 4). **Wolverhampton's first health facility exclusively for women** The Women's Dispensary (later Wolverhampton and District Hospital for Women) in 1866, in St Mark's Place, and then in Park Road West from 1904 (TB Aug 18 2005 p7). **Staffordshire's first synagogue** Perhaps that in Fryer St, Wolverhampton, built 1858 (Wolverhampton City Trail, Wolverhampton City Council, 2006). **First visit to Staffordshire by a Chief Rabbi** Possibly when Rev Dr Adler of London visited Wolverhampton on May 24 1897. He held a reception at the Star and Garter Hotel and afterwards examined the Jewish children at the synagogue (SA May 29 1897 p7 col 6). **Wolverhampton's first ethnic JP** Shu Awath-Bahari (b1933), of Bridgnorth, served on Wolverhampton bench 1969-2003. Dental health practitioner, formerly of South Africa (E&S Feb 1 2003 042p). **First British town centre to get CCTV cameras** Wolverhampton, 1988 (HOWU p166). **First British Police Force to wear head webcams** West Midlands

Police, 2007, and the film is then transmitted on the internet (BBC Midlands Today May 23 2007). **Worst Youth Offenders Institute in the country for drug use** Featherstone YOI, sometime before 2006 (BBC Midlands Today Sept 4 2006). **First hospital in UK to contract out its paperwork to India** New Cross Hospital (BBC Radio 4 News April 14 2006). **Place where the National Older Peoples Day was conceived** Bilston, and the idea was taken to Government by Bilston MP Pat McFadden and his predecessor Lord Turner; the first National Older Peoples Day was on Oct 1 2007 (TB July 21 2005 p23. Sept 6 2007 p19). **Britain's dimmest city** Wolverhampton in 2003, as revealed by an internet quiz involving more than 200,000 people in total, with Wolverhampton participants answering only 36% of the questions right (E&S Feb 28 2003 pp1,4). **Britain's best unfashionable town or city** Wolverhampton as voted on BBC's Breakfast News (BBC website Jan 6 2006). Wolverhampton was **the most-populated Staffordshire parish in 1801** with 24,632; it was also **1st in 1811** with 30,249; **1st in 1821** with 36,937; **1st in 1831** with 48,184; **1st in 1841** with 70, 370; **1st in 1851** with 92,287; **1st in 1861** with 11,3832; **1st in 1871** with 12,2881; **1st in 1881** with 13,1587; **1st in 1891** with 14,1832; **1st in 1901** with 15,9227. Wolverhampton (borough & urban areas) was **2nd most-populated area in the West Midlands conurbation in 2001**; **13th largest city in England in 2004** with a population of 251,462 (Wikipedia, 2007). **Wolverhampton's largest non-white population in 2001** People who described themselves as of Indian ethnicity, at 12.3% of the overall population (Wikipedia 2007).

Bilston...

One of the largest villages in England by 1790 Bilston, until converted into a market town by an Act of 1824 (HOBLL p170) (TB Aug 16 2001 p15). **'the Acropolis of a hundred collieries'** Bilston in the later C17 (SA Oct 6 1849 p7 col 1). **'Epidemic centre of the Midland Coalfield'** Bilston, where in the cholera outbreak of 1832 742 died out of a population of 14,492 (WP p126). **"one of the most ignorant, brutal, depraved, drunken, unhealthy populations in the kingdom, unless it be a set of people in the same occupations in the neighbourhood of Manchester!!"** Samuel Sidney in 1851 on unsanitary conditions at Bilston in the wake of the cholera epidemics (Bilston Town Trail, Wolverhampton City Council, 2006). **'Bilston stands by its faith and industry'** The Bilston motto (Staffordshire Handbook c1966 p43). **First chairman of Bilston Improvement Commissioners 1850** William Baldwin, ancestor of Earl Baldwin (Staffordshire Handbook c1966 p43). **Bilston's oldest building** Greyhound Inn High Street (BCOPP p23pl). **First market hall to be lit electrically in England** Reputedly, Bilston Market Hall opened on Aug 9 1892 (BOP p23p). **One of the worst Bilston pits for colliery accidents** Messrs Baldwins, which had fatalities in Nov 1850, Oct 1851, Jan 185, April 1856, Aug 1858, July 1859 (which took the life of the third member of one family all killed in Mr Baldwin's service), and Sept 1868 (SA Jan 23 1859 p2 col 7). **Last chairman of Bilston UDC, first Mayor of Bilston Borough**

Herbert Beach, who served as mayor from Bilston Charter Day on Sept 28 1933 to 1935 (TB March 22 2007 pp20-21ps).

Transport...

'**Wolverhampton 21**' Refers to the 21 locks on the Birmingham Main Line Canal to the north of Wolverhampton. **Staffordshire's most-important centre of carriers, 1834** Wolverhampton (The Staffordshire Atlas, 2008). **First tram to run in Wolverhampton** An horse-drawn service of Wolverhampton Tramways Company (formed 1876), between Queen Square and Newbridge, May 1 1878 (TB Jan 11 2007 p26). **Last tram to run in Wolverhampton** Aug 26 1928, thereafter the service was replaced by trolley buses and motor buses (TB Jan 11 2007 p26). **First and last Wolverhampton trolley buses** The first was a Telling Stevens T6 which ran on Nov 29 1922 between Wolverhampton and Wednesfield; the last ran on March 5 1967 between Wolverhampton and Dudley (TB Feb 3 2007 p25. Feb 22 2007 p13il). **Biggest trolley bus system in the country in 1930s** Wolverhampton (The Black Country. Edward Chitham. 1972 p167). **Last trolley bus cable pole still in situ** Walsall Rd, Sandbeds, Willenhall (TB Aug 17 2000 p13p). **First experimental traffic lights in Great Britain** Were set up for a one-day trial in Princes Square, Wolverhampton, on Nov 5 1927 (WF p25) (WOLOP p121p) (BCP p112p). **Most cars converted to lead-free petrol on a single site** 1,115 cars at Wolverhampton on April 30 1989 (GBR 1990 p113).

Sport...

ATHLETICS World record for billiard table jumping Joseph Darby (1861-1937) of Windmill End, Netherton, 'Great Spring-jumper the World has ever known!' at Roland's Circus, Wolverhampton on Feb 5 1892, when he cleared a full-sized 12 feet billiard table lengthways, taking off from a four inch high solid wooden block (TB June/July 1972 p5. March 1994 pp1,36p. Aug 5 2004 p13) (GBR 1980 p218) (MMBCC pp38p-45). **World record for 880 yards** Brian Stanford Hewson at Wolverhampton with one minute 47.8 seconds on June 14 1958 (GBR 1966 p251). **UK men's running record** Peter Frank Radford at Wolverhampton on May 28 1960, running 100 yards in 9.4 seconds, 220 yards (turn) in 20.5 seconds, and 200 metres in 20.5 seconds (broken in 1972) (GBR 1970 p235. 1974 p330). **100 metres running record** Peter Frank Radford on June 18 1960 at Wolverhampton with 10.3 seconds (GBR 1966 p251). **Staffordshire Six Mile track champion 1954, Staffordshire 15 Mile road champion 1957-60** Colin Kimball (1928-2004) of Goldthorn Park (TB April 329 2004 p25p). **Only British athlete to compete at five Olympic games** Tessa Sanderson (b1956) of Wednesfield, 1976-92 (The Guinness International Who's Who of Sport. Peter Matthews, Ian Buchanan, Bill Mallon. 1993). '**the White City of the Black Country**' Aldersley Stadium, as described in one venue programme (TB May 17 2007 p35). **BOWLS 'one of Staffordshire's best known greens'** Was at the Molineux Hotel, Wolverhampton (TB June 21 2007 p33). **First meeting of Staffordshire Association**

for Bowling The Ring 'o' Bells Inn, Wolverhampton, 1902 (TB June 21 2007 p33). **The first British Individual Merit Crown Green Bowls Champion** Enoch Peers, born Hall Street, Wednesfield, 1910; the first Crown Green championships were held at Fleetwood, Lancs, 1877 (TB Sept 1983 p1p. June 21 2007 p33). **CYCLING Staffordshire's/ Wolverhampton's earliest cycle racing** Perhaps that on July 27 1869 at Vauxhall Gardens, Cannock Rd, held by the Velocipede Club, described in 1869, as recently established. There were three races - firstly the 'Velocipede Derby' (won by G Tolman who covered 2 miles in 9 mins 57 seconds, out of six entries), secondly the 'Carlton Cup,' and a race to see who could go at the slowest speed (SA July 31 1869 p5 col 1). **British League of Racing Cyclists (1942) founder, 'man responsible for bringing cycle sport into modern times'** Percy Stallard (1909-2001) of Wolverhampton; represented England five times on the continent in World Championships (E&S Jan 10 2003 p27p) (BBC website, 2006). **World amateur pursuit bronze medalist 1963, Commonwealth gold medalist 1966, Cycling Individual Pursuit World champion 1968, 1970, 1972, 1973 (only man to hold this title four times)** Hugh Porter (b1939), Wolverhampton-born cyclist (TB Oct 20 2005 p30. July 27 2006 p35). **British record for cycling (professional unpaced standing start) for 20 km** Set by Phil Bayton at Wolverhampton on June 10 1975 in 27 minutes 24.4 seconds (GBR 1980 p265). **FOOTBALL Most goals scored in League matches by 1974** George Arthur Rowley, born Wolverhampton 1926, scoring 434 for West Bromwich Albion, Fulham, Leicester City and Shrewsbury Town between 1946-65. He had also scored 32 goals in the FA Cup and 1 for England 'B' (GBR 1974 p269). **World record for highest women's score in a (football?) match** Willenhall Town Ladies who beat Burton Brewers Ladies 57-0 at Willenhall, March 4 2001 (GBR 2003 p209). **HORSE RACING 'Father of the Turf'**, founder the Jockey Club, Oaks winner 1787 Richard Vernon of Hilton Hall (1726-1800). **First Derby winner 1780** Was Diomed belonging to Sir Charles Bunbury trained at Hilton Park (VB p126). **Wolverhampton's most famous horse 1978** Pennwood Forge Mill (E&S Sept 15 1978 p23p). **MOTOR SPORT One of the oldest Speedway tracks in the world** Wolverhampton Speedway, opened 1928, originally for Wolverhampton Dirt Track Motor Cycle Club (BBC website). **Wolverhampton Speedway's first World Speedway Champion** Ole Olsen at Gothenberg, Sweden, 1971 (BBC website). **Wolverhampton Speedway's saddest accident** The death at the Monmore Green track of rider Gary Peterson killed whilst competing in Heat 11 of the 2nd Leg of the Midland Cup Final, Oct 17 1975 (TB Sept 14 2006 p31p). **Most British Senior Team Championships (instituted 1950) in Cycle Speedway** Is six by Wednesfield Aces (1974, 1976-8, 1981, and 1983) (GBR 1985 p265). **Le Mans 24 Hours winner 1970** Richard Attwood (b1940) of Wolverhampton, Formula One driver, in a Porsche 917; in the same race 1971 Attwood and his co-driver Hans Herrmann came 2nd (Wikipedia, 2007). **OTHER Britain's leading fighting cock trainer, c1824** 'Cockie' Potter,

Bilston native, of the Britannia Inn, Moxley, Cock-Master General to Lord Derby (MR2 p39). **British Junior Champions (Rifle Marksmanship) 1950** Wolverhampton Junior Rifle Team (TB April 1 2004 p35p). **UK male Hammer field event record** Set by Martin Girvan (b1960) who achieved a distance of 254 feet five inches at Wolverhampton on May 12 1984 (GBR 1995 p227). **UK's oldest golfer** Possibly Charles Viner (b1907), of Shropshire, but former Art teacher at Wolverahmpton Grammar School (BBC 1 Midlands Today Dec 4 2007). **PRIZE FIGHTING Wolverhampton's greatest ever bare knuckle fighter, 'The Champion of America'** Joe Goss (b1838), who was brought up in Wolverhampton, he won his American title in 1876 against Tom Allen (born Birmingham) on a foul (TB June 1 2000 p32il. Aug 19 2004 p31p). **Another Wolverhampton pugilist** George Bonny Evans, still being pushed into ten or 12-round fights when he was going blind (E&S March 12 2008 p9). **Bilston's pugilists** Ellis Richardson and Richard Wilkinson (alias Dicky Drybread), fl1865 (TB Feb 26 2004 p27). **First ever World Light Weight champion** Abraham Hicken (alias Abe Ikin) (1840s-1910) of Wolverhampton, emigrated at some point to USA, title holder 1868-72 (TB Jan 24 2002 p35. Feb 23 2002 p35. May 16 2002 p35).

Wolverhampton Race Course...

First meeting under Jockey Club rules Took place on Aug 13 and 14 1888, when the course was officially opened by Mr Staverley Hill. On the first day an estimated 15,000 paid for admission. The first race - The All-Aged Maiden Plate of 100gs of five furlongs - was won by Silver Spur ridden by T Loakes (SA Aug 18 1888 p6 col 4). **The only Staffordshire course to stage flat racing** Wolverhampton at Dunstall Park in 1895 after the closure of the course on Whittington Heath. **One of the first all-weather horse race courses in UK** Wolverhampton Racecourse (take a brain sip website 2006). **Britain's only floodlit horse race track** Wolverhampton Racecourse (Wikipedia, 2007). **One of Wolverhampton's best races** The 2030 BST, the Weatherby's Dash (BBC website, 2001). **The best performance by a British correspondent in horse race tipping** Is seven out of seven winners for a meeting at Wolverhampton on March 22 1982 by Bob Butchers of the Daily Mirror (GBR 1994 p262). **World's first betting shop millionaire, whose final horse in his accumulator was at Wolverhampton** Freddie Craggs of Bedale, N. Yorks, who placed 50p on eight horses to win races in a multiple bet on odds of 2,798,000 to one at William Hill at Thirsk on Feb 23 2008. His final horse was A Dream Come True in the 9.20 at Wolverhampton, by which point his state was worth £399,975.46. It came in first at 5/2 (The Sunday Telegraph Feb 24 2008 p17. The Daily Telegraph Feb 25 2008 p2p).

Wolverhampton Wanderers...

The two boys who formed St Luke's FC, which, with another club, formed Wolverhampton Wanders 1877 John Brodie and John Baynton (TB Jan 16 2003 p18). **First official game at Molineux** Sept 2 1889, a friendly against Aston Villa (TB Aug 7 2003 p13). **One of the 12 original members of the Football League** Wolverhampton Wanderers (TTTD p293). **Olympic Gold Medalist London 1908, FA Cup Winner's Medal 1908** Rev Kenneth Hunt (d1948), of Wolves, resident at St Mark's Vicarage, Chapel Ash (TB March 17 2005 pp18-19p). **First English team to play in the Soviet Union** (take a brain sip website, 2006); **'The Unofficial World Champions'** after one of their most famous victories, against Honved of Hungary (take a brain sip website, 2006). **Wolves' first appearance at Wembley, biggest shock in FA Cup final history** When Wolves lost to Portsmouth 4-1 on April 29 1939; the team were presented to George VI (TB Feb 12 2004 p35) (E&S Nov 15 2005 p11) (WOLOP p88p). **War League winners 1942** Wolves. **Only England match on Staffordshire soil** Perhaps that at Molineux when England played Denmark Dec 5 1956, presumably in a qualifier for the 1958 World Cup. England's captain was Wolves' own Billy Wright. England beat Denmark 5-2 (TB June 22 2000 p10). **Player who became Mayor of Wolverhampton** Tom W Phillipson (b1899), Wolves 1923-28, mayor 1944-45 (TB March 23 2006 p4p). **FA Cup medallist 1949** Bert Williams, goalkeeper, when with Wolves; he was born in Bradley, Bilston, in 1922 (Wikipedia 2007). **'The Dustbin Final'** FA Cup final 1960 when Wolves beat Blackburn Rovers, so described by Daily Telegraph's Laurie Pignon for the shoddy, ordinary play littered with ugly challenges (TB March 23 2006 p35). **First player in history to win 100 full caps** Billy Wright (b1924) of Wolves, when he led England against Scotland at Wembley 1959 (TB July 27 2006 p35). **Greatest total of full international caps in Association Football by 1969** 105 by Billy Wright, who had 38 international championship appearances (1946-1959) and 67 foreign international and world cup matches (1946-1959) (GBR 1965 p276. 1969 p311). **First team to have been champions of all four English league divisions by 1988, only club to have won five different League titles (Divisions 1, 2, 3 (and 3 (North), 4)** (take a brain sip website, 2006). (Wolverhampton the 1930s and 1940s. Elizabeth Rees. 1988. pl 52) (WF p61). **Wolves' greatest manager** Stan Cullis (1916-2001), manager 1948, sacked Sept 16 1964. Statue of him was unveiled outside the ground on Aug 8 2003 (E&S Aug 8 2003 p6) (TB April 19 2007 p19). **Wolves' greatest player** Peter Broadbent of Bilston, in the opinion of Steve Gordos, E&S sports editor (Peter Broadbent. Steve Gordos. 2007) (TB April 19 2007 p19p). Or perhaps Steve Bull of Tipton (TB Dec 7 2006 p23). **Wolves' oldest player** Archie Goodall, 41 years 170 days when he played against Everton on Dec 2 1906. **Wolves' youngest player** Cameron Buchanan, 14 years 57 days when he played against WBA in Sept 1926 (TB Aug 23 2007 p30). **'The most charismatic man in English football'** Derek Dougan, alias 'the Doog' (1938-2007) in the opinion of sports presenter, Ian Winter (BBC Midlands Today 25 June 2007), originally of Belfast; memorably he scored a hat-trick in his first home game for Wolves in 1967; was their top scorer in 1967, 1968, 1972 (Daily Telegraph June 25 2007 p25) (The Sash He Never Wore. Derek Dougan. 1972). **British transfer records**

When Wolves sold midfielder Steve Daley to Manchester City for £1,437,500 (including VAT & levy charges) on Sept 5 1979; on Sept 8 1979 the club smashed this record by signing striker Andy Gray from Aston Villa for £1,469,000 (including extras) (TB July 27 2006 p35). **Club of the Year 1969** Wolves Social Club, built 1964/5, awarded by the national trade publication 'Club Mirror' and presented to the then chairman John Ireland by Miss World 1969, Penny Plummer, Australia's first Miss World (The Wolverhampton Wanderers Football Book. Phil Morgan. 1970 pp106-109p). **Biggest advert in British football** A 20 by 12 metre poster erected between the Jack Harris and Billy Wright stands in Feb 2008 for the 2008-09 season, by Morgan Est, promoting a career in engineering (E&S March 12 2008 p23p). **First female appointed to the Board of Directors** Rachel Heyhoe Flint, former England Women's Cricket Captain of Tettenhall, in Sept 1997 (TB Aug 11 2005 p30).

Work...

Where Jack Sheppard's 'irons' were made Wednesfield manufactured the leg irons which manacled highwayman Jack Sheppard at Newgate Prison; these specially-designed 'irons' were used in H.M. Prisons throughout England (TB Aug 17 2006 p23il). **Wolverhampton's first 'great' industrial exhibition** The South Staffordshire Industrial and Fine Arts Exhibition, opened May 11 1869, in the grounds of Molineux House (TEBC2). **Largest integrated works in Staffordshire by 1895** Spring Vale Furnaces, which then produced steel (BOP p126). **'last of the Black Country towns to undergo the drastic transformation of Industrial Development'** Wednesfield, which, according to the Staffordshire Advertiser, was until c1895 a type of the towns of South Staffordshire as they appeared at the beginning of the C19, due to lack of coal to be mined in the area (SA July 21 1900 p4 col 5). **'one of the largest manufacturers of aluminium foil in Britain'** Star Aluminium Co. Ltd, Wolverhampton (Staffordshire Handbook c1966 p79). **Supplied components to the 2nd largest power station in UK** Richard & Ross Ltd, Wednesfield, for the Blythe Power Station (TB July 31 2003 p21). **'the British Empire's largest manufacturer of paints, printing inks and varnishes'** Mander Brothers of Wolverhampton by the late C19 (Daily Telegraph Aug 25 2006 p31), **'one of the largest, and reputedly the most technologically advanced of such firms in the whole of Britain'** Mander-Kidd Ltd (Mander Brothers successors) at Heath Town in 1950s (TB March 15 2001 p21). **One of only six UK companies to hold all four royal warrants** Halcyon Days Enamels made by Bilston & Battersea Enamels (formed 1969) granted warrants from The Queen, The Queen Mother, Prince Philip and The Prince of Wales 1972-78. They are the first ever and only 'Suppliers of Objets d'Art' royal warrant-holders (An Introduction to Halcyon Days Enamels website 2008) (MIW p121 - says seven warrants). **UK's leading specialist mortgage lender** Edeus, which has its HQ in Wolverhampton (sign leading into Wolverhampton, 2008). **First firm in the world to recycle plastic from mixed plastics** Omnia Recycling, Wolverhampton, using newly-developed technology which recycles different types of plastic in one go by early 2008 (BBC Midlands Today Jan 25 2008).

Iron working...

'the father of the South Staffordshire coal and iron industry' John Wilkinson (DNB); the first biography of him, incidentally, appears in 'Price and Beebee's History of Bilston' (1868) (BCM Spring 2002 p34). **Third iron barge launched in world** Bradley, Bilston, 1787 (Staffordshire County Handbook c1958). **First blast furnace in UK** Bilston, 1767 (Staffordshire County Handbook c1958). **UK's highest concentration of blast furnaces by 1790** Bilston, which had 15 of 21 then in Britain (Staffordshire County Handbook c1958). **One of the first blast furnaces to work on the principle of High Top pressure, the Black Country's biggest blast furnace** 'Elisabeth' at Stewart & Lloyds, Springvale (the Bilston Steelworks), 1954-80 (TB Feb 10 2000 p20. Nov 21 2002 p5p). **The man who patented 'a new or improved steam boiler to be heated by the waste heat of pudding or mill furnaces'** George Jackson of Bilston (SA Nov 22 1856 p5 col 2). **Man who invented the shoe buckle** Thomas Beebee of Bilston, locksmith, fl 1686 (SARA March 29 1956). **Bilston Steelwork's final cast** Read:- 'BILSTON Iron and Steelworks 1768 to 1979 last cast X21402A "B" Furnace 12th April 1979 2.50pm' (TB April 11 2002 p17). **First manufacturer of steel ironing tables in UK** Beldray Ltd of Bilston, originally Bradley & Co. Ltd, established 1872 (Documenting the Workshop of the World Nov 2007). **First British modular storage system produced** The 'Spacesaver' 1961 by Beldray Ltd of Bilston (Documenting the Workshop of the World Nov 2007). **Most efficient and modern steel distribution centre in Europe** Steelpark, Steelpark Way, off New Wednesfield Way, off Neachells Lane, opened 1999 (BBC Midlands Today Oct 29 1999) (E&S Oct 29 1999 p1. Oct 30 1999 p18). **'Wolverhampton's prince of the pumps'** Joseph Evans of Joseph Evans & Sons Ltd, Culwell Works, Wolverhampton, makers of pumps and pumping machinery in the inter-war years (TB Feb 5 2004 p19).

Locks & traps...

Producers of 90% of UK's locks, latches and keys by late 1950s Willenhall (Staffordshire County Handbook c1958 p149) (TB Jan 3 2002 p21). **'more locks, of all kinds, are made here than in any other town of the same size in England or Europe'** Willenhall (TB July 10 2003 p22). **First quadruple lock** Designed 1823/4 by Joseph Duce, Snr, of Joseph Duce & Son of Dudley St, Wolverhampton, and thus made 1824 a Vulcan Medalist by The Society of Arts (later The Royal Society of Arts) (BCM Oct 1986 pp6-11. Jan 1987 pp20-25) (TB April 19 2001 p20il. April 26 2001 p13). In 1842 Joseph Duce, the younger, was granted a patent for a local and key mechanism (VCH vol 2 p252). **First large lock-making factory in Willenhall early C19** Messrs Carpenter & Tildesley, S side of Wolverhampton Street, Willenhall (Willenhall (SW) 1901. Old OS Maps. Godfrey. 1996). **'one of the first to apply machinery to aid in their (lock) production'** James Carpenter (d1844) of Willenhall (BCM Spring 2003 p75). **Supplied the lock to the very**

first post office letter box Chubb of Wolverhampton, 1851. **Largest lock producer in the district 1851, first lock manufacturer in the area to use the Nasmyth steam hammer** The Albion Works (founded 1790), Walsall Road, Willenhall, who started using the Nasmyth in 1856 (Willenhall & Darlaston Green 1885. Old OS Maps. Godfrey. 2001). **First Willenhall lock factory** 1856 (Staffordshire County Handbook c1958). **Largest factory of its kind (locks) in Great Britain 1962** H&T Vaughan Ltd of Willenhall, who were acquired by Yale Co. in 1929 (TB Jan 3 2002 p21). **Oldest firm of locksmiths in Britain** James Gibbons Ltd, St John's Works, Wolverhampton (Staffordshire County Handbook c1958 p51). **'largest and best-equipped contract tool-room in Willenhall'** The Nicor Co. (Willenhall) Ltd, Park Rd, Willenhall, formed 1950 (Staffordshire Handbook c1966 p83). **Home of the UK's National Lock Museum** Willenhall. **Only place in England where large (animal) traps are made** Perhaps Wednesfield (Staffordshire County Handbook c1958). **Largest padlock in the world by 1974** ERA No. 1212 Close shackle 6 lever lock made by JE Reynolds of Willenhall. It weighed 100 lb 45 kg 30, and was used for locking dock gates and boats (GBR 1974 p157p). **Prime Minister John Major's great-great-grandfather** Joseph Ball, a master locksmith of Willenhall in 1855 (BCM Spring 2003 p75). **'Humpshire' 'Upshire'** Local reference to Willenhall on account of locksmiths there developing humped banks bending over their work.

Cars & bikes...

'one of the largest bicycle manufacturing towns in England' Wolverhampton in the late 1900s (Discover Your Heritage, Wolverhampton City Council, 2006). **Sixth largest car-producer in Great Britain by 1910** Star Co. of Wolverhampton; they were taken over by Guys in 1928 (PVBC pp39-45) (Wolverhampton Chronicle July 11 1997 p24. April 16 1999 p5). **First Sunbeam (of Upper Villiers Street) bicycle** 1887. **First Sunbeam car** 1899. First Sunbeam motor cycle 1912. **First British car to top 70 mph** A Sunbeam, 1911. **French and Spanish Grand Prix winners 1923** Sunbeam, when it was also the first British car to win the French Grand Prix (Wolverhampton (SW) 1901. Old OS Maps. Godfrey. 2004). **First man to drive a car at over 200 mph** Henry Seagrave in a Sunbeam V12 on March 29 1927. **The Wolverhampton company that made bamboo bicycles** The Bamboo Cycle Co. of Holborn, London who had works in Petit St, off Pountney St, 1895-7 (TB March 8 2001 p26). **Britain's first bubble car and 'one of the most unusual, and possibly one of the last, mass produced vehicles to be made in Wolverhampton'** The 'Frisky' made by the firm of Henry Meadows, 1957 (TB March 8 2001 p1p). **The Graiseley** A hand-operated three-wheeled electric vehicle used by milkmen produced by Diamond Motors Ltd of Upper Villiers St, Wolverhampton, 1935-75, named after the nearby place Graiseley (TB Aug 15 2002 p14p). **World's fastest petrol run street car** A converted 1981 Vauxhall Victor called Red Victor 2 as claimed by its owner Andy Frost, a 34 year old Wolverhampton engineer. The car can do 0 - 60 mph in one second and reach a speed of 183 mph in 7.8 seconds (BBC Black Country website, 10 Nov 2006).

St Peter's church...

St Peter, **one of 15 such county dedications** (of ancient parish churches); **77th= oldest ancient parish county church** dating from 1290. **Staffordshire's earliest metal monumental effigy in a church** That of Sir Richard Leveson in bronze, 1605 (BAST vols 69-71 p27). **Staffordshire's only ancient stone pulpit** That at St Peter's, possibly by the same artist as the one who did the font; the very quaint lion seated on the balustrade of its stair is perhaps a unique feature (SHOS vol 2 p155) (GNHS p176) (W p80) (LGS p258) (CHMS p75). **Also note** The lectern may be from Halesowen Abbey (CHMS p75). A marble slab to Thomas Pilkington (d1654), one of the Queen's musicians (WA vol 1 No. 5 p148). A floorslab memorial to Rev Thomas Hayes (d1731), rector of Tixall, also his eldest son John Hayes (d1777), Capt in his Majesty's Marine Service (SHOSA vol 2 p18). **In the porch** in 1910 was the epitaph of Charles Claudius Phillips (d1732), born in Wales "whose absolute contempt of riches and inimitable performances upon the violin made him the admiration of all that knew him". Dr Wilkes wrote some verses to his memory (SHOS vol 2 p161) (SHOSA vol 2 p18) (W p91) (LGS p259). **Oldest grave in the churchyard** Is to Walter Southall and is dated AG 18. 1441, but the date should be 1741. He died aged 78. It rested against the western wall of the N transept (WA vol 1 No. 12 pp390-393). See also the grave of Joseph Jones (d1690) who died from over-eating (SJC p11) (WA No. 1 vol 1 p5) (TB Aug 1981 p23). **First dean of Wolverhampton to be also dean of St George's chapel, Windsor Castle** Master William Dudley, appointed probably in 1457, resigned 1476; in 1480 the union between the two deaneries was made permanent (VCH vol 3 pp325, 330). **'one of the largest Anglican Church choirs in the UK'** The choir of St Peter's (Wikipedia, 2007).

Other churches...

In **WOLVERHAMPTON** The **'resurrection' church** St John (1758-76), alias St John in the Square from 1980s, St John's Sq, Snow Hill. So called because of its ability to come back from the brink, almost burnt to the ground in a fire a year after it was built and surmounting a string of calamities since (E&S ?April 5 2008). **One of the most famous organs in England** An original Renatis Harris of c1633 at St John's (Staffordshire: Shire County Guide. Peter Heaton. 1986). **Staffordshire's only classical Commissioners' church** St George (1828-30), Bilston Rd, closed 1978, incorporated into a supermarket in 1987 (BOE p34). St Silas (1901-), mission church of St Matthew (GTS1 p48). St Mary (records from 1843), Stafford Street. **Earliest-known Wolverhampton R.C. priest** John Milward 1692, **longest-serving priest** John Carter for 27 years 1776-1803. **'largest and oldest established black church in England and Wales'** The New Testament Church of God, a fundamental Pentecostal church. It was founded in Wolverhampton in September 1952 when seven brethren got together and hired the YMCA hall in Stafford Street. In 1962 purpose-built premises opened in Nursery

Street. In 1973 the Harvest Temple, Wednesfield Road, Heath Town opened. The Church became part of the international 'Church of God' with its HQ in Cleveland, Tennessee (E&S Jan 29 1962. Aug 29 2003 p25) (Wolverhampton Archives website, 2002). On **ASHMORE ESTATE** is St Alban (1967), Griffiths Drive, Ashmore Park. At **BENTLEY** is Emmanuel (1932, 1956); a plaque with a bust of the church's founder Alfred Owen (d1929) has been moved inside the church for 'security reasons' from a wall in the Memorial Garden (TB June 10 2004 p23p). At **BILSTON** is St Leonard (C12, rebuilt 1825), Walsall St. **First person buried in the church** Sarah Ames, buried Nov 25 1732 in the chancel (SR p108). St Luke (1851-2, now closed), Market St. St Mary (1827), Oxford St. Bilston Primitive Methodist church, knocked down and amalgamated with Swan Bank Methodist church in 1963 (TB April 6 2000 p26p). R.C. Holy Trinity (1834), Oxford St. **In Bilston Cemetery?** - The wooden grave of Ivy M Owen, d1930 aged 20 (TB July 27 2006 p18ps). At **BLAKENHALL** is St Luke (1860-1), Upper Villiers St. At **BRADLEY** is St Martin (1866-8), corner of King and Slater Streets. At **BUNKER'S HILL** St Chad. At **CHAPEL ASH** is St Mark (1848-9). At **EAST PARK** is St Matthew (records from 1849). At **GRAISELEY** is St Chad (1907-8), Owen Rd. At **HATHERTON** - St Saviour. At **HEATH TOWN** Holy Trinity (1850-2), Church St. **In the churchyard** The grave of Daisy Alcock (1903-96), Calligrapher of New Cross Farm, Wednesfield. At **HORSELEY FIELD** St James (1843, now closed), corner of Horseley Field and St James's St. St Matthew (1849, now closed), corner of Lower Horseley Fields and Walsall St. At **LONG KNOWLE** St Gregory the Great (1966), corner of Blackhalve and Long Knowle Lanes. At **MERRIDALE** is St Paul (records from 1835). At **MONMORE GREEN** is All Saints (1877), Steelhouse Rd. At **NEWBRIDGE** St Jude (1867-9), St Judes Rd. At **NEW INVENTION** All Saints Worship Centre (1984), Beacon School, Davis Rd. At **PELSALL** St Michael and All Angels (1843-4). **In the churchyard** The epitaph on Sarah Rowley's grave (1755-85), interested the historian Stebbing Shaw (SHOS vol 2 p61). Memorial to the 22 who died in the Hall Colliery disaster Nov 14 1872. Grave of George Hall killed on the level crossing at Heath End, Pelsall by a train July 9 1887 aged 1 year & 7 months (WOb July 9 1887. July 12 1987). Graves to members of the Charles family of Pelsall Hall. At **PERRY HALL** St Augustine and St Chad (1955), Stubby Lane (TB Aug 23 2007 p5). At **ROUGH HILLS** is St Martin (1938-9), Dixon St. At **SHORT HEATH** is Holy Trinity (1855), Church Rd. Furzebank Worship Centre (1985), Stroud Ave. At **SPRING BANK** is St Anne (1856-8), St Ann's St, Lichfield Diocese Best Kept Churchyard winner 1999. The non-conformist Church of God, of Prophecy (1873), St Ann's Rd. At **SPRINGFIELD** is St Barnabas (1892-3), Wednesfield Rd; St Stephen (1907-9), Hilton St. At **WEDNESFIELD** St Thomas (1751, rebuilt 1903), Church St. At **WHITMORE REANS** is St Andrew (1865, rebuilt 1965-7), St Andrew's Cl, Hunter St. At **WILLENHALL** is St Giles (C13, rebuilt 1867), Walsall St. **One of the first christenings in Staffordshire in C21** Amelia Spittle, aged four and half months, at St Giles' on Jan 2 2000 (E&S Jan 1 2000 p6). St Stephen (1854, rebuilt 1979), Wolverhampton St.

The area...

Wolverhampton is the county's 5th largest parish, consisting of 17,490 acres; **81st= closest parish to the county town**, 12.8m S; **extremist length** 5.3m, making it **27th= longest parish in the county**; **extremist width** 7m, making it **9th= widest parish in the county**. **Chief settlement** Wolverhampton, a very large, proud corporate market town. **Wolverhampton's river** Smestow Brook, according to Angus Dunphy (BCM Winter 2007 p61).

Altitude Records...

Highest points FEATHERSTONE - 427 feet W of Featherstone Hall. **HILTON** - Portobello Tower at 590 feet. **PELSALL** - Pelsall Wood at 499 feet. **WOLVERHAMPTON** - 577 feet on Bushbury boundary N of Ashmore Lodge. **Lowest points FEATHER-STONE** - 358 feet by the brook on the N boundary. **HILTON** - M54 interchange at 440 feet. **PELSALL** - 410 feet on the Walsall Wood boundary by Ford Brook. **WOLVERHAMPTON** - 345 feet by Smestow Brook, S of Newbridge. **World's highest altitude record** by 1862 Henry Coxwell and James Glaisher (d1902/3) who ascended to at least 25,400 feet (perhaps 37,000 feet) from Wolverhampton Gas Works, Stafford Rd, Sept 5 1862 (GBR 1974 p216).

Wombourne
Did you know that...

Largest village in England Sometimes claimed of Wombourne; but there are also 18 other UK contenders, including Gnosall (Wikipedia 2006). **The house that's never sold** The Wodehouse (Wombourne 1900. Old OS Maps. Godfrey. 2000). **Best spear truss in Staffordshire, possibly in the country** That supporting part of the roof at The Wodehouse (info Mr & Mrs Philips). **Deepest well in Britain** A bore-hole near Smestow Bridge built by Germans in 1912, at 2842 feet (TB Jan 1991 p6p) (GBR 1996 p79). **Wombourne's oldest pub** The Red Lion, Battlefield (Wombourne 1900. Old OS Maps. Godfrey. 2000). **The house made from 'one of the last and also one of the greatest half-timbered mansions in Britain'** Lymore at Greenhill, Wombourne, built practically wholly from Lymore Hall, described as the above, near Montgomery, demolished in the early 1930s. Lymore was designed by Canadian-born architect Major Kenneth Hutchinson Smith (d1945); properties in Castlecroft Gardens, Penn, also utilise salvaged timbers from the hall. He is responsible for many mock Tudor houses in the Midlands, collectively dubbed **'The most honest fakes in the business'**. Another house by him is Tinker's Cottage at Prestwood, Kinver, 1934 (WP&P p157) (TB Sept 30 2004 p16p). **Computer Weekly and Digital Equipment Company National Schools' computer competition winners** Ounsdale Comprehensive School on May 25 1976, beating off competition from 100 other schools to win a computer for their school then costing £8,000 (E&S May 26 1976 p). **Britain's number one volleyball tournament host** Ounsdale Comprehensive School if it hosts the Tachikara '4' contest with over 100 international entries proposed for 1977 (E&S June 4 1976). **First event in Wombourne new Civic Centre** The annual dinner hosted by the Chairman of Wombourne PC (Ted Waterfield) in May 1977 (Wolverhampton Chronicle May 27 1977 p). **'one of Britain's top volleyball teams', under-19 National Schools volleyball champions 1978** Ounsdale (High School) Junior Men (Wolverhampton Chronicle Aug 12 1977 p. Nov 11 1977. April 21 1978). **One of the oldest and most respected hockey clubs in Staffordshire** Wombourne (Staffordshire Handbook c1966 p24). **Best Devon Rex cat breed in the world 1978** Sirafen Jaunty Jon, a Devon Rex bred by Cllr Viv Wakeford of Rushford Ave, Wombourne, winning the Class of Honour, a competition between international grand champions and international grand premiers to find the best cat (E&S May 5 1978). **Longest continuous sausage by 1995** One of 21.12km made at the premises of Keith Boxley at Wombourne in 15 hours 33 minutes on June 18-19 1988 (GBR 1995 p214). **Staffordshire's newest permanent maypole** That at Wombourne (TB May 1 2003 p7p). **Staffordshire Best Kept Village (Large Village category) winner 1971 (jointly with Whittington), 1973 (with Hammerwich)** Wombourne.

People...

Wombourne's most famous old worthy Sir Samuel Hellier (?1736-1784). Sheriff of Worcestershire 1762, promoter of music in Wombourne, and creator of pleasure grounds for tourists at The Wodehouse. Whimsical follies in woodland began to appear after 1763, twelve years after his succession to the Wodehouse estate. "Such who come in coaches and appear as people of fashion" could see a hermitage with a life-size hermit called Father Francis, a music room with an organ, Handel's Temple, a druids' temple and a root house. He died unmarried. **Woodford Grange's most famous old worthy** Hugh Lee (d1576). Clerk at the royal armoury at Greenwich. He was tenant and then owner (1554-76) of this extra-parochial estate. **Wombourne's villain** George Thomas, born at Battlefield Terrace, Wombourne, in 1822. Along with fellow Pickford's boatman, William Owen, he raped and murdered Christina Collins as she travelled on a cargo-carrying barge between Liverpool and London at Hoo Mill Locks near Great Haywood on June 17 1839. They were hung at Stafford in April 1840 (TB July 1998 p25). **Wombourne's bravest** Julie Jones, 17 of Bratch Lane, who in Sept 1975 grabbed a prisoner trying to escape from a prison van at Red Lion Street Police Station in Wolverhampton. The man was 6 feet 3 inches and yet she at 5 feet 7 inches, weighing 11 lb, held him in a bear hug until police came to her assistance. The Chief Constable of the West Midlands awarded her bravery with a silver bracelet and a thank-you letter (E&S Dec 8 1976 p). Stephen Lockitt, of Wombourne Park, 11, was first at a road accident and gave urgent first aid to the injured motorist, receiving the Scout's meritorious conduct award (Wolverhampton Chronicle

Joanna Southcott. Staffordshire's only case of a prosecution and conviction for rick-burning was at Wombourne. St Benedict Biscop church at night, this is a unique church dedication

July 22 1976. Aug 5 1976). **Chief custodian of 'Joanna Southcott's Box'** Rev Thomas Philip Foley rector of Old Swinford (1797-1835) and vicar of Wombourne and Trysull (1801-35). In 1801 he travelled to Devon as **one of 'The Chosen Seven'** to examine and appraise the prophecies and teaching of Joanna Southcott (b1750). The Black Country Bugle says her 'activities were creating sensational waves of religious fervour and unease in many parishes, as news of her 'gospel' spread. He was so impressed and captivated by his findings that before returning to the Midlands, he declared his utter loyalty and devotion to 'the cause' and promised to use all of the influence at his command to found the first chapel for her followers... and was a prime mover in the construction of her first chapel, in London where, in Autumn of 1802, she announced that in the compass of a dozen years she would become the Mother of Shiloh (The Second Christ). When she died of 'brain fever' in 1814, the Rev Foley was nominated custodian of her box of Prophecies. This became famous (or infamous) as 'Joanna Southcott's Box' and it remained with him until his death in 1835 (TB Nov 1993 p5). The Panacea Society, founded at Bedford in the WW1 becoming perhaps the **strangest minority religious sect in Britain**, had custody of her Box by 1964 (Sunday Express July 26 1964). **Strange but true!** Mr Parker of Chasepool Lodge ordered his own post-mortem believing he had been poisoned, 1808, which indeed he had with White Mercury; the poisoner was his coachman William Hawkeswood (TB Sept 1998 p25). **'The Wombourne Vagrant'** John Mason, who lived in a sandstone cave beside the Bridgenorth Road. His stomping ground was Wordsley, Wall Heath and Kingswinford. He died of exposure in 1963. His body was found in a railwayman's tool shed near the A449 at Himley, and is buried in a unmarked grave in Himley churchyard (TB April 12 2001 p5p of cave. April 13 2007 p19ps). **'Tommy Gas-Tar'** Tommy Tucker who ran a smallholding at Smestow, was accused of adulterating the milk he sold with water. When asked how he pleaded at Tettenhall magistrate's court he stated "That cow's bin outside, all winter, yer honour, an' her must rain in but I'll gas-tar her back when I gets wum - an' see as it don't happen agen..." The magistrate thought he was simple-minded and left him off with a warning. Thereafter the nickname stuck (MMBCC p104). **2 litre class speed record on longest hill climb course in the country** Will Cole of Wombourne in 1975 in his V12 Jaguar in 63.67 seconds at Loton Park, near Shrewsbury, beating the old record by a fraction of a second (E&S June 17 1975 p). **World's youngest most-travelled person** Perhaps Matthew Harding (b1971) of Wombourne, who by Sept 1975 had, since joining the Junior Jet Club, clocked-up 60,000 air miles. His parents married at St Benedict Biscop (his grandparents the Beddalls resided in Red Hill Ave) before taking up teaching posts in the Bahamas, later starting a new life in Australia, when that did not work out they returned to England (Wolverhampton Chronicle Sept 11 1975). **Wombourne's youngest parish council chairman** Jerald Smith, 36, a school teacher of Richmond Gardens (E&S May 12 1981 p10). **Royal Horticultural Society service bar medalist** Herbert A Butcher of Wombourne for his long service (50 years) as gardener at The Wodehouse in 1976 (E&S Sept 23 1976). **Miss Beautiful Eyes 1982, Miss Beacon Radio 1984** Linda Ashmore (b c1982), of St Benedict's Rd, Wombourne (E&S date ? p24. March 31 1984 p4p) (Wombourne Library press cuttings in WSL). **Wombourne's historian** May Griffiths, of Giggetty Lane, Wombourne, author of 'Wombourne What Was' (1990), 'Around Pattingham and Wombourne' (1992), according to Angus Dunphy (Wombourne 1900. Old OS Maps. Godfrey. 2000); she is also a local civic campaigner (Wolverhampton Chronicle July 1 1977). **'richest man in Wombourne'** By his own definition Jimmy Reynolds, aged 25, hair shirt occupier of a makeshift tent in Himley Wood, who had turned his back on modern life in 1982, but then threatened with eviction by the owners of the wood Woodland Trust (E&S April 8 1982 p6p). **Wombourne's kindest** John Smith who had property in Wombourne by deed 1715, and had two almshouses built in Rookery Road. Also Sir Samuel Hellier (d1784) who left £100 - the income to be distributed among the poor of the parish. **Wombourne's poorest** The almshouses built in Rookery Road in 1716 seem to have become a parish poorhouse by the late C18. In 1828 there was mention of the upper and lower poorhouse (VCH vol 20 p217). From 1836 the poor went to Seisdon Union workhouse. **Wombourne's earliest recorded will** Belongs to Robert Smythe, and is dated May 2 1522. **Choicest quote** W Byford-Jones (Quaestor in E&S) devotes the last chapter of his 'Both Sides of the Severn', 1930s, to Wombourne, and completes the book with "I walked up the road to a slight hill and then, turning, I looked back towards Wombourne. The church was not visible for darkness had fallen but the red curtains of the cottages were lighted by oil lamps, and here and there I could figure out the curling smoke above the cottage chimneys. There was something delightfully English about Wombourne on that Autumn evening!"

Agriculture & work...

County's 5th earliest commutation of tithes when they were dealt with under a parliamentary enclosure act The impropriate and vicarial tithes of Wombourne, by allotments of land, 1793. **Only Staffordshire case of a prosecution and conviction for rick-burning** When John Swatkins, 22, and Thomas Lloyd, 53, Thomas Timmins, 19, and Thomas Wilcox were charged with setting fire to a stack of barley of Richard Powell Williams at Swindon on Jan 14 1831 in protest at increased mechanisation of agricultural implements. Timmins was acquitted and Wilcox was exonerated. The other two were executed at Stafford (Wolverhampton Chronicle Jan 19 1831) (International Review of Social History xix (i) pp86-99) (TB June 1978 p38. June 1986 pp10-11) (VCH vol 6 p120). **First smelt from the Ferro Enamels Company's first furnace** Oct 14 1935, Ferro (Great Britain) Ltd's factory was at Ounsdale (Pocket Images: Wombourne. D Thomas & J Bowler 2005 p68). **Queen's Award to Trade and Commerce** Midland Designing and Manufacturing, of London and Wombourne, makers of mobile floodlighting units 1977 (Wolverhampton Chronicle May 6 1977).

Church...

At Wombourne is St Benedict Biscop, **a unique church dedication** (KES p240) (BOE p326); **54th last AP county church built** dating from 1400. **One of the best sets of C19 church plate in Staffordshire** Dated 1812; along with that of Wednesbury (BAST vol 73 1955 p1). **Also note** a C16 Italian relief carving illustrating the parable of the Good Samaritan, brought from Italy c1720 (LGS p260) (CHMS p57). At Swindon is St John's (1854). **In the churchyard** In the NE corner 'E.R. July 23, 1854, Aged 101 The first in this ground' (Elizabeth Reynolds of Hinksford) (TB April 1 2004 p21). **Wombourne's longest-serving vicar** William John Heale, who served 49 years, 1849-1898.

Canals...

James Brindley's first attempt at combining a lock and a bridge on a public road Awbridge Lock (VCH vol 20 p201). **Unique canal locks** Those three on the Staffs & Worcs Canal at The Bratch, being an embryo form of staircase (IAS p205).

The area...

Wombourne is the **county's 59th largest parish**, consisting of 4360 acres; **46th= fartherest parish away from the county town**, 17.2m SSW; **extremist length** 4.7m; **extremist width** 3.3m. The name **Wombourne first appears** in Domesday Book, 1086. **Geology** Bunter (most), Keuper Sandstones (Orton Hills). Wombourne village lies in a hollow in the red Triassic rocks so has extremes of temperature. On Jan 10 1982 it - but for the absence of an official meteorological recorder in the area - may have had a lower temperature than that recorded at Newport, Shrops, at -26.1C (-15F), making it the **place with the lowest temperature ever recorded in England** (TB March 15 2007 p11). **Highest point** Orton Hill at 535 feet. **Lowest point** 197 feet by the Smestow at Greensforge. Wombourne was **50th most-populated Staffordshire parish in 1801** with 1,170; **56th in 1811** with 1,136; **49th in 1821** with 1,478; **47th in 1831** with 1,647; **48th in 1841** with 1,808; **48th in 1851** with 2,007; **47th in 1861** with 2,236; **55th in 1871** with 2,080; **58th in 1881** with 1,986; **59th in 1891** with 1,910; **60th in 1901** with 1,856.

ABBREVIATIONS

Can be found on the **NEW** The Staffordshire Encyclopaedia Website
at
http:// www.the-staffordshire-encyclopaedia.co.uk/

The Staffordshire Encyclopaedia Website. Is a free on-line service from February 2007. Collected historical information about Staffordshire. The site, constantly is updated and expanded. It contains folklore, day-to-day facts, railways, sheriffs and much, much more. Users can word search any topic, and a search-engine finds that word in any context on the site. The site can be found with a Google search and is at
http://www/the-staffordshire-encyclopaedia. co.uk/

Available from Malthouse Press

DID YOU KNOW THAT... SERIES

Tim Cockin's Did You Know That....
paperback

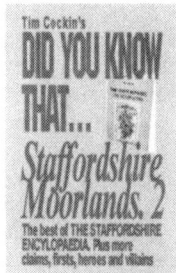

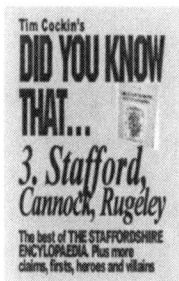

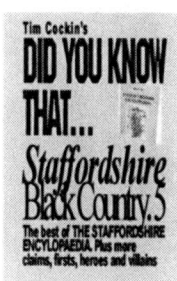

Tim Cockin's Did You Know That....

The best of The Staffordshire Encyclopaedia for the general reader. This series strives to put into print Staffordshire's claims for future substantiation. These little guides, illustrated with lively 'cartoons', contain claims, firsts, lasts, bests, worsts, heroes and villains, plus many additional facts found since The Encyclopaedia was published.

Number 2 the **Staffordshire Moorlands** appeared in September 2007. **£4.50.**
Number 5 **Staffordshire Black Country** is out now. **£7.99.**
Number 3 **Stafford, Cannock & Rugeley** is due out Winter 2008.
Number 1 **Staffordshire The Potteries** is due out 2009.
Number 4 **Lichfield, Burton, Tamworth** is due out 2009.

Available from Malthouse Press

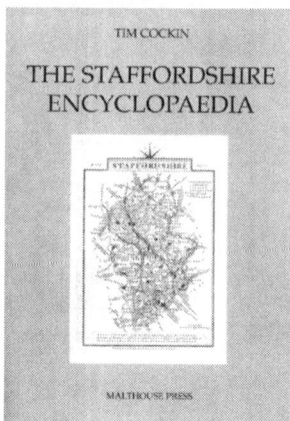

The Staffordshire
Encyclopaedia
paperback

£40.00

The Staffordshire Encyclopaedia. PAPERBACK edition of the acclaimed First edition. By Tim Cockin. Over 40,000 entries. Corrections to the First edition. pp680. 8 inches by 12 inches. Published 2006 and available now. **£40.00.**

Old Parish Boundaries of Staffordshire.
Volume 1: Pirehill Hundred. By Tim Cockin.Hardback. Detailed study of ancient parishes, townships, municipal wards in NW Staffordshire. Each parish is minutely subdivided according to boundary changes, and the history and changing hierarchal layers of local government responsible for that area are sequenced in indexes. Hitherto unknown boundaries of townships are shown by new research. In addition there is all sorts of 'Parish Chest' information from registers to vestry books, and the volume concludes with a comprehensive roll of M.Ps for all Staffordshire constituencies from the Middle Ages to the present, and peers in the House of Lords. The series is in abeyance until there is enough interest in subsequent volumes. 48 Illus. pp364. **£10.00**.

**The Staffordshire
(parishes) Map**
1400 x 1000 mm

£12.00

The Staffordshire Map. WALL MAP By Tim Cockin. 4 feet six inches by 3 feet three inches. Faithful copy of the Ordnance Survey 1875-86 Six Inch to One Mile maps. Showing old parish boundaries, canals, railways, woods and water features the Map is proving to be of great interest to family historians. The Map is part of Biographical County Maps series: Surrounding the map are biographical details on famous persons from every parish. Published 2006. **£15.00.**

An Eccleshall & Mucklestone Country Life, by a Land Girl. A collection Jessie Edwards' farming and countryside stories written for national newspapers in the 1920s and 1930s. 8 inches by 5 inches. Paperback. Illustrated with simple line sketches. Due out 2008. The collection follows the farming year through the seasons in the areas of her homes Park Springs and Eccleshall Road Farms. This is also the story of how a farming girl strove to become and became a freelance journalist for national newspapers in the 1920s under the pen name Jessie Frederick. The collection has been saved by her family and it is now brought to publication by her nephew Geoffrey Edwards of Ellenhall.

189

Available from Malthouse Press

THE POCKET SERIES

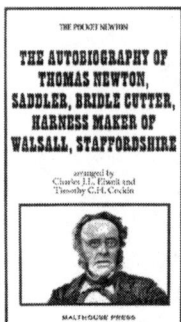

The Autobiography of Thomas Newton, Saddler, Bridle Cutter, Harness Maker of Walsall, Staffordshire Paperback. Arranged by Charles J.L. Elwell and Tim Cockin. This is the first in this new series - The Pocket Series - reproducing the work of great and lesser-known Staffordshire historians in affordable, manageable size. Walsall is known throughout the world as the principal seat of the Saddlery and Harness industries. One of its pre-eminent pioneers was Thomas Newton. Over a hundred years ago the Walsall Observer serialised this man's extraordinary life story; his extensive travels for business and pleasure; his royal commissions; luminaries he met in the Arts and Science; personal sorrows and triumphs. In his own words Thomas Newton has given us a unique Victorian social history. It was inevitable one day somebody would republish his story in book form. Here is that book. pp174. Illustrated with a number of pocket illustrations. **£9.99**

The Natural History of Staffordshire. Reproduced from the original. 8 inches by 5 inches. Paperback. Illustrated. pp464. Projected 2009-10. Dr Robert Plot's Natural History of Staffordshire, was the first-published Staffordshire history when it appeared in 1686. A great work, it is often cited. The 1973 facsimile edition is now rare and expensive; the first edition can fetch in excess of £1,000 at auction. This is your chance to own a pocket copy. Prepublication subscriptions taken at **£10.00** by 31 March 2009.

AVAILABLE FROM MALTHOUSE PRESS
BY SUBSCRIPTION
The Staffordshire Encyclopaedia
HARDBACK edition

This is a secondary source index tome on the history of the old county of Stafford, celebrating its curiosities, peculiarities and legends. It is arranged under place headings in a gazetteer, and draws on some 1,200-1,500 works of reference. 8 inches by 12 inches. Colour dust jacket, stitch binding, tail bands. with over 1,000 additions, corrections and fully illustrated. Prospective 50,000 entries, pp900. Projected for Autumn 2010. Prepublication subscription rates are £60.00 if received before 31 March 2009, £75.00 if received after to 1 September 2010. Projected retail price on publication will be in excess of £90.00.

Printed in the United Kingdom
by Lightning Source UK Ltd.
129321UK00001B/70-309/P

9 780953 901845